Praise for *The Accidental President of Brazil*

"[Mr. Cardoso] . . . deserves enormous credit, not least for the intellectual honesty that allowed him to abandon collectivist ideals as the world changed."
—*The Wall Street Journal*

"In this most engaging and very personal history of twentieth-century Brazil, a genuine philosopher-king recounts how he combined principle and pragmatism to transform a harsh military dictatorship into a hopeful, modern democracy. . . . Readers with even a passing curiosity about Brazil will enjoy—and all aspiring Latin American politicians should study—this rare 'lessons learned' memoir by one of the foremost statesmen of our times."
—*Foreign Affairs* (Editor's pick)

"Honest, personable and engaging."
—*Washington Post*

"[A] charming account of the life of a sociology professor turned unlikely leader. . . . Cardoso shaped Brazil for years to come."
—*Providence Journal*

"In [*The Accidental President of Brazil*] . . . the ex-president . . . uses his life story to illuminate Brazil's ongoing evolution. . . . Along the way, he offers revealing vignettes of his dealings with two American presidents, sounds a cautionary note about China, and offers a surprising conclusion about his homeland's future . . . Cardoso's personal journey in the past half century mirrors the changes in Brazilian society. . . ."
—*USA Today*

"First-rate . . . [Cardoso has] the panache of a seasoned history writer . . . [while] Cardoso's family history would seem to have predisposed him to the role of public man, his story is that of a maverick whose curious mind and love for his country helped bring Brazil into the twenty-first century as a formidable economic and political power."
—*Publishers Weekly*

"An engaging and thoughtful look at the turbulent history of government in Brazil. . . . Cardoso has a deep and intimate perspective on that nation's politics. . . . Readers interested in the political history of this fascinating nation, of huge importance on the American continent, will enjoy this book." —*Booklist*

"A candid memoir about Cardoso's successes . . . and failures . . . provides a context for studying Brazil's political evolution in recent years and will be particularly useful for public and undergraduate libraries." —*Library Journal*

"This is a book about the art of politics and the craftsmanship of governing. The political trajectory of Fernando Henrique Cardoso has important lessons for countries struggling to consolidate their democracies and stabilize their economies . . . it offers insights into how political and economic change occurs in a country renowned for its instability." —*Development Policy Review*

"Fascinating. . . . This entertaining memoir brings together the best of Cardoso's insights as sociologist, politician, president, and elder statesman. It is must-reading for everyone interested in Brazil's past or concerned about its future." —Professor Ted Goertzel, *InfoBrazil*

"Possesses the seductive prose of someone who likes, and knows how, to tell a good story . . . Fernando Henrique Cardoso's story, with his experiences and ideas, is a book full of love for Brazil." —*O Estado de São Paulo*

"A captivating narrative for those interested in history, politics, and sociology." —*El Diario/La Prensa*

"*The Accidental President of Brazil* comes on the scene as a petite classic . . . mixing personal confession, historical thriller, and hard truths." —*Exame*

THE
ACCIDENTAL PRESIDENT
OF BRAZIL

FERNANDO
HENRIQUE
CARDOSO

THE
$\mathcal{A}$CCIDENTAL $\mathcal{P}$RESIDENT
OF
Brazil

·

A MEMOIR
with Brian Winter

PublicAffairs

NEW YORK

BOOK DESIGN AND COMPOSITION BY JENNY DOSSIN. TEXT SET IN ADOBE GARAMOND.

Library of Congress Cataloging-in-Publication data

Cardoso, Fernando Henrique

The accidental president of Brazil: a memoir / Fernando Henrique Cardoso.—1st ed.

p.   cm.

ISBN-13: 978-1-58648-324-1

ISBN-10: 1-58648-324-2

1. Cardoso, Fernando Henrique. 2. Brazil—Politics and government—20th century. 3. Presidents—Brazil—Biography. I. Title.

F2538.5.C37A3 2006

984.064092—dc22

[B]

2005056385

ISBN-13: 978-1-58648-429-3

ISBN-10: 1-58648-429-x

10 9 8 7 6 5 4 3 2 1

CONTENTS

To my grandchildren

Joana, Helena, Julia, Pedro, and Isabel

FOREWORD BY PRESIDENT BILL CLINTON

In the 1990s, for the first time in history, more than half the world's population lived under democratically elected governments. This democratic revolution swept across our hemisphere. As never before, the Americas came together to embrace common goals and common values. My friend, President Fernando Henrique Cardoso, both symbolized and led this movement. He endured arrest, blacklisting, and exile without giving in to despair. His office was bombed, and his friends were tortured, but he never wavered from the ideals of tolerance and understanding.

We have a special responsibility and a special ability, Brazil and the United States, to work together with the other countries of the Americas to maintain the democratic momentum and to expand its benefits to those who have not yet felt them. Our nations have the largest populations and the largest economies, rich natural resources, and enormous diversity among our peoples. Most importantly, we both cherish the same values: freedom and equality, respect for the individual, the importance of the family and community, social justice, and peace. President Cardoso and I forged a close friendship and productive working relationship because of these shared values.

Brazil faced a series of daunting challenges during President Cardoso's terms and, with his leadership, overcame many of them. Brazil emerged from dictatorship only 20 years ago, thanks in part to Cardoso's efforts. He worked as a senator and government minister to consolidate and steady Brazil's fledgling democracy, and then as minister of finance, he strived to stabilize his nation's economy.

Cardoso's economic strategy as finance minister, the *Plano Real*, succeeded in curbing the hyperinflation that was crippling Brazil's economy. Halting inflation dramatically boosted the real incomes of the poor, created a solid foundation for economic growth, and protected the country from many of the financial crises that have afflicted other developing nations.

The *Plano Real* was so successful that the people of Brazil elected Cardoso president. A highly regarded sociologist before embarking on his political career, Cardoso brought academic rigor and policy expertise to his governing style. He continued to work hard on economic and trade issues to bring prosperity to his people, embarking on a privatization effort that has raised billions of dollars. He also understood that globalization could help Brazil, and by pursuing free trade agreements between the nations of the Americas, he increased exports and expanded his country's economy.

Most importantly, President Cardoso was committed to seeking prosperity the right way, with all citizens having a chance to participate in the wealth that the global economy generates. He knew that an increasingly global economy requires deepening democracy and the rule of law, protecting workers, and educating the young people who embody the future of our countries. Under President Cardoso, Brazil spent nearly six percent of its GNP on education and worked hard to increase enrollment and to help more children complete their early years of school. His "Bolsa Escola" initiative is a model for developing nations throughout the world, and we formed the Partnership for Education to work together to prepare our children for the future.

President Cardoso's dedication to justice goes beyond his own country. He ensured that, during his presidency, Brazil was a responsible global citizen. He worked against international threats like crime, drug trafficking, and terrorism. Brazil was a signatory of the Nuclear Non-Proliferation Treaty, the Comprehensive Test Ban Treaty, and the Kyoto Accords. The nation also took a forward-thinking, aggressive approach to combating the HIV/AIDS pandemic, providing anti-retroviral medicines to all Brazilians who needed them.

For two terms as president, Fernando Henrique Cardoso navigated his country through a potentially perilous landscape with courage, foresight, and grace. He assumed the presidency of a young democracy with an unstable economy, and he transformed Brazil into a mature and prosperous nation respected around the world. His memoir tells the story of his remarkable leadership as president, his fascinating personal life, his remarkable encounters with other historical figures, and perhaps most movingly, his lifelong love for Brazil. No one has served Brazil better or more faithfully than he has.

THE FAMILY BUSINESS

POLITICS FIRST INTERRUPTED my life on a crystalline beach in Niterói, across the bay from Rio de Janeiro. It was May 1938, and I was just six years old. My family had been enjoying a typically carefree vacation of tropical sun and surf when, late one night, a jangling telephone jostled us awake. My father lifted the receiver from the wall, listened, said nothing, and then slammed the phone down. Hurriedly, he changed into a military uniform, grabbed a revolver, and rushed out the door.

It was the night of the coup attempt by the *integralistas,* a rather bizarre band of fascists who spewed hatred against Jews and Communists under the motto "God, Fatherland, Family." They received funding from Mussolini and envisioned themselves as the heirs to Hitler, but the integralistas were unmistakably, uniquely Brazilian. They raised their right arms to salute like the Nazis, but instead of *"Sieg heil!"* they shouted *"Anauê!"*—an Indian word of murky meaning that was supposed to reflect the group's nationalist leanings. Shoved out of power soon after the president had ordered Congress closed the year before, a small band of integralistas had panicked and made a daring, foolish attack that May night on the presidential palace.

With the palace unguarded, President Getúlio Vargas had no choice but to try and repel the attackers himself. The paunchy, cigar-smoking strongman appeared in the palace window with a handgun and took potshots at the rebels outside, while Alzira, his twenty-three-year-old daughter, frantically telephoned military commanders and begged for reinforcements. The integralistas, who turned out to be no experts in combat themselves, haplessly returned fire from behind exploding flowerpots and sculptures. The battle turned decisively when someone mounted a submachine gun in the palace window. In one of the most surreal moments in Brazilian history, Getúlio himself then proceeded to blaze away at the attackers, keeping them at bay for several hours until my father and other soldiers arrived.

A dozen of the integralistas were killed, and the rebellion was summarily crushed. From that point on, Getúlio established a personal squad of bodyguards who accompanied him at all times, reflective of a deep paranoia that would eventually lead to his death.

When my father returned home the next day, he was sweaty and exhausted, but unharmed. "Everything's fine now, Fernando Henrique," he told me with an easy smile. "We can go back to our vacation."

That night at the beach, I realized for the first time that, in Brazil, a government sometimes had to defend itself with guns. This was a hugely disturbing revelation because, in my young mind, Brazil's government was altogether inseparable from my family; they were one and the same. My great-uncle, Augusto Ignácio do Espírito Santo Cardoso, had been Getúlio's minister of war. My father worked in the ministry with him. Several other family members were also generals and officials intimately tied to the regime; one of my cousins later followed his father as war minister, and another cousin became the government-appointed mayor of Rio. A coup attempt was therefore akin to an assault on all of my family.

To a six-year-old, it was a vivid political baptism.

As the years went by, I realized such episodes were hardly an aberration. I grew up hearing fantastic tales about my great-grandfather, a provincial governor on the parched, backward Brazilian high plateau; about my grandfather, a general who had helped found the Republic; and about my father, a general also, who had been imprisoned twice for joining doomed rebellions in the 1920s. Politics, it seemed, was both a life-consuming passion and an unwelcome, violent intrusion for generations of my ancestors. There was a certain inevitability about it. "Always try to make casual conversation with your jailer," my father once instructed me. "Make yourself seem as human as possible. You must always talk. And with the guard, not with the captain." I couldn't have been much older than ten when he said this. Yet I never once questioned why he would be telling me such a thing. His fatherly advice would, indeed, prove indispensable later on.

Still, if politics seemed to be the Cardoso family business, then I took the route of many favorite sons—I spent my early life trying to avoid it. Some of my friends (and more than a few of my critics) scoff at this notion, believing I was naturally drawn to power at any cost: It was said that "Fernando Henrique couldn't be pope, so he settled for being the president of Brazil." But the fact is that I was always more interested in quietly reading books in the sun, preferring the world I had known before the phone rang that autumn night in Niterói.

People forget this: Back when the job fell to me, who in their right mind would have wanted to be president of Brazil?

Following twenty years of military dictatorship, which finally collapsed in 1985, I was Brazil's third civilian president. One of my predecessors had died before he could be inaugurated. The other was impeached for allegedly embezzling millions of dollars. Look further back in time, and the stories of Brazilian heads of state get even bleaker. One ended his presidency by shooting himself in the heart; another died heartbroken, bankrupt and exiled in a Paris hotel room; still another resigned out of the blue one day, got rip-roaring drunk, and boarded a boat for Europe.

Failure alone does not drive men to such extremes. It could only be the special kind of failure that results when tantalizing potential falls tragically short of expectations. That is the kind of failure that Brazil has always specialized in.

At first glance, it is easy to be dazzled. When we travel abroad, Brazilians are gently mocked for our habit of using superlatives to describe our country. We cannot help it. Brazil is the world's fifth-largest country in terms of both size and population, with 185 million people spread over an area larger than the continental United States. It has the biggest economy in Latin America, and the ninth largest in the world, putting it ahead of Russia and just behind Italy. It is the world's number one producer of sugar, oranges, and coffee, but it's not just a producer of commodities; it's also one of the world's top ten makers of airplanes and automobiles. Its rich ethnic diversity can be matched only by the United States: According to rough estimates, Brazil boasts at least 25 million people of Italian heritage, 10 million of German descent, and more than 10 million Lebanese. Brazil has more people of African descent than any country besides Nigeria. There are more ethnic Japanese in São Paulo than in any other city outside Japan. Brazil is the number one beef exporter, the planet's most populous Roman Catholic country, and so on.

All of this abundance sits on a gorgeous and varied landscape of white beaches, emerald forests, and fertile plains. Brazil possesses a quarter—a quarter!—of the world's arable land. The country is practically self-sufficient in oil, and over the centuries it has yielded vast quantities of gold. There is seemingly no limit to the natural and human riches that lie within its borders.

So surely Brazil is a paradise? It could be, were it not for hellish problems of an equally superlative nature.

Despite its abundant natural resources, Brazil is probably most notorious for having one of the world's largest gaps between rich and poor, with 10 percent of the population earning about half of the country's wealth. One in four people earn less than $1 a day. Despite Brazil's vast farmland, there are still pockets of malnutrition. Thousands of abandoned street children roam our cities. The murder rate is so high that it meets the United Nations' definition of a low-grade civil war. We have the world's highest number of gun deaths. São Paulo and Rio de Janeiro have morphed into veritable "cities of walls," with the middle class seeking refuge in compounds that resemble penitentiaries more than apartment blocs. The legacy of slavery, which saw more African slaves brought here than anywhere else in the Western Hemisphere, left one of the world's most unjust traditions of brutality, exclusion, and exploitation. The world's highest foreign debt, coupled with chronic budget deficits, has left the government's finances in a permanent state of crisis.

Politics in Brazil is about trying to reconcile these monumental contradictions. The scale of the challenge is hard to appreciate. Every new president, an optimist on his first day in office, thinks he can pull it off. But in the past, by the time many of these men left the job they were reduced to a bitter shadow of their former selves. What happened in the middle was rarely a pretty story.

Bill Clinton once told me that every country has one great fear and one great hope. Russia will always fear foreign invasion, for example, whereas China will always fear disintegration from within. I told Clinton that, in Brazil's case, the fear and the hope are essentially one and the same.

Our hope is to become a prosperous and just world power, worthy of our continental size. We have always believed this is our destiny. The almost childlike obsession with our potential, and the belief that we will one day achieve greatness, are even emblazoned in our national anthem:

Brasil, um sonho intenso, um raio vívido
De amor e de esperança à terra desce,

Se em teu formoso céu, risonho e límpido,
A imagem do Cruzeiro resplandece
Gigante pela própria natureza,
És belo, és forte, impávido colosso
E o teu futuro espelha essa grandeza

Brazil, an intense dream, a vivid ray
Of love and hope settles on the earth.
As in your beautiful sky, smiling and serene
The image of the Southern Cross shines.
Strong, an intrepid colossus,
A giant by nature, you are beautiful,
And your future will match this grandeur.

Powerful words, never realized. As I told Clinton, the reality in Brazil has been much closer to our national fear: that we will never realize our destiny, that we will remain imprisoned by the memorable line from Stefan Zweig: "Brazil is the land of the future, and it always will be."

Brazilians have always resented that cliché. We have equal distaste for the way the world sees Brazil: as a country of frivolous, perpetually beach-bronzed youths, reveling in an eternal Carnival, partying hard with the Girl from Ipanema without ever having to worry about the hangover. Not so, we protest, desperate to be taken seriously. But there *is* some truth to the way the world sees us. Brazil *does* have to overcome an irresponsible, almost clownish streak of character that has sometimes made the country look ungovernable. History offers some clues as to why, but understanding this instability and conquering it are two different things altogether.

I have spent most of my life as a professor of sociology, trying to explain the way complex social forces cause countries to change. In fact, this is the thirtieth book that I have participated in writing. This book, however, is vastly different from the rest. It is not a detailed discussion of my academic career; nor is it an exhaustive policy analysis of my government. That information can be found elsewhere. Rather, this is mostly a book about people. And, somehow, I think the story is best told this way. Looking back on my life, I find it stunning—and more than a bit scary—how individual personalities can have such a profound effect on a country. This is a book about the people, some of them famous, others less so, who have shaped Brazil over the past century.

It tells the story of how Brazil took a step toward its great hope—a shaky step, but a step nonetheless. It is the story of my life, my family, and my country—all of which, through chance or fate, have been intertwined in the most personal and improbable ways. It is the story of my great love for Brazil: a love that has had dizzying ups and downs, but has survived them all. And it is the story of my unlikely journey to the top, which was aided by good fortune, good friends, and, yes, more than my share of lucky accidents along the way.

CHAPTER

2

THE EMPEROR AND THE GENERAL

I N A PALACE nestled in the emerald hills outside Rio, there hangs a lithograph depicting the moment in 1889 when Dom Pedro II, the second and final emperor of Brazil, was ordered into exile. The scene represents a moment of truth, the kind of high-stakes confrontation that can alter a country's history forever.

On the right-hand side of the image, three stern military officers deliver a letter instructing the emperor to leave Brazil within twenty-four hours. To the left stands the royal court, a sea of dismayed faces. And in the middle, slumped in a chair, sits Dom Pedro II. He was a frail, sixty-three-year-old man by the time they finally came for him, a coarse white beard cascading down his chest, his once-striking six-foot-four frame wracked by diabetes and old age. In the lithograph, he appears curiously calm; he limply extends his hand to take the letter, and his handsome, sparkling blue eyes have an air of tired disinterest. He looks every bit like a man resigned to his fate.

Perhaps Dom Pedro II had been expecting a more dignified sendoff. The emperor had ruled for nearly half a century, spanning the lion's share of Brazil's history since it won independence from Portugal in 1822. Dom Pedro II, himself a descendant of the Portuguese royal family, had inherited the Brazilian throne under less than ideal circumstances. His predecessors had enjoyed mixed results in taming the wild young country; his great-grandmother had been known simply as "Mad Maria"; his grandfather, Dom João, fared better as a ruler, but his merits were nearly overshadowed in the public imagination by his notorious appetite for fried chicken, chunks of which he was known to hide in the pockets of his flowing dress uniform. Dom João also had to lock the queen in a convent when she was found to have arranged for the murder of her boyfriend's wife. This kind of scandal rocked the royal court from its inception, eroding authority that was already tenuous in a vast and chaotic country.

It was under this dubious legacy that Dom Pedro II inherited the Brazilian throne at the tender age of five, when his father returned to Portugal to seek the more prestigious throne there. A regency was meant to run the day-to-day affairs of Brazil until Dom Pedro II became an adult, but fate intervened; he was rushed into full governing duties at just fourteen in an attempt to preserve the unity of the country, which was threatened by regional revolts. Having a teenager in charge was hardly a recipe for success for a fragile country that was almost as young as he was, but Dom Pedro II eventually blossomed into an enlightened and accomplished leader, by the standards of his time.*

The emperor spoke or read ten languages, including English, French, Spanish, Greek, Latin, Sanskrit, and Hebrew. One of his favorite diversions was traveling abroad under an alias, wandering into synagogues, and reading aloud from the scrolls. He ordered an astronomical observatory built in his palace, and with his love for opera,

---

*Much more information on the life of Dom Pedro II can be found in the book *Citizen Emperor: Pedro II and the Making of Brazil, 1825–91*, by Roderick J. Barman (Stanford, Calif.: Stanford University Press, 1999).

painting, sculpture, and the theater, he single-handedly sparked a cultural boom in Rio. In his spare time, he amused himself by penning poetry and translating foreign texts, or by sending letters to his numerous friends abroad, who included Louis Pasteur, Victor Hugo, Alexander von Humboldt, and Henry Wadsworth Longfellow. A man of incurable wanderlust, he traveled widely throughout Europe and the United States, helping give rise to the enduring image of the amiable Brazilian abroad.

Dom Pedro's most high-profile voyage was in 1876, when he became the first foreign head of state ever to set foot on U.S. soil. This seems incredible in retrospect, but both Brazil and the United States were still relative pretenders in a world dominated by the monarchies of Europe. In fact, the emperor's royal bloodlines arguably bestowed his country with more prestige than the United States had, according to the backward calculus of the times. He was anything but traditional, however. Dom Pedro II raised more than a few eyebrows when he timed his visit to coincide with the hundredth anniversary of U.S. independence—which, after all, celebrated overthrowing a European monarch to establish a republic. The symbolism could not have been accidental, and it foreshadowed the changes to come.

The centerpiece of the emperor's trip was the Centennial Exposition in Philadelphia. There, Dom Pedro II sought out a young, relatively obscure teacher at the School of the Deaf named Alexander Graham Bell, with whom he had exchanged letters. Trailed by a phalanx of reporters, the emperor strolled up to Bell's exhibition booth, which was buried in a poorly lit corner of the fair. Bell excitedly told Dom Pedro II of his newest invention, which had received scant attention thus far, and asked the emperor to help demonstrate it to the growing mass of curious newspapermen.

The emperor picked up the strange "telephone," then dropped it in astonishment when he heard Bell on the other end, reciting Hamlet's soliloquy: "To be or not to be?"

"My God!" Dom Pedro II exclaimed. "It speaks!"

Thanks to the publicity, Bell's invention became the sensation of the fair.

The seemingly tireless Dom Pedro II made the most of his journey throughout the states, attending a Shakespeare play in New York, visiting Niagara Falls, and taking a steamboat ride down the Mississippi River to New Orleans. He met President Ulysses S. Grant, whom he later privately described as "uncouth." Along the way, the emperor often seemed to behave less like a foreign dignitary than a travel writer; when his train was late leaving New Jersey, for example, he declared: "What an active people—when it is a question of making money! In other respects I find them lazy."

From the United States, the emperor continued on to Europe and the Middle East. He saw the Acropolis bathed in moonlight, sailed down the Nile, and visited his relatives in the royal courts of the Old Continent. "It cannot be said *what* he has not seen and done!" the amazed Queen Victoria of Britain noted in her diary. "He begins the day at six in the morning and remains up late at parties!" Indeed, it would take quite a bit of partying before Dom Pedro II had his fill. He finally returned to Brazil in September 1877—after an astounding eighteen months abroad.

If the length of his trip makes it seem like Dom Pedro II was running away from home, well, that's because he was. During his long journey abroad, the emperor had left his daughter Isabel in charge back in Brazil, instructing her to contact him only in case of an absolute emergency. Upon his return, the emperor turned uncharacteristically churlish, even depressed. He lashed out at his family and lost much of his famous zeal for life. It seemed as if reassuming the daily responsibilities of governing Brazil represented just too enormous a task. He would not be the last man to feel that way.

For all of his personal enlightenment, Dom Pedro II was flummoxed by the same dilemma that would bedevil all of his successors: There were at least two Brazils, of which one was very rich, and one very poor. Beyond the gilded courts and museums of imperial Rio, there laid a vast and untamed land of ramshackle villages and abject rural poverty. Only a tiny percentage of the population knew how to read, and there was little access to medical care. Dom Pedro II certainly recognized the problem; he had spent many of his years in power opening schools, building hospitals, and promoting culture. But despite his efforts, Brazil's misery seemed intractable.

There was, of course, a reason for this. Dom Pedro II had utterly failed to address the main root cause of Brazil's inequality: the institution of slavery. On a personal level, the emperor had a strong distaste for slavery, but he had been unable to summon the political strength to abolish it. Brazil's economy revolved around the sugar *fazendas,* or plantations, of the northeast and the coffee farms around São Paulo and Rio. The plantation owners depended on a steady supply of slave labor to harvest their crops. In terms of economic structure, much of Brazil thus resembled the southern United States, where a civil war had proven necessary to change the status quo. Until a similarly dramatic transformation took place in Brazil, the country was damned to perpetual inequality, no matter how many schools or hospitals the emperor opened in Rio.

Around the time that the emperor returned from his trip, a tenth of the population was still enslaved. More than half of Brazilians were black, most of them freed slaves or their descendants; despite their free status, they routinely suffered from discrimination that kept them stuck at the bottom of the economic ladder.

Discontent over the situation had been brewing for years. Between 1864 and 1870, Brazil had fought a brutal war with its neighbor to the southwest, Paraguay. To address the shortage of "qualified" soldiers, the army had no choice but to fill its ranks by drawing from the slave population, guaranteeing freedom to those who fought. Brazil triumphed, but the costs were enormous. A country that was deeply ashamed of its African population had to send a largely black army to repel a foreign invasion. When the "savage" troops fought with remarkable bravery, skill, and patriotism, the mostly white elite found itself confronted with an even more difficult and soul-searching set of questions: How could Brazil ever become modern if part of the population was enslaved? Would such a nation ever be capable of defending itself? *Was it even really a nation?*

Nowhere were these questions asked more loudly than within a progressive group of young veterans who had just come home from the war. These veterans had seen firsthand how unjust their country really was, and they had no easy answers. They only knew that they did not want to live their lives in a perpetually backward society; they had witnessed the volatility that inequality wrought. Brazil needed to make a great leap forward to catch up with equally young but more modern countries such as Argentina and the United States. In these veterans' minds, there was only one clear solution: to get rid of the emperor.

Thus, Dom Pedro II was stuck between an elite determined to defend its survival and a growing segment of the population that demanded change. Many future Brazilian leaders would find themselves trapped in the same situation, but tragically, the emperor proved unable to resolve these competing claims. On May 13, 1888, when Brazil finally abolished slavery, Dom Pedro II wasn't even personally responsible. Serious health problems, including diabetes and a minor stroke, had forced him to make another, far less glorious trip to Europe to seek medical treatment. In his absence, his daughter Isabel signed the decree of abolition. Under dubiously legitimate circumstances, Brazil became the last country in the Western Hemisphere to free its slaves.

With one of the most overdue decisions of its history up to that point, the empire thus sealed its fate. The hastiness of Isabel's decision enraged the country's powerful plantation owners, who had been Dom Pedro's last remaining pillar of support. Meanwhile, sensing their moment was finally at hand, and unsatisfied with the emperor's gesture, the progressive young veterans began speaking openly of revolt.

By November 1889, Dom Pedro II had returned from his convalescence in Europe, but a conspiracy to oust him was already taking shape. The progressive young officers rallied around Manuel Deodoro da Fonseca, a respected general who had served in the Paraguayan War.

Several of the rebels gathered at the home of Benjamin Constant Botelho de Magalhães, a highly regarded professor at the military school in Rio, to plot the emperor's overthrow.

"The old man should go into exile," declared one of the young officers present. "And if he resists, he should be shot!"

The professor shook his head and admonished the fiery youth. "On the contrary," Benjamin Constant said firmly, "the emperor will have a guarantee of safe passage, and further considerations."

On the evening of November 14, the young officers sprang into action, fearing the government might otherwise catch wind of their plans and attempt preventive arrests. The column of rebels, led by Deodoro, marched out of their barracks and toward the Ministry of War in Rio. At dawn the next morning, rebel troops deployed in a line facing the building. The political head of government, the viscount of Ouro Prêto, arrived at the army headquarters and ordered the soldiers loyal to the emperor to charge outside and capture the rebels' artillery.

"In Paraguay, our soldiers captured artillery in much worse conditions!" the viscount pleaded.

"Yes," replied Floriano Peixoto, adjutant-general of the army. "But there, we had enemies in front of us, and here we are all Brazilians."

The palace doors were thrown open, and Deodoro rode gallantly inside on a horse, accompanied by the young officers. At that moment, all resistance collapsed.

As all this transpired, an oblivious Dom Pedro II was enjoying a quiet day at his palace outside Rio. In the morning, he had received an urgent telegram from Ouro Prêto describing the standoff and pleading for instructions on how to act. The emperor read the message calmly, folded it up, put it in his pocket, and proceeded as if nothing had happened. After a morning mass to commemorate the anniversary of his sister's death, Dom Pedro II received a second telegram: The rebels had successfully taken over the military school, and Deodoro had declared a new cabinet, effectively establishing a new government.

This was finally enough to spur the emperor into action—of a kind.

Dom Pedro II boarded his personal train, which chugged down the mountain to Rio. There he was met by the imperial coach, drawn by six horses, which whisked him unimpeded through the capital's streets to his palace. Following an afternoon of busy but ultimately ineffectual meetings, the emperor's family joined him, and they all sat down for a leisurely dinner, brought in from a nearby hotel. When the meal ended, the emperor dispatched a messenger to Deodoro to open negotiations. Then, he retired to bed.

At seven in the morning, newspapers arrived at the palace reporting that a new republic had been formed. Cavalry detachments and infantry patrols were placed at every door of Dom Pedro's palace. All access was forbidden, and the members of the imperial family found themselves prisoners in their home. Dom Pedro II woke up late and quietly read his scientific journals. At three o'clock in the afternoon on November 18, 1889, three officers entered the palace and presented a message ordering the emperor and his family to leave.

Upon hearing the ultimatum, Dom Pedro II glumly replied: "I am leaving and I am leaving now." With that, Brazil's imperial era was over and its rebirth as a republic guaranteed.

That is the moment captured by the aforementioned lithograph that hangs in the palace outside Rio. On the frame, a caption lists the names of the three officers who are depicted in the image delivering the message to the emperor. One was a major named Solon Ribeiro. Another was a young lieutenant, Sebastião Bandeira. The third officer was the same fiery young man who, as the revolt was being planned, had hotly urged the execution of the emperor. His name was Joaquim Ignácio Batista Cardoso—my grandfather.

Joaquim Ignácio was born in 1860 in Goiás, a hardscrabble gold-rush town and provincial capital in the dusty Brazilian interior, to a family that was no stranger to palace intrigue. His father, Felicíssimo do Espirito Santo Cardoso, was a captain in the National Guard who had been banished to the far western reaches of the province when the politics in the city had taken an unfavorable turn. In this desolate savanna, Felicíssimo's job was to teach basic reading skills to Indians who had been recently converted to Catholicism—virtuous work, perhaps, but not a plum assignment. By the time his son was born, the political winds had shifted again, and the Cardoso family was back in power in the capital, which was about 300 kilometers west of modern-day Brasília. Felicíssimo was appointed the governor of the province, and he dedicated much of his life to making sure his children would become part of the Brazilian elite for good.

That meant military school. For families who were on the cusp of prominence, but who couldn't quite afford to send their children to college to study law or medicine, the army offered the best chance for social ascendancy. Joaquim Ignácio showed great promise early in life—he was articulate and intellectually curious, and by age sixteen he was giving Latin classes to other students. He was tall, agile, solidly built, and brilliantly skilled on a horse: in other words, a natural candidate for the army. He left Goiás for Rio in 1881 to begin preparatory classes for entry into the military academy at Praia Vermelha, or "Red Beach," on the edge of the city.

Rio must have seemed like an oasis of modernity compared to Goiás, but even by those relative standards, the *cidade maravilhosa,* or "Marvelous City," was still very much a work in progress. To get to the school from downtown, one had to ride a streetcar that was pulled down Rua do Ouvidor by a team of donkeys. The final stop came in front of Rua da Passagem, where rowboats awaited to take professors and officers further down the shore to the academy. Students, however, had to go by foot on a long, rustic path on the edge of Praia da Saudade. Once they arrived, the amenities didn't exactly improve— there wasn't a whole lot to do besides train and study. People like my grandfather who didn't have family or friends in Rio entertained themselves on weekends by climbing the Sugar Loaf Mountain, or riding their horses to Copacabana Beach, which was a far cry from the high-rise condominiums and hotels of the modern day. Rather, on the empty stretch of sand, the students could pick wild cashews and other fruits, or rent a boat and go fishing in the bay. On Saturday afternoons the academy hosted the *caroço,* a kind of improvised dance in which the students (all males) danced with each other in pairs.

If the social life wasn't always thrilling, the academic life certainly was. The military school indoctrinated its students in a new philosophy known as positivism, which elevated science above religion as a way of seeing the world. This scheme of values, developed by the French philosopher Auguste Comte, did not glorify poverty in the same way that Catholicism did, instead emphasizing the virtues of order and progress. These young students dreamed of turning Brazil into a positivist utopia, a perfect society made up of philosophers and historians, with the military in charge. Their vision was at once authoritarian and egalitarian; they believed that only a strong state could guarantee the social equality that had thus far escaped Brazil.

As an outsider among the entrenched Rio elite, Joaquim Ignácio already possessed a natural egalitarian streak. But his teachings at the academy inflamed his passions, and he became a fervent preacher of the cause. Believing his long last name too pretentious for this brand-new era, my grandfather dropped "Espirito Santo" from his last name and shortened it to simply "Cardoso." He also became a dedicated disciple of one of positivism's main proponents at the university, the professor Benjamin Constant—and the two formed a strong bond that would, years later, lead to my grandfather's participation in the coup.

Despite his studies and the formidable obstacles, Joaquim Ignácio managed to marry up. His fifteen-year-old bride, Leonídia Fernandes (nicknamed Linda), was the daughter of a Portuguese business magnate who earned a small fortune paving the streets of Rio. She had grown up attending glamorous royal balls, and her family was quite close to the emperor's court. However, wealth and privilege could not guarantee everything in rough-and-tumble nineteenth-century Brazil;

Leonídia would eventually give birth to sixteen children, only nine of whom survived into adulthood. This was not entirely unusual back then, even for the families of the elite. Tropical diseases and numerous other scourges claimed lives indiscriminately. It was still, by any measure, an enormously difficult country to live in.

My grandmother found out just how difficult around 1886, just a few years before the emperor was ousted, when she made the first trip of her young life outside Rio. My grandfather took her to Goiás to meet his family. They began their journey by boarding a train from Rio to São Paulo—that was the easy part. Then came a 700-mile trip on horseback across the savanna to Goiás, which probably took about a month. They would have traveled with servants; nobody well-off would dream of making such a journey alone. But I imagine that a month on a horse is still a month on a horse, no matter how many servants rode with them. By the time she arrived in Goiás, she was exhausted and eager for the luxury she believed awaited her in the provincial capital, where her father-in-law was still the governor.

She was more than a little disappointed. The governor's palace was the only building in the entire province with a real floor; everywhere else just had dirt. Her in-laws spent their days smoking and making candles to use later that night. There were no sewers, not even running water. Servants carried water back and forth. For bodily needs, there were pots, which the servants also took away. People would frequently spit on the dirt floor and rub their foot over the stain until it disappeared. To the rich girl from Rio, Goiás must have seemed like a different planet.

The British writer Peter Fleming visited the interior a half century later and chronicled his travels in the book *Brazilian Adventure*. Apparently, little had changed, and he would likely have sympathized with my grandmother. He wrote:

> There is nothing at all to do in Goiás. . . . There are no trams, no skyscrapers, and the cinema functions once a week. The gables are gar-

goyled with vultures, and small wild boys on small wild ponies clatter inconsequently over the cobbles, with huge spurs strapped on their bare feet. . . . All day long the women sit at their windows and stare, in an ardent and provocative manner, at the empty street. All day long the men, with the air of philosophers in training, sit on little chairs outside the front doors, wearing straw hats. . . . Occasionally one of them gets up and goes indoors, to lie down. Nothing else happens.

My grandparents spent an entire year in Goiás. For my grandmother it must have been a very, very long year. In reality, life was a bit better than Fleming presented it—the elite, of vaguely European origin, had created an improbably vibrant cultural life in the small frontier town, complete with Baroque music, renowned painters and sculptors, and literary circles. Nevertheless, when my grandmother became pregnant, she steadfastly refused to have their first child in Goiás. She was quite far along in her pregnancy by the time they made the arduous trip back to Rio. It was probably just as well. Her husband had a coup to plan.

When my grandfather and the other officers came for him, Dom Pedro II was too exhausted to put up a fight. He had dedicated his life to the dream of a better Brazil, an idea that inspired the men who now stood before him, but the emperor realized that his time was up. Any effort to cling to power would only provoke another of the bloody confrontations that had so plagued Brazil's young history. Instead, the emperor dedicated what time he had left to penning one last love letter to his country. He agreed to relinquish control of Brazil to Deodoro and his young officers, amicably adding that there were no hard feelings. "In thus departing," he wrote, "I, in common with all the members of my family, will conserve for Brazil the most heartfelt memories, with ardent wishes for its greatness and prosperity."

The message was sincere. But the emperor also knew perfectly well the scale of the task that awaited whoever dared to try and govern Brazil after him. He kept his mouth shut about it until he was boarding the boat to Europe. Only then did he turn to his military escorts and permit himself a moment of sincerity: "You are off your heads," he told them, and with that he took his leave.

Deodoro, who was quickly declared president of Brazil, would have done well to heed the emperor's words. Much to the dismay of my grandfather and the other young officers who had pushed for change, the Republic was an instant disaster. Within two years, Deodoro was stuck in a deadlocked confrontation with Congress. He tried to grant himself dictatorial powers, and the country teetered on the verge of chaos. Some among the Brazilian elite began whispering about a restoration of the monarchy.

As bad as things had been for Brazil, those two years were even worse for Dom Pedro II and the deposed royal family. Within a month of their arrival in Europe, his wife of fifty years passed away, sickened by the tough transatlantic journey—and, more than likely, a certain amount of heartbreak as well. Queen Victoria confided to her journal that she was "greatly shocked" to hear of the empress's death. "The Revolution doubtless killed her. It is too sad," the queen wrote.

With his pension revoked, Dom Pedro II skipped from one hotel to another in France and ran up debts he knew he could never repay. His diabetes often rendered him too weak to walk, and he slept fitfully at night. He was depressed, and for the first time in what had long been a charmed life, he was often alone. He ruminated in his diary that he could talk only with his books, and even that pleasure was soon deprived from him as diabetes robbed him of his vision as well. By the time a Paris newspaper caught up with him to sound out the possibilities of returning to Brazil, Dom Pedro II was, perhaps for the first time in his life, a bitter man—although he did his best to hide it.

"During what is now a long life," he told the French reporter, "I have applied all my forces and all my devotion to assuring the progress and the prosperity of my people. It seems that I have not succeeded!

"I am termed down there the philosopher emperor, which is a consolation for everything! This philosophy lessens, in reality, the pain which I feel at seeing myself thus misunderstood by those whom I would consider to be my children; but nothing will ever console me if I see an entire people become the victim of its own mistakes."

He concluded, "I would be sufficiently repaid if I might sleep my last sleep in my well-beloved country."

It was not to be. In late November 1891, on a day trip outside Paris, Dom Pedro II felt a chill as he left a heated building. He was initially diagnosed with the flu, but the infection spread to his lungs and became pneumonia. Nineteenth-century medicine had no answer for this, especially not for a diabetic. His fever spiked to nearly 106 degrees Fahrenheit, and his remaining family gathered by his bedside. Just before Dom Pedro II passed away at thirty-five minutes past midnight on December 5, 1891, it is said that he muttered something about Brazil.

Thirty years would pass before the emperor's body was allowed to return to his beloved country.

Once, on a visit to Paris as president, I met the great-granddaughter of Dom Pedro II. She was very old by the time I saw her. Her grandfather was the Count d'Eu, of the family Orleans, which would have made her part of the French royal family—if such a thing still existed. I remember she had kind eyes and was still able to speak Portuguese, although with a strong French accent. "My family is very happy," she told me, sweetly.

When the smoke cleared after revolts in Brazil, life often went on much as before. Even when Brazil won its independence from Portugal, it was a member of the Portuguese royal family who became Brazil's first emperor—such seamless continuity would be impossible to imagine in most other countries, but this was the Brazilian way. For all of the violent conspiracies that Brazil endured over the years, very little of substance ever actually changed at the top. When the dead were finally counted, the elite classes were always still in charge—a different faction of the elite, perhaps, but the elite nonetheless. Sins in politics tended to be forgiven quite quickly, and the status quo returned. Dom Pedro II had surely known this. My grandfather, who had his own hopes and dreams, would soon discover the same frustration the hard way.

By 1891, my grandfather was the *ajudante-de-ordens* to President Floriano Peixoto. It was a position of considerable influence, a mix of chief aide, personal secretary, and political adviser, and my grandfather and his young family lived in the presidential palace, where they could be kept close to power. When the navy took up arms against Floriano that year, the president and his aides gathered their families on the beach and watched, enraptured, as gunboats shelled forts loyal to the government on the other side of the Guanabara Bay. My father, then a toddler, later remembered standing in the surf, witnessing the loud booms and the clouds of smoke that peppered the blue horizon.

The naval revolt against Floriano, like so many others, was eventually put down. But establishing the new Republic's authority over a deeply diverse and often anarchic country would prove to be a massive chore, one that would consume much of my grandfather's life. In some quarters of Brazil, powerful landowners or military officers took up arms to resist the federal dictums from Rio; they, however, could be dealt with rather straightforwardly. Far more problematic were the vast swathes of the country where people simply shrugged.

A beautiful Portuguese word was used to describe the popular reaction to the new Republic—Aristides Lobo, a journalist, said that the masses heard the news *bestificados*. That is, they reacted "like beasts," thoroughly unable to process how this change would impact their lives.

And, usually, it didn't. Most Brazilians lived their lives weeks or even months distant from the capital, reachable only over shoddy jungle roads or rough seas. It took years for some people to hear about the coup that deposed Dom Pedro II. This was an era before radio, before any kind of mass communication, and word of the Republic was received in far-flung provinces as little more than a vague rumor.

In Goiás and other small cities and towns, the great landowning families were able to sustain their centuries-old monopoly over political control while offering no resistance at all. My grandfather received a sardonic letter to that effect from his father, by then no longer governor, shortly after the emperor was ousted. "You all created the Republic, but nothing has changed," the letter said. "Here, just like before, the Caiado de Castro family continues to be in charge."

The same was true in Manaus, the biggest city in Brazil's Amazon region, where my mother grew up. Manaus was then in the midst of a boom fueled by rubber exports, over which Brazil enjoyed a global monopoly at the beginning of the twentieth century. The city seized on the sudden bonanza and transformed itself into an oasis in the middle of the jungle, fully independent from Rio. Fabulously wealthy rubber barons financed the construction of the Teatro Amazonas, a marvelous opera house with gold-leaf ceilings and marble-tiled floors, designed after La Scala in Milan. The extremely wealthy lived in European-style mansions and imported their clothes and wine directly from Paris or Lisbon, which in practical terms, because of the Amazon, which could be traveled by boat, were then closer to Manaus than Rio was. In such places, government buildings often flew the local state flag, while the yellow, blue, and green Brazilian flag was nowhere to be found. Orders from Rio did not need to be openly defied—they could simply be ignored.

Meanwhile, other *caudilhos,* or regional strongmen, sensed the fragility of the Republic and saw an opportunity to grab power. In 1894, my grandfather was dispatched to help put down a long and bloody civil war in Rio Grande do Sul, a limitless expanse of grassy plains bordering Uruguay where cattle and *gaúcho* cowboys roamed with equal freedom. He spent months crisscrossing the area by horseback, battling a rebel army of 3,000 men with plans to march on São Paulo. While there, my grandfather took orders from General Manoel do Nascimento Vargas, whose son Getúlio would become president of Brazil almost four decades later. While my grandfather and the elder Vargas rode about the plains, the rest of the young Cardoso family took up residence in the nearby town of Porto Alegre, living in constant terror they would be found by the rebel army, which was rumored to be composed of *degoladores,* ranchhands cum assassins-for-hire who killed their human prey just like their sheep—with a swipe of the machete to the throat. My father remembered that, when he was a child, the family would blockade the front door every night with dressers and other pieces of furniture to keep the invaders out.

Building a country required more than force. My grandfather never forgot the idealism that had inspired the Republic in the first place, or the positivist motto of "Order and Progress" that the young officers had emblazoned on Brazil's new flag. He realized that his country would prosper only under a more educated, less hierarchical society, based on the rule of law and firmly controlled from Rio. When he was posted to São Paulo, he helped organize the state's first division of military police. When he was made a general, he commanded the northeastern state of Pernambuco, where he created the local league against illiteracy. The league created twenty-two schools, one of which still bears his name, Joaquim Ignácio Cardoso. To this day, most people in the region have no idea that he was my grandfather. Later, in the 1950s, my grandfather would be honored with a statue in a public park in Goiás. There is also a statue of him in Rio.

As they grew into old men, however, my grandfather and many other founders of the Republic feared they would never live to realize their vision for Brazil. By then they knew their coup had only replaced one oligarchy with another. Under the Republic, Brazil was almost as plagued by inequality as it had been under Dom Pedro II.

Hope followed by disappointment is a particularly Brazilian cycle, but the rapid, unexpected changes that rocked the Republic in the early twentieth century would have ruined even the best-laid plans. Roughly 5 million immigrants entered Brazil between 1820 and 1930, with by far the largest influx arriving around the turn of the century. About a third of them were from Italy, and another third from Portugal; the rest hailed from places as diverse as Spain, Germany, Japan, Ukraine, Russia, and Lebanon. Most of the newcomers took jobs that had been occupied by the recently emancipated slaves, primarily working on coffee farms in and around São Paulo. They were treated little better than their predecessors had been, running up huge debts and living worse than they had in their home countries. As disease ran rife, boats leaving Europe for the more temperate and prosperous destination of Argentina began advertising "no stops in Brazil." The economy soured as the rubber boom turned to bust, and the Republic was burdened by heavy debts, budget deficits, plummeting exports, and the lowest exchange rates in three decades. In economic terms, Brazil was little closer to an egalitarian society than it had been under the emperor.

Meanwhile, to quote the historian E. Bradford Burns, "democracy under the Old Republic played as farce." The presidency alternated between leaders from just two states, São Paulo and Minas Gerais, after they formed a power duopoly that came to be cynically known as *café com leite,* or "coffee with milk," which the two states produced, respectively. Because of wealth and literacy requirements, fewer than 3 percent of the adult population was eligible to vote in elections. Not even a third of Brazilians older than fifteen knew how to read. Worse, officials showed a wanton disregard for the "egalitarian" principles that the leaders of the coup had claimed to represent. One particularly outrageous example occurred in 1904, when a street demonstration against compulsory vaccination in Rio was bombarded by artillery. More than 300 of the detainees were deported, without any judicial proceedings, to a distant camp in the Amazon.

So much for "Order and Progress." By the 1920s, a sense of depression washed over Brazil as many intellectuals realized their country lagged behind other, more enlightened places in the hemisphere. The problem was unchanged: Brazil's elite had displayed an appalling unwillingness to assimilate those at the bottom rungs of society. Those at the top continued to live the good life, failing to commit money to the education, health care, and land reform that would produce a more equal nation. Until this imbalance was addressed, neither stability nor progress would be possible. Unfortunately, another seventy years would pass before the lesson would be properly learned.

In the meantime, something unusual happened. Already well into old age, and endowed with the comfortable rank of general, my grandfather became a rebel one last time.

At an army fort on the tip of Copacabana Beach in Rio, a barracks revolt broke out in July 1922. The culprits, as they had been a generation before, hailed from a young group of military officers. These men, popularly known as the *tenentes,* or lieutenants, were not just unified by formal rank—they would come to represent an important new ideological current within Brazilian politics. In broad terms, they shared the ideas that the Republic's founders had promoted a generation before: the hope for a more just society, through their enlightened, although authoritarian, rule.

Their first foray into armed resistance was an unmitigated disaster. Other units throughout Rio were supposed to join the rebellion, but they lost their nerve at the last moment. The rebels in the fort at Copacabana got off only a few ineffectual cannon shots before they were quickly surrounded by troops loyal to the Republic. Eighteen of the rebels then emerged from the bombarded fort, guns blazing, and bravely marched down the beach. Most of them were quickly shot dead.

My grandfather was one of only two Brazilian generals who supported the tenentes. With a place in history already assured, he took a tremendous risk. He was fully aware the revolt would fail. But he was so heartbroken by the state of the Republic that he took up arms anyway. At the agreed-upon hour of the doomed uprising at the fort at Copacabana, my grandfather, unlike most other officers, kept his word. He took a tram across town to the Vila Militar, home of several regiments' residences and barracks, with the intent of rallying support for the tenentes' cause. On his way there, he was arrested. The government then ordered General Joaquim Ignácio Cardoso into indefinite solitary confinement on a boat moored in Guanabara Bay.

Dozens of other rebels were also jailed, including my father, who was by then a young officer. But putting these men in prison together was one of the worst decisions the Republic ever made. For most of the tenentes, their incarceration offered an excellent if squalid opportunity to spend time together and to bond. Being military officers, they even enjoyed certain privileges. There is an old photo from the era that shows several of the tenentes, my father among them, gathered around a piano, singing songs—while still, theoretically at least, in jail. After a few weeks, all of the young lieutenants were released. Some of them were punished with distant postings in the Amazon or in the far west. But that was as severe as it got.

The tenentes would be back. In 1924, they mounted another revolt, and they also led other, more imaginative forms of resistance to the decaying Republic in the years that followed that first attempt. The most spectacular example was the so-called Prestes Column, a band of tenentes who undertook a 24,000-kilometer, three-year march through the interior of southern and western Brazil. Their primary goal was to thumb their noses at state and federal authorities by eluding capture during that entire time. They thus demonstrated the weakness (and often nonexistence) of government authority in large parts of the country, and the rebels earned a revered place in the public imagination. Although the revolt might have been a spectacular short-term failure, it set events in motion that would soon culminate in Brazil's most dramatic revolution.

In fact, after the gunfire halted on Copacabana Beach, there would be only one other casualty caused by the tenentes' uprising. Indignant that his distinguished career as a servant of the Republic had seemingly ended in prison, my grandfather spent most of his time in captivity standing up, performing his own eccentric, silent protest. He refused to walk on the ship's deck for exercise, adhering to a strict military protocol stipulating that officers could walk only in the company of someone of equal or superior rank. I suppose that his stubbornness resulted from the great anger and frustration he must have felt.

Whatever the reason, he developed a blood circulation problem in his legs that plagued him even after his release from jail a few months later. Like the emperor, my grandfather might have recovered from his physical ailment, were it not for the broken heart he suffered at the hands of Brazil. Joaquim Ignácio Batista Cardoso died the following year, disappointed and disillusioned with a country he felt had betrayed him.

CHAPTER

3

ALL BUBBLES MUST BURST

I WAS BORN in my grandmother's house in Rio de Janeiro on June 18, 1931, into a world that was rapidly collapsing. The city still clung to its dreams of tropical splendor and middle-class insularity, and long, breezy afternoons were spent at cafés or in the surf. When I was very young, I took gym classes on Copacabana Beach, and my friends and I would run and play up the green mountains dramatically jutting up from the city, which were still free of the *favelas,* or shantytowns, that have climbed their slopes ever since. Back then, the problems that haunted Brazil beyond the Sugar Loaf Mountain remained just a rumor to many of Rio's residents. It was an idyllic, slightly delusional existence, but reality would come barging into our lives soon enough.

In the meantime, the middle class happily preoccupied itself with a vibrant cultural life. Rio had always looked to Paris as its guiding light, and its citizens engaged in a painstaking, often amusing imitation of the Old Continent. When my aunt took my sister and me to the opera during Rio's tropical "winter," she and the other women insisted on donning ostentatious fur coats. They would nearly sweat to death, of course, because the temperature only rarely dipped below 60 degrees Fahrenheit—a reality accented by the fact that, during the summer, the coats were stored in specially made icehouses to keep them from disintegrating in the tropical heat. Rio was not quite Paris, but that didn't stop it from trying.

Just beneath the surface, however, Rio was starting to suffer the same problems as the rest of Brazil. The Great Depression broke the backbone of the Brazilian economy, sending the global price of coffee plummeting by 65 percent. At first, farmers elected not to sell their crop at such abysmal prices, and by 1930, more than 26 million sacks of coffee laid untouched in Brazilian warehouses, a staggering amount equivalent to the entire world's consumption the year before.

While the powerful landowners waited in relative comfort for a recovery that never came, hordes of suddenly desperate, jobless souls roamed Rio's streets. Widespread hunger in rural areas fed Brazil's first great wave of urbanization as peasants sought refuge in the cities. But they found little relief in a country that lacked any semblance of a safety net and was unwilling to help new arrivals become part of a productive society. In the 1930s, more than half the adult population still did not even know how to sign their names.

This reality surrounded me at all times, but I have to admit that I first understood poverty from books. I remember that John Steinbeck's *The Grapes of Wrath* had a particularly deep impact on me. This might seem shocking—that a Brazilian who grew up in Depression-era Rio needed to acquaint himself with poverty through a tale about California, told by an author from the United States, no less. But it is the truth. I knew there was poverty in Brazil—but to feel it, to really understand it, was very difficult. To draw a modern-day, North American parallel, a privileged child on Manhattan's Upper West Side might be aware of poverty just a few blocks away in Harlem, but does he know what hunger really feels like? Probably not. For me, literature was the best available portal into this world. We also had marvelous Brazilian authors, such as Jorge Amado, José Lins do Rego, and Graciliano Ramos, whose books illustrated the hardscrabble life of hunger, droughts, and revolts in the arid northeastern plains of Brazil. Their vivid accounts of rural poverty were instrumental in fostering a social awareness, however incipient and generalized, in a generation of young people like myself.

Of course, as I grew older and more aware of my surroundings, the legacies of Brazilian poverty started materializing before my eyes, and their links with the past became obvious to me. Some of the signs had been there all along. In my parents' house, there was a woman named Alzira. She was the daughter of my great-grandfather's former slave. It is difficult to describe the role she played in our home. She was more of a nanny than a servant. She lived with us, almost like a member of the family, but not quite.

The relationship between us was complex, straddling two very different eras in Brazilian history. It embarrasses me a great deal to admit this, but when I was very young, and I wanted Alzira to get me something to drink, for example, I would loudly declare, "I want water!" I would not look at her, or anyone, as I said this. I simply expected that she would be present and that she would hear me and comply. That was how things were done back then. On the other hand, Alzira often sat at the dinner table and ate with us, as an equal. In some houses, this would not have been allowed. But in our family's, it was.

I was the eldest child, and under the tutelage of my mother and grandmother, I learned to read by the time I was three years old. Later, I had a private French tutor. It was, in sum, a perfect upper-middle-class existence. But as I grew older and started paying attention to the conversations at the dinner table, I began to realize that a much harsher, more dangerous world lurked just beyond our front door.

A year before I was born, Brazil had finally succumbed to the revolution that my grandfather had yearned for. The tenentes had failed in

1922 and 1924 to bend the country to their vision, but their moment finally arrived in 1930, when the Old Republic brazenly attempted to rig a presidential election. The outraged lieutenants joined forces with the apparent loser of the vote, Getúlio Vargas. A band of his supporters rode triumphantly into Rio, hitched their horses to a monument in the middle of downtown, and declared Getúlio the president of Brazil. This dramatic bit of gaúcho showmanship was the boldest challenge yet to the frail and discredited power elite. After a halfhearted flurry of skirmishes, President Washington Luís glumly declared that he had no desire to start a civil war, and off into exile he went. The old Republic was over.

Getúlio filled the ranks of his government with the tenentes and their sympathizers, among them my father, who left our house every morning for his job at the war ministry to guard against the constant threat of new revolts. After the infamous palace siege at the hands of the integralistas, when my father hurried off to Rio in the middle of the night, I immersed myself in the adult world—the world of politics, violence, and Getúlio Vargas—determined to anticipate the next threat to my father's existence. There would certainly be no shortage of palace intrigue in the years to come.

Our dinner table was a staging ground for all the great debates that divided Brazil. A steady stream of intellectuals and politicians held court in our family home. They allowed me to sit in and participate as they argued the future of the country into the early morning hours, drinking coffee after coffee. I liked our discussions, and I also discovered that I immensely enjoyed winning debates. I triumphed in a fair share of them with some of Brazil's greatest intellects—at least, in my seven-year-old mind, I did. In retrospect, it is far more likely that they just grew weary of bantering back and forth with such a precocious little boy. In the end, my father would just smile, with a certain measure of pride, and gently urge me to go to bed.

My father, General Leônidas Cardoso, was a fantastic storyteller, a handsome and dignified Renaissance man who held the center of attention at any dinner table. Refined and soft-spoken, liberal and tolerant, he was the antithesis of the commonly held stereotype of the brutish Latin American soldier. He never wore his military uniform at home, and he did not encourage me to follow him into a career in the armed forces. Instead, he only expected his children to be as intellectually curious as he was—and that was a challenge in itself. Being an officer in those days was not a full-time job, so my father earned his law degree and became a practicing lawyer. He wrote political columns for the newspapers in Rio. He also briefly attended medical school, apparently just for the hell of it. Drawing on this knowledge, every winter he gave my siblings and me injections of codfish oil, believing it would protect us from sickness.

By the time I was born, my father had the air of a man who had lived a full, sometimes contentious life, and he took great joy in aspects of domestic life that his peers might have considered mundane. He often helped my mother clean the house, which was absolutely scandalous in an era when it was considered inappropriate for men to so much as enter the kitchen. I think his long bachelorhood, spent in postings all over Brazil, must have mellowed him a bit; he had not married until age forty-four. Because of his age, he often seemed more like a grandfather figure, and he was wonderful with children. With his own hands, he made us kites and spinning tops that we shared with other kids in the neighborhood. My childhood friends absolutely adored him. He went by the somewhat whimsical nickname of *Sapo,* or "Frog," derived from his birth in the southern state of Paraná, where frogs are quite literally everywhere in the spring. I loved and revered my father; his influence on me was immeasurable.

His legendary charm had been born partially out of necessity, a product of troubled times. He had been imprisoned twice during revolts against the Old Republic in the 1920s. In both cases, he developed a good rapport with his jailkeepers, which allowed him to communicate with the other prisoners, including his brother. My father's good-natured demeanor, plus Brazil's rapidly emerging capacity for forgiveness, meant that his punishment was always light. After the 1924 revolt, he was removed from Rio and posted to Óbidos, in the northern state of Pará. From there, they sent him to the Amazon city of Manaus, where he met my mother. He often teased her that she was his punishment for having been a rebel.

Like most jovial men close to power, my father could also turn deadly serious at the drop of a hat. He distrusted big business, financial markets, or any kind of profiteering, as he believed that money corrupted people. He had no tolerance whatsoever for idiots, and if a dinner conversation turned overbearing or dull, he would turn his bad ear toward whoever was droning on. My father never drank, and he exercised regularly, believing that a healthy body equaled a healthy mind. An agnostic in an overwhelmingly Catholic country, he could be a bit defensive when the topic turned to religion. Whatever gulf existed in his spiritual life he filled by reading voraciously. I still have some of his books. He enthusiastically consumed French literature, enjoying authors such as Victor Hugo and Anatole France. He also devoured philosophers such as Herbert Spencer, a principal proponent of the theory of evolution, and Auguste Comte, the father of the positivist creed the tenentes held so dear. Politically, he took after my grandfather, passionately believing in the construction of a strong, centralized state that existed to do good for Brazil.

My father was an intelligent man, but I think my mother, Nayde, was even smarter. She was fiercely independent; in an era before feminism, she was determined to live life her own way. She was much more perceptive than my father was about other people's intentions; she could always tell the good from the bad. Later on, when my father went into politics, my mother was the driving force. At one political meeting, when another politician was speaking ill of my father, she went after him, swinging an umbrella. Most of the time, luckily, she was a bit more reserved, although she always wore her emotions on her sleeve. She could not read French, but she still pored over translations of romance novels that were fashionable during the era. Even by today's exacting standards, my mother was a modern and formidable woman.

Even under my parents' enlightened watch, however, a midnight coffee at the Cardoso house could still turn ugly. As I approached my teenage years, scars still ran deep in our family over a revolt that had transpired in 1932, when Paulistas took up arms against the federal government, afraid their region was losing influence in the inner circles of Rio and that Getúlio was taking Brazil ever more distant from democracy. This kind of regional revolt is almost impossible to comprehend in the modern era, but it shows just how tenuous federal power remained in Brazil deep into the twentieth century. Local factories in São Paulo produced their own tanks, and rich housewives sold jewelry to fund the rebellion. Combat raged for three months, and the death toll ran into the thousands. Families were torn apart, including our own. Some of my cousins took up arms in sympathy with São Paulo, and my great-uncle, the war minister, found himself in the awkward position of having to imprison a few of his relatives. As a result, the extended Cardoso family splintered for good. Some family members never spoke to each other again.

Other families close to us suffered much more serious consequences from the constant turmoil. In 1935, the Communist Party mounted an armed revolt against Getúlio, marking the first time in the Western Hemisphere that Communists directly funded by Moscow attempted the violent overthrow of a government. The leader of the coup was Luís Carlos Prestes, who a decade before had been the hero of the eponymous Prestes Column, the group of tenentes who had tormented the Old Republic and evaded authorities with their long march through the countryside. Prestes was an old friend of my father's, although their ideologies had diverged by the 1930s, when Prestes went into exile in the Soviet Union. When Prestes decided to return to Brazil, determined to spread Stalinism in South America, he was assigned a beautiful female bodyguard named Olga Benário, a German Communist Jew. On the boat sailing for Brazil, they fell in love. When the revolt failed, Prestes was sent to prison. Getúlio's police captured Olga and deported her to Nazi Germany, where she was killed in a gas chamber in a concentration camp.

As I heard such stories, and the names of Hitler and Mussolini began to echo in the ears of the world, I began to wonder what kind of man my father was charged with defending. But, although Getúlio was capable of shocking brutality, he preferred to co-opt his enemies and rule through alliances rather than terror. That, more than anything, allowed him to stay in power for fifteen years, from 1930 to 1945.

By that point in Brazilian history, the threat of violence colored every decision in political life. No one wanted to see a repetition of incidents such as the Canudos Massacre or the regional wars and revolts. The country's leaders' priority was to avoid such ignominious events. Thus, a penchant for compromise became perhaps the most glorified and necessary trait among Brazilian politicians. Getúlio was probably the first president to appreciate this and to implement consensus-building as the main philosophy of his government. With the two extremes of communism and fascism locked in a death struggle, each attempting coups against him at different times, Getúlio was able to stick around by navigating squarely down the middle.

Like all dictators, he knew how to play the good guy. Short, handsome, and somewhat plump, always with a cigar in hand, Getúlio spoke with a soft, squeaky voice that would have suited a professor better than a strongman. The historian Thomas Skidmore has described him as "about as uncharismatic a dictator the world is likely to see," and in a traditional sense, this was true. But Getúlio was enormously appealing in his own way. He dressed splendidly, always in a blazer and a hat, even in the tropical heat. People saw him as very kind and very competent, the sort of sober father figure they wanted running a tumultuous country.

Behind the benevolent public façade, however, resided a much darker, more anxious man. Since so many members of my family worked in his government, our dinner table buzzed with talk of

Getúlio's hidden fears and eccentricities. Those who knew him best said Getúlio became surprisingly reserved when the spotlight dimmed, mistrusting even his closest circle of advisers. He seemed lonely, perhaps even depressed. He was a gaúcho, from a family of ranchers, and this made him somewhat of an outsider in Rio's high society, which never really accepted him. Given the circumstances, one could forgive Getúlio for seeing conspiracies around every corner; his diary was a veritable laundry list of supposed military putsches seeking to oust him from power. Many of them were imagined, but many others were true.

To fight off the plotters, Getúlio also often relied on naked nationalism. As a small child, I remember attending a giant parade to support the government. It was called "Patriotism Day." My entire school was there in a plaza in Rio, and we sang songs about the greatness of Brazil. Flags hung from the buildings. Getúlio and his top aides stood on a giant stage and waved as the children paraded below. He employed similar tactics with other sections of society; once a year on Labor Day, thousands of factory workers would gather in a soccer stadium to hear Getúlio give a speech.

This was part of a greater change—the twentieth century saw massive growth in Brazil's economy. Between 1900 and 1982, only Japan's economy grew at a faster pace than Brazil's. The fallout from the Depression waned rather quickly, and workers streamed into the cities to fill new jobs. Their children would become part of an expanding middle class and began to hunger for a political voice to accompany their newfound wealth. Industry expanded at a torrid pace once the Depression ended, and factory output more than doubled during the 1930s. Getúlio realized that, by co-opting the new urban working classes, he could gain a powerful, up-and-coming ally and stoke the engine of economic growth.

Although Getúlio may not have always governed in their best interest, he was at least smart enough to acknowledge the workers' presence—and that was largely enough. For the first time in Brazil, a labor ministry was created. State policy was guided by a new form of social organization, called "corporatism," that sought to facilitate the adoption of modern-day capitalism while avoiding both a completely laissez-faire approach and total state direction. Syndicates were established to represent certain economic sectors for both workers and business, and it was the government's role to negotiate disputes between competing syndicates. Put a different way, the state was expected to solve all economic problems—a legacy that would be no small headache for future leaders down the road.

Ultimately, the comparisons to Mussolini and Hitler were inaccurate. Certainly, Getúlio was an autocrat, and his government was capable of deploying an intolerable degree of torture, imprisonment, and censorship to stifle its opponents. He closed Congress in 1937, and he spoke gleefully of the "decadence of liberal and individualistic democracy." But to put Getúlio in the same league as the material authors of World War II would be disingenuous. Even though the military was his power base, specifically the tenentes during the early years, Vargas himself was not a military man. He cultivated close political ties with the Catholic Church and discouraged political parties of any kind. He was, to almost an extreme degree, the emerging face of Brazilian compromise. He was a master in the calculus of building and maintaining power.

Ironically, Getúlio's sympathies for the Allied cause in World War II led to his downfall. When the war broke out, it was at first not at all clear which side Brazil would support. My father initially supported the Axis powers because of his deep distrust of Great Britain, which he saw as an imperialist power. However, he and the rest of the military elite eventually came around, owing in part to a skilled U.S. lobbying effort for Brazil to join the war. Washington dispatched a group of Portuguese-American military officers to Rio to cultivate the military and cultural elite. I remember these officers coming to our house on several occasions to have dinner with my father. These efforts—along with the promise of generous U.S. financing to help Brazil create a steel industry—eventually won Getúlio over. Brazil committed 25,000 troops to the Allied effort, sending the only Latin American army that fired a gun. By the time the war ended, 500 Brazilians had died fighting for the liberation of Italy.

For me, the war was a vivid reality, not at all distant from our shores. In 1942, German submarines sunk numerous Brazilian ships just off our coast, killing hundreds of people. I was just eleven years old, but my father allowed me to accompany him late at night to the docks in Rio, when Brazilian ships sailed under the cover of darkness. I stayed up late at night listening to the radio and tracking the movements of the Allied and Axis armies on a large map in my parents' bedroom, using buttons to pinpoint troop locations. I am at a loss to explain why, but I also distinctly remember clambering about on a playground while wearing a gas mask. Members of my family wore pins that said "Royal Air Force" or "I gave to the Allied cause." Innumerable donation drives and military parades united Brazil in a way that nothing else really had before.

For a while, at least. When Brazil's troops came home from Europe after the war was won, they took a good long look at Brazil—and at Getúlio—and realized that it was time for change. After years of spilling blood in the name of democracy, and confronting the Holocaust and the other horrors that Europe's fascists had wrought, these officers believed the dictator at home also had to go. The middle class concurred. In October 1945, just a few months after the war in Europe ended, the Brazilian military, with no sense of irony or inappropriateness, staged a coup—a coup in the name of democracy. Getúlio was informed that, unless he resigned immediately, the army would surround his palace and cut off power, water, and all other supplies.

This time, with the deck stacked against him, Getúlio opted to leave the presidency just like his predecessors had: without much of a fight. He muttered vaguely of a global conspiracy to depose him, but in the end he went quietly. "I was the victim of agents of international finance who intended to keep our country simply as an exporting colony for raw materials and a purchaser of industrial goods," he declared.

The military handed over the presidency to the head of the Supreme

Court, who organized elections that would be relatively fair and open, inaugurating universal suffrage in Brazil for the first time. Meanwhile, Getúlio was spared exile and retired to his ranch in Rio Grande do Sul, where he immediately started laying the groundwork for another act that would become quite familiar in Brazilian politics: the comeback.

Shortly before the war ended, my father was transferred from Rio to São Paulo, which the British travel writer Peter Fleming visited during the same era. "The air is brisk," Fleming wrote. "The streets clang; electric signs challenge the stars with hyperbole. . . . As you watch the straw hats bustling in and out of Woolworth's you feel—with satisfaction or regret, according to your nature—that here is the South America that matters, the South America of the future."

A travel guide from Great Britain from the same era was no less enthusiastic. "São Paulo bears the impress of energy. . . . The City indeed represents that solid core of well-based economy, industry, agriculture, export and import which lies behind the façade of romance which is usually associated in the visitor's mind with Brazil."

Well, maybe. But to me, having grown up among the finer trappings of Rio, São Paulo was a frightful shock. I had never seen unpaved roads before; in our new neighborhood, all the roads were made of dirt, and cows still walked through the streets. In just three decades, São Paulo would become the largest city in South America, but at the time I felt as if we had moved to Siberia. I hung on somewhat pitifully to the traditions of Rio, continuing, for example, to wear the same white-and-black shoes to school that Rio kids wore. I despaired when my prized footwear became ever filthier from those awful muddy streets. My schoolmates insisted on calling me *carioca*, the term for someone from Rio. I spent several sleepless nights plotting a daring escape by night from my family's home so I could somehow rejoin my good friends on Copacabana Beach.

Thankfully, as on so many other occasions in my life, I made friends and adapted quickly. In fact, I would spend most of the rest of my life in São Paulo, and I have always felt more *paulista* than *carioca*. I eventually shunned my Rio shoes and adopted the formal coat, vest, and tie of São Paulo, then perplexed my parents by insisting on wearing the ensemble to the beach on visits to Rio. The truth is that I was an oddball in São Paulo, and I was an oddball in Rio; it didn't really matter where we lived. Luckily, I had friends and family that were willing to tolerate and even encourage my eccentricities.

I rapidly discovered the pros of living in a bona-fide boomtown—circuses and movies, museums and book clubs. Most schools were divided by gender in those days, but my friends and I nevertheless acquired girlfriends at a very young age—aided by the fact that my parents' house was strategically located around the corner from a girls' school. My friends came over and we would spy on the girls for hours on end. Swing dancing came into style, and we struggled to master it. Some had more success than others; I was a less than brilliant dancer. But at least I tried. It was, overall, a quite idyllic upbringing, a solid, happy foundation for the rest of my life.

In one of the military parades during the war, I was allowed to climb into one of the tanks that rumbled down the boulevards in Rio. Influenced by the drama of war and the example of my father, I decided that I wanted to be either a general or a cardinal.* For the only period in my life, I became intensely religious. My sister remembers walking by my bedroom door at night and listening as I kneeled on the floor and fervently prayed for God to save my family of heathen nonbelievers.

As an adolescent, I began to enjoy participating in everything. I had a broad range of friends—not all of whom liked each other. This was probably why I began to develop skills as a diplomat. Years later, Celio Benevides de Carvalho, a close childhood friend of mine, describing me for an interviewer, said:

*Rather than just a "soldier or a priest." I suppose I have always had an appreciation for hierarchy.

He wasn't someone who was necessarily *always* leading the group. He wasn't the leader, but more the man of consensus, who made alliances. He went and talked to everybody. His leadership was of a different nature. It was he who coordinated, who articulated. He already manifested a pronounced taste for politics that was unmistakable. He also punctuated everything he said or did with a good dose of humor, which was sometimes ironic or malicious. He knew how to find the funny side of things, and his ironic observations always ended up tearing down his worst adversaries.*

I think that description makes me sound a bit too much like a fourteen-year-old Machiavelli. I say that with the benefit of hindsight, because I never aspired to be "political" as a child, but the description is nevertheless essentially accurate. The truth is that our pursuits were usually quite trivial, or at least typically adolescent. We organized an art appreciation group, a reading group, and even took a shot at starting a literary magazine. All of us were desperate to be writers, and we penned poetry. We took ourselves extremely seriously. Some of the poems I wrote have, regrettably, survived for posterity and surfaced in biographies of me, including this one:

Ai, os agudos acordes do violino
Soando nos meus ouvidos,
E eu que perdi o ritmo da vida
Na luta com os demonios
Criança sem vida
Amiga perdida.

Alas, the violin's acute harmonies
Echoing in my ears
And I who lost life's rhythm

*Quoted in Brigitte Hersant Leoni, *Fernando Henrique Cardoso: O Brasil do Possível* (Rio de Janeiro: Editora Nova Fronteira S/A, 1997).

In the struggle with the demons
Lifeless child
Lost friend.

The world is probably a better place since I stopped writing poetry. That piece appeared in the first edition of a magazine called *Revista de Novíssimos*. Three of the young writers for the magazine would later go on to become accomplished poets, but apparently the contributions of the less gifted among us deprived them of earlier fame. *Novíssimos* never managed to publish a second edition.

Our youthful enthusiasm, if nothing else, reflected the excitement of living at the time of São Paulo's burgeoning growth. We lived in an area, Perdizes, that was on the outskirts of the city when we arrived but is considered part of downtown today. With such rapid change, it became a city of apparently limitless potential, quickly transforming itself into one of South America's main centers of thought. People were practically elbowing each other out of the way to get noticed. Aspiring thinkers all knew each other and crossed paths constantly at bookstores, teahouses, and cocktail parties. São Paulo also enjoyed an economic boom, as the war in Europe fed the need for factories in Brazil to meet demand at home and abroad. Following the coup of 1945, liberal democracy took hold in Brazil for the first time, empowering more people than ever before. Ultimately, all these factors made São Paulo a turbulent microcosm of the class conflicts and ideological debates rocking Brazil, and the world, at the time.

The man who replaced Getúlio was Eurico Gaspar Dutra, who had been an aide-de-camp to my grandfather and a close friend of my father's as well. In the mornings during the 1930s, Dutra had often stopped by our house, and he and my father walked to work together at the war ministry. Dutra offered the country a totally different political program in theory—which turned out, typically, to be all too familiar in practice. It was, in that strange Brazilian way, fitting that the man who led Brazil through its first steps of democracy was a general who, at the beginning of World War II, was so retrograde that he had opposed aligning Brazil with the Allies against Nazi Germany. When he came to office, he quickly outlawed the Brazilian Communist Party. He supported the United States in the opening salvos of the Cold War, and he exchanged official visits with President Harry Truman, asking him for U.S. economic aid.

How to understand all of this when you're just a teenager? Inspiration struck me in an odd place: by the swimming pool. On a vacation in the mountain resort of Lindóia with my friends, I struck up a conversation with an elderly gentleman who was reading books that interested me. He turned out to be a distinguished professor of literature named Fidelino de Figueiredo, a Portuguese exile. Poetry was a shared interest of ours, although, as previously illustrated, my talent in that field probably did not impress him. After a brief chat, he suggested that I apply to the brand new College of Philosophy, Sciences, and Letters at the University of São Paulo (USP).

I already knew I would attend USP, but I had not defined my field of study. My father had never imposed a military career on me, and I was more interested in the world of words and ideas. Law seemed like an appropriate choice, or at least a popular one—fully a quarter of Brazilian university students in those years became lawyers, reflective of the enduring bureaucratic legacy from the imperial era. But, in one of those tiny random acts that changes the course of one's life, I failed the Latin portion of the entrance exam for law school.

So off I went to the philosophy school, as Figueiredo had suggested. Once there, I instantly gravitated toward sociology. If the field was not quite as respected in Brazil as law and medicine were back then, it at least was not as dull or dogmatic as it might seem now. In the 1950s, sociology was a fresh, exciting field of study. It taught us how to understand society in order to change it. Sociology incorporated a bit of politics, economics, culture, and social life, and it offered the opportunity to study the present just as much as the past. We were taught, in a very scientific manner, to analyze hard data and apply what we found to a dynamic and shifting world. All of us who entered the school were motivated by a desire to change Brazil. Most of us were from the ideological left, perhaps more interested in being socialists than sociologists. But the rigor of the school would soon discipline us. The sociology department at USP created a remarkable generation of young thinkers who would become some of Brazil's most prominent leaders.

Eager to show that we were neutral, objective scientists, we wore white lab coats around campus, as if we were medical doctors. The field of study was rigorous and comprehensive—my first paper was on a pre-Socratic Greek philosopher, Parmenides.* The prosperity of São Paulo had allowed the department to import several fine French professors, and many classes were taught in French. Meanwhile, the intellectual life outside class was also stimulating. We had imposed on ourselves a rigorous set of rules that theoretically forbade us from participating in daily life with the "subjects" of our studies; sociologists were supposed to operate in a world apart, dedicated to science. Of course, this was impossible in practice, and I might add that these rules fell apart entirely in the 1960s, when students and professors alike were drawn to the glamour of street demonstrations or to the guerrilla movements themselves.

I soon decided that I wanted to be a professor. I was sure that I wanted to spend my life researching, writing, and trying to understand the world—and teaching was the best avenue available for doing that. I was also good at it, despite my bad grade on that first paper. When I was twenty-one, still an undergraduate, I was asked to teach a course in European economic history. That was the first paycheck I ever earned. I received my degree in 1952 and was hired as a teaching assistant in the sociology department the following year. My lectures generally were well-attended, my first books were judged important, and I climbed in the leadership structure of USP.

In some countries, academics are perceived as people who have

---

*I got the Brazilian equivalent of a D, not exactly an auspicious start. I also had a rather difficult time with economics, ironic given my later career path.

failed in life, unable or unwilling to participate in the real world. But in Brazil in the 1950s and 1960s, this could not have been further from the truth. The intellectual elite was unbelievably small—there were only about 100,000 university students in a country of 65 million people. So men and women with degrees were accorded almost reverential importance. Top academics had an influential role in government and business. Universities were seen as the perfect place to educate oneself in preparation for a full, active life. It was like being in training; we just didn't know for what exactly. After twenty years, a professor could go on to become a senator or a business executive. As a young professor, I had no intention of entering politics; I was happy to teach and to learn. But I always felt that I was preparing myself for *something*.

In the meantime, we sociologists felt as if we were investigating an exciting mystery. Studying sociology required us to try to explain the larger forces driving everyday events in our society. In Brazil, this meant looking into a whirlwind—everyday events for us would have been national traumas in some other countries! Why was Brazil in such turmoil? What were the structural reasons for poverty? What was it that drove people from the countryside into the cities? What were their stories? These were the questions that motivated our research.

From the very beginning, I honed in on one topic that seemed to lie at the heart of it all: race.

Back in the 1950s, race was something no one talked about in Brazil. The subject was completely taboo. When someone did bring it up, it was only to parrot the socially acceptable, official line: that Brazil had a "racial democracy." For decades, official Brazil—the government, the media, and most literature and music—had promoted a popular image of our country as the world's leading model of harmony between the races. Nowhere else, the official line went, had blacks and whites blended their cultures and their families into such a peaceful melting pot. Nowhere else was slavery more benign over the centuries. Nowhere else had there been such an absence of discrimination, or such an abundance of opportunity for people of African descent.

There was *some* truth to these ideas. For example, race relations in Brazil were always less confrontational than those in the United States. Blacks and whites could live together, and interracial violence was rare. There were no laws sanctioning institutional racism along the lines of the "separate but equal" statutes in the United States. The blending of the races was widely accepted, which had the corollary effect of making it difficult to create and enforce legislation on the matter. Put another way, there was no way to define who was black and who was white; almost everyone in Brazil has some African and indigenous blood. Occasionally in Brazil, a dark baby is born to fair-skinned parents, and no one really bats an eye, just because a few generations back, who knows what happened?

And yet, in general terms, to be black was to be poor in Brazil. This could be summed up in one word: *favela*. The favela was really much more than a shantytown or a very poor neighborhood—back then, it was a cluster of homes that didn't have basic sanitary services, didn't have a police presence, and didn't even appear on maps. In the Brazilian public imagination, it was a place that *didn't technically exist,* populated by people whose role in society could, unfortunately, be compared to untouchables. Favelas started to proliferate in earnest following World War II, most famously on the green hills overlooking Rio where I had run and played as a child.

Anyone who entered a favela or any poor urban neighborhood in Brazil in the 1950s could plainly see that most of its inhabitants were black. However, there were no official government statistics on the matter because the subject was so taboo. So we sociologists decided to go study the situation ourselves. We felt that, if we could understand the dynamics of race, we could gain unique and unparalleled insight into the forces that were transforming Brazil.

The leaders of the study were Roger Bastide, a French professor, and Florestan Fernandes, the son of humble Portuguese immigrants. Florestan would be the greatest influence on my development as an intellectual. Following research done under their guidance in São Paulo, a group of us, all assistant professors, started our own surveys in the southern states of Brazil: Paraná, Santa Catarina, and Rio Grande do Sul. Over the course of five years, from 1954 through 1958, we asked several questions in these areas over and over again, trying to get to the bottom of the mystery.

They were simple questions: Are there many blacks here? How do you get along with the whites? Do your children play with friends from other races? Do your children attend school? Are you discriminated against in your job? All of our queries sought to decipher how blacks and whites interacted in Brazil.

We must have been quite a bizarre sight. We were young, relatively wealthy white men, wearing white lab coats and carrying clipboards, entering some of the most dire neighborhoods in Brazil, mazes of houses made of wood, tin, and cardboard. We sometimes had to wade through ditches or trudge through seas of mud, since the blacks were always clustered in the worst part of the favela, often pressed up against the banks of a river. We sometimes had difficulties communicating— Bastide, for example, when researching in São Paulo's slums, spoke with a thick French accent that was rendered even more incomprehensible by his ever-present cigar—but people were exceedingly patient with us.

Despite our odd appearance, and the intrusive nature of our questions, the people we encountered were simply wonderful. Nowadays, it can be very difficult to enter a favela because of the violence, but back then people were softer, less angry. Everywhere we went, people answered our questions with enthusiasm and honesty. They were docile, articulate, and direct.

Slowly, surely, a portrait of the region emerged. The racial patchwork in Brazil's south was far more complicated and fascinating than anything we had expected. We discovered that there was a black petit bourgeoisie—largely made up of people whose grandparents had been free blacks. The members of these families had worked for generations in manufacturing, often at the dried meat factories in southern cities.

They attended black social clubs. I went to one of these club gatherings when I was invited there by a friend. It was held at a place in Porto Alegre called "Floresta Aurora."

The name of the club was in itself odd—*floresta* means jungle, and *aurora* means dawn. I discovered the significance of the name only later, while doing research in the city of Pelotas, when I came across old copies of a nineteenth-century newspaper by the same name that had been written by and for freed slaves. There was another club called "Marcílio Dias" that was named after a mulatto marine hero during the Paraguayan War. Both names spoke to a vibrant and distinct black Brazilian culture that was, to a large extent, kept underground in those days. I realized that this was yet another hidden aspect of the myth of "racial democracy"—in a society of supposed equals, a separate black culture was in itself controversial.

Meanwhile, the mere need for black social clubs reflected the discrimination that existed in day-to-day life. They were among only a few places where blacks with a certain degree of education and culture could establish a social network. Understandably, those who went to these events often felt frustrated by their limitations. I will always remember a gorgeous young mulatta woman, a high-school teacher whom I met at Floresta Aurora. She pointed at the crowd of young black men on the dance floor. "You know, I will end up marrying one of these," she told me with a look of disgust on her face. "And they are far less educated than I am."

In one favela after another, we saw the structural causes of Brazil's poverty. Slavery had left an unquestionable legacy of violence and inequality. This was the basis for a presentation I gave at a United Nations Educational, Scientific and Cultural Organization (UNESCO) conference in Rio. The conference was held at Itamaraty Palace, the former presidential residence my father had grown up in as the son of a presidential adviser. UNESCO had partially funded our efforts. When I was finished, the leader of the seminar, a respected elderly Brazilian lawyer, approached me.

He was furious. "I was ready to throw you out of the room," he seethed.

"Why?"

"Because you didn't have the right to speak the way you did in the presence of foreigners. You said we have racial discrimination, and there is none. We are a racial democracy."

I was astonished. "I would love nothing more than to live in a racial democracy," I replied. "But my data show just the opposite. What would you have me do? Not tell the truth?"

He said nothing and walked away. The honest answer, of course, would have been a resounding "yes." The persistence of the myth depended on it.

Understanding race, and thereby the history of slavery, completely transformed the way I looked at Brazil.

The problems were nothing new; in many ways, nothing in Brazil had changed in the previous four centuries. By the mid-1950s, half of Brazil's 61 million people still suffered from chronic malnutrition. Half were barefoot, and more than half were illiterate. Only one out of three children went to school; one out of six made it to high school. One out of three Brazilians hosted intestinal hookworms. In some remote areas, every other baby died before turning one year old. The average life span was 46 years, versus 69.4 in the United States. All of this misery was as old as Brazil itself.

So what was the big change, then? In a word: urbanization. As the poor masses fled rural discrimination and moved to the city, a process that began in earnest after World War II, Brazilian politics would be turned upside down. This is what the changes in the twentieth century were all about. These new city dwellers would justifiably demand health care, education, jobs, and a political voice. The percentage of the population living in cities would skyrocket to 41 percent in 1955, 62 percent in 1975, and 79 percent in 1995. These newly enfranchised Brazilians would multiply in number as well. In the course of those same years, the total national population would grow from 59 million in 1955 to 107 million, then 172 million.

The bubble was bursting.

During those years, the country came face to face with what it had always been. The poor saw the rich, and the rich saw the poor. Brazil would never be the same.

Still, most of the Brazilian elite remained completely in the dark about the reality in the country. The old guard would try to govern the country the same way they had before, and then fail miserably. No one discovered this quite as completely as Getúlio Vargas, who staged a doomed return to the presidency in 1951.

Getúlio was vaguely aware of the rapid social changes, but not quite sure how to harness them, and his second coming was more precarious than his first. His labor minister, a young fellow gaúcho named João Goulart, terrified the business elite. Goulart recommended a 100 percent increase in the minimum wage, which had not been raised for several years. The uproar from the conservatives was so loud that Goulart was forced to resign—but Vargas announced that the wage increase would be implemented anyway. Some employers then refused to honor the decree, leading to a wave of strikes across the country. With labor unrest growing, whispers that Getúlio had become a Communist grew louder and louder.

Then onto our national stage strode Brazil's answer to Joe Mc-Carthy. A city councilman in Rio and the owner of an influential newspaper, Carlos Lacerda would play a major role in the downfall of three Brazilian presidents, including Getúlio. Though he had been a Communist during the 1930s, Lacerda turned on his roots with a vehemence that suggested no small amount of self-loathing. His newspaper focused almost exclusively on attacking communism and populism of all forms, using every means possible to defame Getúlio and his ministers. He became the best-known voice of the opposition, openly calling for the military to overthrow the president and "save Brazil."

Getúlio was desperate to silence his new foe, but he had no idea how to go about it. In his first, more authoritarian term, censorship would have been the likely recourse, but the new spirit of democracy made that impossible. Getúlio tried to fight back at first by building up his alliances in the media, engaging in a competition with Lacerda that resembled an epic arms race—but this was a race for newspapers instead of nukes. Brazil became more polarized. In the end, Lacerda's guns proved bigger and louder. His *Tribuna da Imprensa* newspaper published lurid accounts of corruption. Getúlio was shaken by the revelation that a journalist friend of his, Samuel Wainer, had gotten sweetheart loans from the Bank of Brazil. The president later lamented: "I feel like I am standing in a sea of mud."

The palace was in constant turmoil. Getúlio became withdrawn and more depressed. One of his most faithful followers, Gregório Fortunato, the president's black bodyguard and chauffeur, decided to help out his beloved boss—by contacting a professional gunman and telling him to eliminate Lacerda.

Early on August 5, 1954, as Lacerda pulled into his apartment on Copacabana Beach, his car was showered with bullets. Somehow, Lacerda suffered only minor wounds in the foot. But a heinous sin had been committed anyway: Rubens Vaz, an air force major riding in the car with him, was killed while trying to escape. The armed forces were livid, along with the rest of Brazil. Lacerda resumed his attacks, now even more virulent, from his hospital bed. Although it could not be proven that Getúlio had personally sanctioned the hit, the die had been cast. Twenty-seven army generals signed a manifesto demanding the president's resignation. Vargas holed up in the presidential palace, silent.

On the morning of August 24, with a coup imminent, Getúlio sat down to write a letter. "I have fought against the looting of Brazil," he wrote. "I fought against the looting of the people. I have fought bare-breasted. The hatred, infamy and calumny did not beat down my spirit. I gave you my life. Now I offer you my death. Nothing remains. Serenely I take the first step on the road to eternity and I leave life to enter history." He then withdrew quietly to his bedroom, closed the door, and shot himself through the heart.

For eighteen months after Getulio's suicide, the country suffered a period of uncertain transition as various politicians and military figures wrestled for power. A democratic successor to Getulio was finally assured by the intervention of the minister of war, Marshal Henrique Teixeira Lott, who guaranteed the army's support for Juscelino Kubitschek. Kubitschek's name alone was an indication of a Brazil that was changing fast: he was the offspring of Czechs who were part of relatively recent immigration from Europe, the first president whose origin was not Portuguese. Others would follow in the future. Juscelino helped promote change at an even faster pace during his term, which lasted from 1956 to 1961.

JK, as he was known, left a legacy of respect for democracy and tolerance that was hardly matched by any other president. Two small military upheavals tried to oust him. He not only dismantled these coup attempts, but granted amnesty to his enemies. Faced with harsh opposition throughout his tenure in office, he managed both to formulate and implement—a novelty in Brazil—a very ambitious plan that laid the pillars for the industrialization and basic infrastructure of the country, all that in partnership with foreign investment. He was also the visionary who built Brasília, the new capital, in the geographical center of the country.

Yet, and possibly on account of the enormous tranquility he ensured for the country, that was the period in which I was possibly most distant from politics. I remember visiting Congress only twice during all those years. My children were very young. When I was not with them and Ruth, I was either traveling extensively into Southern Brazil to undertake my field research or organizing the Marx seminar sessions. The Left did not regard JK favorably, given his efforts to strengthen a free market economy with participation of foreign capital. Nor was he much admired by the academy that viewed with suspicion his flamboyant democratic attitude, which usually led him to reconcile conflicting forces. My father was a federal deputy at that time, a member of the coalition of parties that supported the government.

In any event, JK's administration was a landmark in Brazil, a good time for Brazilians. He is still considered one of the top three presidents Brazil has ever had. No one could imagine then the disaster in the making, in the person of his successor Jânio Quadros.

A Recipe for a Coup

BEST KNOWN for trying to ban the bikini and the miniskirt—
in Brazil, of all places—there may not be a more eccentric,
mercurial, or tragic figure in our history than Jânio Quadros.
Our paths crossed in the most extraordinary and unexpected ways during our lifetimes. A high-school teacher who once sold his history of
Portuguese grammar door to door, Jânio was an acquaintance of my father's. He spoke with a high-pitched voice that somehow seemed muffled by his thick eyeglasses and even thicker dark mustache. His left eye
perpetually wandered off to the side, the result of a Carnival celebration gone bad during his youth. *France-Soir* compared him to
"Marx—not Karl, but Harpo." Jânio's own wife described him as "the
ugliest man I ever met."

Luiz Inácio Lula da Silva, popularly known as "Lula," would be
widely hailed four decades later as "Brazil's first working-class president," but Jânio's beginnings were humble as well. He grew up in a

dusty frontier town in the western state of Mato Grosso, where his first home was a rented room above a barber shop. His family bounced from town to town, on the lam from bill collectors, until they finally settled in São Paulo when Jânio was sixteen. Following a stint as a teacher, he got into law school through sheer ambition. There, he was nearly blinded by an exploding bottle of colored ether, which Brazilians habitually shoot off at Carnival. Ashamed of his looks, with an eye that now perpetually wandered off at a 20-degree angle, Jânio withdrew into self-pitying obscurity and whiled away several months obsessively rereading a biography of Abraham Lincoln and writing bad poetry. When he finally reemerged, he decided to run for city council in São Paulo. His wife advised him against it, and sure enough—he finished forty-seventh in the race for forty-five seats. However, the Communist Party was outlawed shortly thereafter, a dozen of the candidates were disqualified, and Jânio Quadros got his first job in politics.

The tall, scrawny young man with the bad eye then enjoyed an un-precedented and largely baffling rise to power. He became mayor of São Paulo in 1952, then graduated within two years to the more presti-gious state governorship. In 1960, at the age of forty-three, Jânio ran for president. His record as a competent civic administrator helps ex-plain some of his electoral success, but it is far more likely that Brazil-ian voters, many of them young and enfranchised for the first time, were simply looking for a *different* kind of politician. And Jânio was certainly that. During campaigns, he gave speeches while waving a gi-ant broom, saying he was going to sweep away graft. He also carried a box with a rat in it and said he was going to get rid of all the corrupt rats in government. When he campaigned in Japanese neighborhoods, he wore a kimono and bound his feet together. On other occasions, he wore a trench coat in the tropical heat.

Somehow, Brazilians found all these eccentricities amusing and de-cided they would make Jânio a suitable president. No one knew what he really stood for—his campaign slogan was simply "Jânio is com-ing"—but the self-described "anti-politician" won the election with the largest popular mandate in Brazilian history up to that point, taking 48 percent of the vote in a field of several candidates. In a public ceremony on January 31, 1961, Jânio Quadros received the presidential sash from Juscelino Kubitschek. Forty-two years would pass before a democratically elected Brazilian president would again hand power to another one in a public ceremony.*

When Jânio moved into the presidential office in the newly constructed capital of Brasília, he hung a portrait of Abraham Lincoln on the wall—and then he decided to get *really* weird. He installed red and green traffic lights outside his office door that informed ministers when to knock and when to wait. Each time Jânio climbed into his presidential limousine, he spent several minutes obsessively positioning himself exactly in the middle of the rear seat. After a trip to Cairo, he announced plans to import Egyptian robes and shawls because they were so comfortable and because Egypt's climate was so similar to Brazil's. In addition to his infamous attempts to ban the bikini and the miniskirt, he tried to get rid of gambling and cockfights.

His prohibitions may have been moralistic in nature, but as usually happens in such cases, the man himself had not a moral bone in his body. He threw himself at women with an unbecoming, even violent zeal. He was also a drunk with a taste for expensive whiskey or port wine, and he was famous for once having declared: "I drink because it's liquid. Had it been solid, I would have eaten it."

Perhaps that explained why he was so combative; whatever the reason, he took the Brazilian talent for compromise and turned it upside-down.

"The rebellion is invincible!" Jânio declared upon taking office. "It is a state of mind, a collective spirit, a fact of life that has already filled the nation's conscience and that no one will compromise or paralyze—I will not be stopped unless by assassination!"

Jânio never really specified whom "the rebellion" was against, and most Brazilians didn't seem to mind. But the rest of the world, partic-

*I handed power to Lula on January 1, 2003.

ularly the United States, was not ready to gloss over these words from the new leader of Latin America's largest country. Just two years before Jânio's inauguration, Fidel Castro had taken power in Cuba. The debut of communism in the Western Hemisphere sent the U.S. government, and all of Brazil's conservatives as well, into a panic. The new president of Brazil was in fact reviled by the Communists, who branded him a capitalist stooge during his campaign. But that didn't seem to matter anymore—Jânio had stirred deep suspicion by visiting Castro in Havana during his campaign.

As president, Jânio did nothing to dispel fears that he was taking Brazil down a radical path. When the U.S. government offered Brazil a $100 million loan to help him through his first ninety days in office—the government was $176 million in arrears on its foreign debt—Jânio dramatically spurned the offer. Instead, he sent delegations behind the Iron Curtain to ink new trade deals, then announced he would vote for debate on the admission of Communist China into the United Nations.

If the Cold War was a giant chess match, players in Washington worried that one of their most important pieces had just been hijacked by a nimwit who might deliver victory to the Communists. "A strong, healthy Brazil does not guarantee democracy in Latin America, but it is certain that if Brazil does not make it, few others will," *Time* magazine presciently opined in a cover story on Jânio in its June 30, 1961, issue. The story listed Jânio's innumerable personal quirks with no small degree of irony, but the author, like everyone else, nevertheless seemed a bit taken with the man and tempted by the idea that he might be leading the country in a positive direction. And who knew, really? The magazine described Jânio as having "burst on the world like Brazil itself—temperamental, bristling with independence, bursting with ambition, haunted by poverty, fighting to learn, greedy for greatness."

The portrait on the cover, situated against a surreal and somewhat silly green and yellow backdrop that must have been intended to invoke the Brazilian flag, made Jânio look almost statesmanlike. He wore a blue suit and tie, and his jaw jutted forward confidently. Both of his eyes even looked straight ahead. That cover was, in fact, about as good as things would ever get for Jânio. Just two months later, his departure would prove even more bizarre than his arrival.

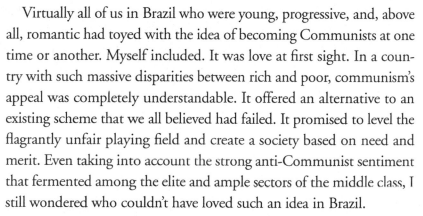

Virtually all of us in Brazil who were young, progressive, and, above all, romantic had toyed with the idea of becoming Communists at one time or another. Myself included. It was love at first sight. In a country with such massive disparities between rich and poor, communism's appeal was completely understandable. It offered an alternative to an existing scheme that we all believed had failed. It promised to level the flagrantly unfair playing field and create a society based on need and merit. Even taking into account the strong anti-Communist sentiment that fermented among the elite and ample sectors of the middle class, I still wondered who couldn't have loved such an idea in Brazil.

For a budding intellectual, it was awe-inspiring to see how many of the influential leaders in Brazil were Communists. They made it look tremendously attractive. Jorge Amado, the Brazilian author and hero from my youth, was a passionate Communist leader. So was Oscar Niemeyer, the architect who designed Brasília. At USP, the Communists were not great in number, but they seemingly held proportionately more key positions—the best physicist, the best philosopher, and so on. A great many of the Communists in Brazil came from the ranks of the armed forces, most notably Luís Carlos Prestes. The Communists also supported my father's successful campaign for Congress in 1954. They formed just one part of a vast coalition of parties that supported him, but I certainly took notice of how the man I had always admired and loved could count on them.

I was never a formal member of the Communist Party, but I certainly had my flirtations. As a university student, I wrote for a journal called *Fundamentos,* which was generally considered a voice of the

Communists—publishing interviews with Joseph Stalin, condemnations of the Korean War, and the like. Many of my sociology classes agreed with the notion that the global capitalist system was headed inexorably for an implosion, at which point it would be replaced by something better. As I conducted my studies in the south of Brazil and became more aware of the poverty and inequality in my country, I became even more taken in by this theory. I considered joining the party. And it was then that I finally decided to take a closer look at what communism really meant.

Stalin horrified me. That is the simplest way to explain why, upon deeper examination, I lost my enthusiasm for communism. As the years passed, details filtered out to the world of how Stalin had murdered millions, using repressive tactics to keep Eastern Europe firmly under his thumb. It became clear that communism was not the economic panacea it claimed to be, and it seemed to be unsustainable without hard-line oppression. I never had any taste for authoritarianism, and I began to believe there might be a better system for helping the poor. I started writing for a different leftist magazine that was critical of communism. By the time the Soviets invaded Hungary in 1956, I had fully turned my back on the party. I was just twenty-five years old.

Shortly thereafter, some friends of mine and I visited Paulo Emílio Salles Gomes, a well-known Brazilian intellectual and film critic. We told him about our cycle of disillusionment, and why we had ultimately decided not to join the Communist Party.

"What, only now?" Salles snorted, teasing us. He said that every generation, including his own, went through the same cycle of temptation and frustration with the Communists. Looking back, I think he was absolutely right.

That didn't stop us, however, from looking for alternatives. Around that same time, I was sunbathing on Copacabana Beach with a group of friends, including my brother-in-law, Roberto Cardoso de Oliveira, and José Arthur Giannotti, a young colleague of mine who had just returned from France. While there, he had been trained in reading classical texts the same way French philosophers did: in groups, poring over the text one word at a time and then discussing the content. Now, he wanted to try the same method with some friends from USP.

"Why don't we try to replicate this in Brazil?" Giannotti asked.

"Sounds fine," I said, a bit lazily. "Whom would we read?"

"Well, what about Marx?"

That this idea originated on the beach in Rio speaks to its modest original intentions. The so-called Marx Seminar would, however, go on to achieve an almost mythical reputation in the decades to come.

In the 1950s, the works of Karl Marx were hardly studied at all in Brazilian academia; he was confined almost exclusively to the dogma of the ideological left. We chose to study him not only because his works spoke to the problems of transforming an undeveloped society, but also because we felt his views had been distorted by the Communists in Brazil. The Communists had a certain monopoly on Marx, and this seemed wrong. So, every two weeks, we met at someone's house and had a thorough reading session using the French style Giannotti suggested. Then we enjoyed a nice long dinner. Marx was not the only author we studied—in fact, we also looked extensively at John Maynard Keynes. That might surprise critics who saw the seminar as a nest of leftist thought. Marx was merely the most notorious of our many subjects, but as a result, I have been regarded as a "Marxist" ever since.

This label is misleading, at least in the traditional sense. Marx's works did inspire me, but more for their rigorous method of analysis than for his dogmatic, nineteenth-century views on capitalism and revolution. We all knew that Brazil in the 1960s was not France in the 1840s. The Soviet invasion of Hungary had crushed any rosy fantasies we might have otherwise had about life in a Communist state. Instead, we focused on the way Marx identified class structures—the various income levels and interest groups of society—and what they strove for, which we found to be extraordinarily lucid and relevant. True to our scientific aspirations, we were enamored with Marx's talent for empirical analysis, even when we didn't agree with his conclusions or prescriptions. In that way, we were inspired to try to undertake the work that Marx might have done had he been alive in the 1950s in South America.

It was a marvelous experience. We often hovered at the dinner table well into the wee hours of the morning, arguing until we turned blue. The discussions were abstract and intellectual in nature, although practical politics was never wholly distant. The Marx Seminar met on and off for seven years. Its legacy in Brazil is relevant not so much because of what we studied, but because of the astonishing number of members of the group who went on to later prominence. Besides Giannotti, the members included Octavio Ianni, who became an influential sociologist; Fernando Novais, one of Brazil's best historians; Roberto Schwarz, a well-known literary critic who taught at Harvard, Brown, and Columbia; Bento Prado, one of Brazil's best-known philosophers; Paul Singer, an economist who later became a top official in Lula's government; Francisco Weffort, who became my minister of culture; and Juarez Brandão Lopes, a famous sociologist.

There was another member of the Marx Seminar who had a particularly strong influence on me. In 1952, the same year I received my undergraduate degree, I married an intelligent, striking young woman named Ruth Villaça Correa Leite. We had met rather inauspiciously, studying together with friends. The possibility of romance was slow to cross my mind, and I must admit that I was rather slow on the uptake. We went to bookstores and museums together, the best of friends. When I finally dared to take her on a date to a theater in São Paulo, I wore a rather drab gray suit and tie. Ruth has never tired of gently poking fun at how ragged I looked that night, much to the surprise and delight of those who knew me only late in life, when I had to pay more attention to how I dressed. At any rate, it was a perfect match and the beginning of a long and rewarding relationship. The following years saw the birth of our three beloved children: Paulo Henrique, Luciana, and Beatriz.

In 1960, while Jânio was out trapping rats and collecting brooms in preparation for his presidential campaign, we reached another kind of intellectual pinnacle. Jean-Paul Sartre, the French philosopher and father of existentialism, visited Brazil and spoke at several universities. He had just completed a trip to Cuba in the wake of Fidel Castro's revolution, and the world eagerly awaited Sartre's evaluation of his experience. Sartre was invited to participate in a debate at a theater. The event was scheduled to last for two hours, and it would be televised live nationwide. The format was like a roundtable, and I was invited to sit at the table and perhaps ask him a question or two.

Just minutes into the debate, it became obvious that the professor who had been selected to translate for Sartre, who spoke no Portuguese, was not doing an adequate job. With the cameras rolling, a call went out for anyone else in the room who could speak French and might be able to translate for him.

I volunteered. For the next two hours, I did the best job that I could. It was quite intimidating. I was just twenty-nine and suddenly found myself attempting to speak on behalf of a legend. It was quite a spectacle: a world-famous, ultra-leftist philosopher and the planet's leading feminist giving televised speeches in a tropical country that was still largely illiterate, with a young translator who had only half an idea what they were saying. Still, the audience was enraptured, hanging on my shaky version of their every word. After the event ended, a friend of mine approached me, astonished. "I didn't know you spoke French *that* well!" she whispered.

I leaned into her ear and confessed: "I don't! But don't tell Sartre!"

I'm sure that I made my share of mistakes, but later in their tour of Brazil, Simone de Beauvoir, his companion and an iconic figure in her own right, gave a speech on feminism and I translated for her as well.

The truth was that I understood *most* of what was being said. I told my friend that translation was really more about communicating the concept than each individual word. By that definition, I thought I had done a decent job. Beyond that, well, I figured that what Sartre didn't know wouldn't hurt him.

I couldn't have been too awful, though, because Sartre was suitably impressed and accepted my invitation to come have dinner with my friends at my house in São Paulo. It was a bizarre night, for many reasons. I lived on Nebraska Street in an area of São Paulo known as Brooklin, reflecting the U.S. influence that had grown in the city since World War II. Under the guidance of President Juscelino Kubitschek, Brazil had experienced a boom of prosperity during the late 1950s. It would later prove too good to last forever; but in the meantime, Brazil busied itself with the idea that it was becoming "American," buying cars, televisions, and other trappings of newfound wealth.

My friends and I were embarrassed by this kind of cultural imitation, believing it showed a lack of originality on the part of Brazil's populace—and we weren't too happy about the growth of American-style capitalism either, of course. Despite Sartre's revolutionary politics, however, he didn't seem to mind. We were mesmerized by him that night. He was an ugly man, cross-eyed and short. But once he started speaking, he revealed a very winning personality—polite and shy. He seemed most at ease talking to young people like us. That was why he had come to Brazil, and that was why his visit was so successful.

Simone was a beautiful, elegant woman with sparkling blue eyes. She treated Sartre more like a baby than a lover. Like many visitors, she also brought a certain prejudice with her to the tropics. In her memoirs, she wrote about the group of young academics in São Paulo who knew what was going on in literature and philosophy elsewhere in the world. She was astonished that we knew so much about existentialism.

The whole episode, for us, was a kind of validation. For the duration of the visit of these most fashionable European intellectuals, we could content ourselves that we were part of the mainstream intellectual world. In Brazil, it was sometimes tempting to succumb to the national inferiority complex, to believe that our isolation and Third World status left us irrevocably on the fringes. For Sartre to come and sing our praises, however, gave us invaluable confidence. I was even more thrilled when Sartre presented me with a letter giving me exclusive rights to translate and publish his works in Brazil. I never took him up on the offer, but it was flattering.

Before he left, Sartre took a small side trip to Araraquara, in the interior of São Paulo state, where he had an unlikely encounter with a Brazilian of truly global stature. The episode is retold in Joseph A. Page's fine book *The Brazilians*: As Sartre stood outside a building conversing with a cadre of intellectuals, down the street came Pelé, the world's greatest soccer star, accompanied by several fans. The two groups converged on a street corner. When they separated, the intellectuals realized they were now following Pelé, and Sartre was walking alone. The intellectuals ran back down the street, a bit embarrassed, and rejoined their French hero. According to Page, many residents still refer to the spot as "Pelé-Sartre Corner."

As much as he loved it, there was one thing that Sartre never was able to understand about Brazil. Over dinner, we spoke about the 1960 election, which pitted Jânio against a retired field marshal and former minister of war named Henrique Teixeira Lott. Sartre was bewildered by our support for Lott instead of Jânio, who had visited Cuba, after all, and on the surface appeared to be more amenable to our progressive ideas.

"Jânio is a populist, and in Brazil, that's not necessarily the same as a leftist," I told Sartre. "Besides, can't you see the man is a clown?"

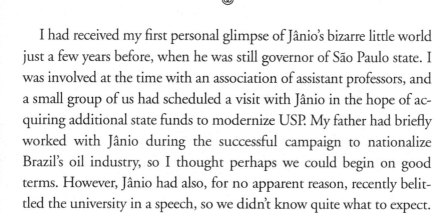

I had received my first personal glimpse of Jânio's bizarre little world just a few years before, when he was still governor of São Paulo state. I was involved at the time with an association of assistant professors, and a small group of us had scheduled a visit with Jânio in the hope of acquiring additional state funds to modernize USP. My father had briefly worked with Jânio during the successful campaign to nationalize Brazil's oil industry, so I thought perhaps we could begin on good terms. However, Jânio had also, for no apparent reason, recently belittled the university in a speech, so we didn't know quite what to expect.

After a long wait on the appointed day, we were escorted into Jânio's office at the governor's mansion. It was a cramped, dark room, and we had to strain our eyes to see anything. At first, I could barely make out a silhouette in the corner; someone seemed to be mumbling to himself in low tones, barely audible.

Once my eyes adjusted, I saw that it was Jânio. He had his back turned to us, and he appeared to be dictating to his secretary. To this day, I am convinced that he was only pretending to talk to her, engaging in a bit of dramatic flair. All of us stood there, thinking we'd found ourselves in the pages of a Kafka novel, and waited until he finished. Then, Jânio ever so slowly swiveled around in his chair and turned to face us, his lazy eye only just visible in the shadows.

"Ladies and gentlemen," Jânio squealed with his high-pitched voice, "what can I help you with today?"

"Well," the head of our organization began, "we are here on behalf of the university and, . . . "

"I have nothing to do with that!" Jânio interrupted with a shriek. "Why are you wasting my time? This is intolerable! Get out of my sight!"

I can count on one hand the times in my life that I have truly lost my temper. When it happens, I see black and I say very strong things that I later regret—as a man who prides himself on being in control and having impeccable manners, I don't allow it to happen very often. But there was something about Jânio, from the very first time I met him, that repulsed me. I lost all regard for protocol.

"You will *not* speak to us like that!" I seethed, jabbing my finger at him. "We are professors! We demand respect from you!"

Jânio sat there for a long while, gaping. He shuffled some papers on his desk and said nothing. Then, all of a sudden, he looked back at us and transformed into a completely different man. From that point on, he was docile, respectful, and receptive—even charming. We left his office with a promise for the money we had been seeking.

A few weeks later, a colleague of mine tried to set up another meeting with Jânio. His apparent response was: "That's fine. But do not bring that man Cardoso."

Given the nature of my first encounter with Jânio, I was shocked by what happened shortly after he became president in 1961. I received a phone call from his press secretary, José Aparecido de Oliveira, who, without elaborating, invited me to come to Brasília to meet with Jânio. And that was how I made my first-ever visit to the Planalto, the presidential palace.

With the memory of my first encounter with Jânio still fresh in my mind, I showed up a few days later in Aparecido's office, nervous and more than a bit confused. To my bewilderment, Aparecido told me that Jânio was going to invite me to participate in the National Economic Council, a board of advisers to the president. It was a very high-level position, even requiring approval by the Senate. I was stunned, given that I knew next to nothing about economics. My first inclination was to turn the offer down. But I said I was willing to meet with Jânio to discuss the matter.

So we waited. Aparecido's office was quite spartan in its decor, reflecting the general newness of Brasília. He had nothing more than a desk and a small, tinny speaker that Jânio used to summon him. Every so often, Jânio's squeaky voice buzzed through: "Aparecido, come here!" he barked. It was a purely theatrical performance. Aparecido would scurry off and disappear for hours at a time, while I just sat there waiting, with nothing to read, no art to admire.

At the end of the day, Aparecido told me Jânio had gone home. He made no attempt at explanation. Empty-handed and more than a bit perplexed, I went with Aparecido to his apartment and slept on a stiff cot in his living room.

The next morning, I finally came to my senses. "Look, Ze Aparecido, I'm sorry, but I'm not going to accept this," I said. I told him that I wasn't an economist, and that I was far more interested in my academic career than in politics.

"You're practically a kid!" Aparecido protested. "The president of Brazil is inviting you to do this! You cannot turn him down."

But that's exactly what I did. I thought I was probably passing up the best shot I'd ever have at a political career. But I didn't care. Additionally, all my instincts told me that Jânio was just too unstable for me to tie my fortunes to him. Inviting the young professor who had confronted him a few years before to join his team was probably just another eccentric whim of Jânio's designed to co-opt an opponent—I doubted I would have any real influence. As it turned out, it would have been the most temporary of appointments anyway.

By August 1961, barely a month removed from making the cover of *Time,* Jânio had become an extravagant caricature of himself, if such a thing were possible. He openly provoked Congress, and he seemed to have a daredevil's penchant for frightening the conservative elite. Carlos Lacerda, the acerbic anti-Communist journalist, abruptly withdrew his support and started loudly clamoring for Jânio to be deposed. Meanwhile, Jânio sent his vice president, João Goulart, on a conspicuous trip to Red China. But the crowning blow came when Che Guevara was invited to Brasília. Jânio decorated Che, just a year and a half removed from the triumph of Fidel's revolution in Cuba, with the Order of the Southern Cross—the highest honor Brazil can bestow upon a foreigner.

That same week, I was in the city of Belo Horizonte doing Jânio a kind of favor. When I turned down the offer to participate in his economic council, I had accepted a much smaller role in helping organize a new, working-class university to be called the University of Labor. It seemed like a worthwhile project that transcended politics. A select group of professors was sitting in a conference room debating how to organize this new school when one of our colleagues barged through the door, white-faced.

"Jânio quit!" the professor blurted out, panting. "He quit!"

"He did *what?*"

"He resigned!"

It was like hearing thunder on a sunny day. All of us just sat there, speechless.

To this day, we can only guess why Jânio left. The economy was in relatively good shape, and there was no specific political crisis to speak of. He simply offered his resignation to Congress, departed Brasília—and then disappeared. Some historians think that Che's visit that same week may have led someone to threaten Jânio. Others believe, far more plausibly, in my mind, that the resignation was really a threat, a political ploy to galvanize support in Congress. Jânio may have believed the legislature would beg him to stay and cede him dictatorial powers—much as had been given to General Charles de Gaulle in France. With his vice president in China at the time, Jânio would have been able to take control of Brazil entirely by himself.

If that was his intention, Jânio's power play backfired badly. The president of Congress, Auro Moura Andrade, took the resignation in hand and told the chamber: "I received this letter from the president and he has resigned. He resigned, it's a personal decision, unilateral in nature, and we're not going to discuss it further." And that was the end of it.

Back in Belo Horizonte, the other professors and I realized that the University of Labor was no longer our top priority.* All of us went to the house of José Magalhães Pinto, the governor of Minas Gerais state. We drank late into the night and discussed this latest absurdity in Brazilian political life. Magalhães Pinto had some of the best political connections in the country, but, like us, he hadn't seen it coming. "I don't believe this," he kept repeating, his hands on his head. "How could something like this happen? I don't believe this!"

The next day, back in São Paulo, a group of us went to the home of Roberto Gusmão, who had been in charge of the University of Labor project. As we entered, Gusmão put his finger to his lips, telling us to be quiet. There on a couch was José Aparecido, Jânio's press secretary who had invited me to Brasília months before. It was a truly bizarre

*In fact, it would never come to fruition.

sight: He lay there, so depressed that he could not sit up. He stared at the ceiling, mute, acting as if we weren't even there.

Hours later, Jânio's labor minister arrived. His mood was the polar opposite of Aparecido's. He stalked angrily about the apartment, yelling, at no one in particular, "Where is Jânio? Where the fuck is Jânio?"

Well, Jânio had flown to São Paulo and temporarily stopped at a military base. Witnesses said he had been drinking heavily, and he had had a fistfight there with the governor. From there, he made a short trip to the port of Santos. Only reporters and a few curious bystanders watched as Jânio boarded a boat for exile in Uruguay. He later went to Europe. A writer for *Time* reported that Jânio "shook with sobs" as he mounted the gangplank and the lines on the ship were dropped.

In one last rambling tirade, Jânio blamed "occult forces" for bringing down his government. "I was compelled to resign," he declared. "But like Getúlio, I shall return one day, God willing, to show everyone who were the scum in this country."

Unbelievably, Jânio was right. He *would* return one day, and he would even win one last election, as I would discover at my cost.

It may be hard to believe that anyone could have done a worse job than Jânio. But Brazilian politics never disappoints with its capacity for theater, and Jânio had, in essence, stacked the deck to ensure that his successor would be even more unacceptable. His vice president, João Goulart, was loathed by the military and Brazil's conservatives. Known popularly as "Jango," he had earned the wrath of the business elite in the 1950s when, as Getúlio Vargas's labor minister, he had proposed the 100 percent minimum wage hike, which had cost him his job and set in motion the collapse of Getúlio's reign. At the precise moment of Jânio's resignation, Goulart had been chatting with Mao Tse-tung on a state trip to Communist China. He started packing his bags to come home and assume Brazil's presidency—until the Brazilian military instructed him not to bother.

Led by the aging war minister Odílio Denys, the steadily growing conservative wing of the military flatly forbade Goulart from becoming president, warning that his plane would be shot down if he returned from China. Tanks moved into battle position in Rio, bracing for all-out combat. "Do you want your children to be brought up Communists?" Denys asked the country. "The time has come to choose."

The only significant opposition to the coup against Goulart came from his home state in the South. Leonel Brizola, the governor of Rio Grande do Sul (where my grandfather had helped put down the Naval revolt seventy years earlier), called his province to arms on behalf of Goulart, his brother-in-law. Brizola blocked the harbor in Porto Alegre, called in the state militia, had trenches dug, surrounded his palace with barbed wire, and put machine guns on the roof. "We are not going to fire the first shot," Brizola declared, "but you may be sure we will fire the second—and many more!"

After a month of negotiations, the military allowed Goulart to take office, but only after he agreed to curtail his powers. The compromise centered on overhauling Brazil's system of government, switching from a U.S.-style presidential setup to a European-style scheme of parliamentary government. This would essentially weaken Goulart by instituting a prime minister—Tancredo Neves, a mild-mannered federal deputy—who would theoretically wield more power than the president. The strategy was half-hearted and ineffective—a typically temporary solution that ended up causing more problems later. Still, the military finally agreed to let Goulart come to Brasília. The new president, taking no chances, waited until after sunset to board a jet to the capital, then ordered the pilots to turn off all the lights until the plane had landed safely.

As the real world spun out of control, I took some shelter in the academic universe. It was really the only period in my life during which I withdrew into something of a shell. I declined invitations to teach at the University of Brasília—it was too close to the eye of the storm. I suppose that I sensed a disaster was inevitable.

Meanwhile, the country grew ever more militant and divided. A few of my colleagues and friends took jobs within Goulart's administration, among them Darcy Ribeiro, a well-known anthropologist, who became his chief of staff. Darcy, who was very close to my family and used to take beach vacations with us, called me one night and said he was going to come to São Paulo to give a speech.

"Look, Darcy, I think it's risky," I told him. "If you come to São Paulo, come with protection."

A few days prior, Goulart's minister of agrarian reform had been to São Paulo and was assaulted by protesters. It wasn't exactly an assassination attempt, but he had been badly mauled. Meanwhile, bands of pro-Goulart militias had formed what were called "Groups of Eleven." The idea, inspired by Brizola, was that groups of eleven people each would form to "protect democracy." It was absurd, but at the time these groups seemed to provide the only reliable source of protection for Darcy and other government figures. It was an indication of how fantastic the country's political life had become.

"Come with the Groups of Eleven," I instructed Darcy, "because otherwise you could get killed here."

I had no idea that my advice to Darcy had been overheard: Our phone conversation was being recorded by the military, and would be used against me later.

Goulart managed to last longer than any of us expected. He was a decent man and a shrewd politician. It is safe to say, however, that by 1964 most Brazilians were terrified of him. A shy man in person, Goulart was all too audacious when it came to wielding power—especially the kind he didn't have. Advised by several Communists, including Luís Carlos Prestes, Goulart made a clumsy attempt at agrarian reform. He also noisily vowed "urban reform"—to this day we have no real idea what he meant, but the mere threat had all Brazilians, in the city and in the country, terrified of losing their homes. Thousands of farmers and others armed themselves and formed militias, prepared to defend their land.

It was, indeed, a recipe for a coup.

What should Brazil have done?

On one hand, it is difficult, in retrospect, to argue in favor of either Jânio or Goulart. Both men made a train wreck of their presidencies. They openly provoked the most powerful sectors of Brazilian society—Jânio with his bizarre flirtation with communism, Goulart with his plans for land reform—while simultaneously doing precious little to help the poor. Inflation soared and investment plunged. From that perspective, the argument for military intervention seems rational. History shows, however, that the military was so agitated that it would swing almost as far to the right as Goulart had gone to the left. The military had intervened several times in Brazilian history, but *never* had it done so to seize power for itself. This time would be different. And the result would be disastrous.

On March 13, 1964, I was visiting my father at his house in Rio. That day, Goulart held a noisy rally with supporters in Rio in front of the ministry of war, perhaps sensing the end was near. As night fell, I left the apartment and saw that the city was illuminated with a new kind of light. All over downtown, candles were placed in windows, a symbol of silent support for a coup against Goulart. In my father's building, only two windows were dark: his, and that of the famous Brazilian poet Carlos Drumond de Andrade.

I went to the train station, which was right by the rally, and ran into a whole circle of young friends who, like me, were taking an overnight train back to São Paulo. It was an eerie, dark, somber ride home. "This isn't going to end well," someone said. The possibility that some of us would have to leave Brazil was broached for the first time.

Most of the time, however, we rode in silence.

A month later, I would be in exile.

THE BITTER CAVIAR OF EXILE

ITHIN HOURS of the coup, the military police arrested a thirty-three-year-old sociology professor named Fernando Henrique Cardoso. Or so they thought. In reality, they detained a younger colleague of mine, Bento Prado, on his way into the university, interrogated him for a while, and then started to take him away to God knows where. Thankfully, he managed to convince them that he was not me, and they grudgingly let him go. But I didn't need a doctorate to understand the message: I was a wanted man.

Bewildered, I spent the next few nights at friends' houses, on couches and cots, changing hideouts every few nights. It didn't feel particularly momentous or even that frightening at the time, though—ridiculous would be a better description. Here I was, a professor on the run, transformed overnight into some kind of Che Guevara in a tweed jacket. I almost felt like turning myself in just so I could get answers to basic questions: Why had I been targeted for arrest? Who had given the order? What law had I broken? And, perhaps most important: On whose authority? Who was in charge of Brazil?

Nobody had any idea what was happening. We knew the military had seized power, but we had only a vague idea of which internal faction would end up running Brazil. On the night of March 31, 1964, hostile troops had approached Rio from Minas Gerais and São Paulo. Goulart had caught wind of the plan and fled for southern Brazil and, shortly thereafter, exile in Uruguay. Just like that, another bloodless coup was completed. This time, however, the change would be more drastic. With Goulart's departure, the military aspired to end once and for all the Getúlio Vargas era, with its focus on the urban working class, and return power to the military and economic elite.

In the days thereafter, Goulart was replaced not by a roar of anger or authoritarianism, but with a vacuum of misinformation. There was no news, only whispered conspiracies. The radio blared little besides rousing military marches. Newspapers were censored and rendered instantly useless. Jittery, baby-faced soldiers roamed the streets toting machine guns. Police cars sped by, going nowhere in particular, their sirens blaring for no other reason than to scare people. It was preposterous, but it worked. There was, in fact, almost nothing happening.

One of the wildest rumors was of a pocket of resistance in the south. A friend of mine was related to a general who was supposedly supporting Goulart, and in a fit of youthful idealism we grabbed revolvers late one night and hopped into a car bound for the airport and—who knows what we had in mind? It was insane. I might have been the son of a general, but I barely knew how to fire a gun. I suppose we were swept up in the moment, horrified by what dictatorship might bring. That night, a military roadblock forced us to turn the car around. It was fortunate; we could have been killed. Thus ended, without incident, my ill-advised foray into armed resistance—the only such attempt I would ever make.

Aside from that one aborted excursion, which no one ever found out about, I've never been precisely sure why the military was after me. I was not a member of the Communist Party, and I had no great affection for Goulart, either. There were, however, a few compelling reasons to try and silence me. The day after the coup, I held a meeting with students at the university where we tried to decipher what was happening and how to act. There were far more questions than answers. Would the coup last? Would there be resistance? Had anybody seen so-and-so? Did you hear who had been arrested? The worst sin we committed was not a call for resistance but, in fact, the very opposite kind of crime: silence. My department, the faculty of philosophy, science, and letters, did not immediately issue a public statement supporting the coup. Since I was relatively influential among the professors, I suppose my personal silence must have seemed particularly conspicuous.

Still, it remains a mystery why the military came for me with such haste and intensity. I suspect that, in the end, politics probably were less of a factor than petty personal rivalries. At the university, I had been part of an effort to transform the *cátedra,* a hierarchical, almost feudal system in which professors received lifetime appointments and wielded absolute power over students, academic studies, and other teachers. Our objective had been to make the system more democratic. Of course, this greatly threatened older professors who had already obtained the rank. All they needed to get rid of me was to make a phone call to the right colonel . . .

Therein lies the insidious nature of coups. They are always portrayed at first as noble, cleansing events but then degenerate into vulgar score-settling by whoever happens to be on the right side. A witch hunt ensues, and the unscrupulous can spit out the names of people who possess no fault other than being their personal adversaries. In those days, Brazil put Salem to shame. Lives were ruined. Careers were ended. And many of the victims never found out why.

Ruth spent hours wandering São Paulo, in and out of police stations, desperate to discover why there was an arrest order over my head. She finally managed to find a family friend who spoke with São

Paulo's secretary in charge of public security, a distinguished professor of law and former *integralista* named Miguel Reale. The friend asked Reale why the police were so zealously pursuing a young professor with no particular political affiliation.

"This man is not just an academic!" Reale exclaimed. "He is a militant!"

This was hardly the case. In the days following the coup, this "militant" was hard at work—on his thesis. I scarcely believe it now, but as I bounced from one house to another, I actually continued writing my dissertation on Latin American businessmen and development. I stayed up late at night in friends' living rooms with one worried eye cast toward the door, the other revising drafts and flipping through academic theses. Not exactly the textbook activities of a guerrilla leader.

As time dragged on and the police closed in, I suppose I adhered to an old stereotype about Brazilians—under duress, I sought refuge at the beach. Accompanied by Ruth, our children, and a friend, Leôncio Martins Rodrigues, I retreated to a tiny apartment that belonged to another friend about 80 kilometers from São Paulo. The apartment was just a short walk from the ocean and, as fate would have it, right behind an army base. There we were, right under their noses as they haplessly knocked down doors looking for us in another city. But the irony did little to lift our spirits, and those were some of the longest days of my life. We were completely isolated, with no newspapers, no radio, and few phone calls. After four or five days, we decided that we looked too suspicious—a man and his kids at the beach in April, which is not vacation season in Brazil—so Ruth and the children returned to São Paulo.

Leôncio and I spent endless hours moping along the beach, worried sick about what was happening to our families and our country. The sun even failed to shine. So I was almost relieved when a phone call came from São Paulo.

"The situation is getting worse here," Ruth said softly, delicately. "All of us think it would be better if you left Brazil for a while."

Her words shattered me. But I instantly knew she was right. Too many of our friends were disappearing, and it was clear that my family connections would not protect me. My father's opposition to the coup, although quiet, disturbed the military hierarchy. By 1964, he was old enough, and quiet enough, to avoid deeper trouble. I would not be granted the same special treatment. Ruth often sees things with more clarity than I do, and in this particular circumstance, her instincts were right on target.

Leôncio and I drove back to São Paulo, where I stayed with an architect who had been building us a house. The architect was good friends with the U.S. consul, a very kind man who came over to the apartment and gave me a travel visa for the United States. Right after he left, however, it occurred to me that if U.S. officials knew where I was, then the Brazilian military certainly would know as well. The coup had been entirely Brazilian—that is, it took place without direct U.S. support—but there could be no doubt whose side the United States was on. So I thanked the architect and got out of his apartment as quickly as possible. I kept the visa.

The only way out now was the airport, but this was a tricky proposition. We had a good friend, Maurício Segall, who had contacts at Air France and, therefore, access to a list the military provided to the airlines of "subversives" who were not permitted to fly out of the country. The list was ever-changing, with a different version at each airport, and Maurício found out that I did not appear on the one at Campinas, just outside São Paulo. He booked a flight for me out of the country on a somewhat disreputable South American airline—here, one deep-seated fear overwhelmed another, and I told Maurício that, if that was the only option, I would rather stay and take my chances with the Brazilian police. Finally, however, we found a more acceptable airline that would take me to Argentina, and it was decided that I would fly out the next afternoon.

I remember very little about the day I left Brazil. My head was spinning from a combination of anger and fear that I had never in my life felt before. All the details about that day have since been pieced together by Ruth. I am told that, first, we stopped at my friend Roberto Gusmão's house to drop off a copy of my thesis, which we hid—hid!—behind a stereo speaker. Maurício had given us these very specific instructions on what to do next, and Ruth used the same system repeatedly in coming months to help others escape from Brazil: I took a bus out to the edge of the city, where I was instructed to wait in a bar on the side of the highway. Meanwhile, Ruth and several other friends drove on to the airport to see if the police presence was heavy that day. When they saw the coast was clear, they came back to the bar to pick me up.

All of us were dressed in our finest, most expensive clothes. I had put on a very elegant three-piece suit, while Ruth and her friends were wearing long, flowing dresses and high heels. The theory behind this speaks volumes about Brazilian society: If we appeared to be members of the upper class, the police would not dare to bother us once we reached the airport. And we were right—no one did. On the afternoon of April 17, 1964, I got on a plane and left Brazil.

There are few things more undignified than exile. I felt emasculated, helpless. I was leaving my family behind, and my country as well—a country that so many ancestors of mine had endeavored to build and improve. I believed my exile would only last a few weeks, perhaps months, but I worried that in the meantime I would lose my job and my friends. All I remember from that day is wanting to cry as I boarded the plane for Argentina. I recall thinking: My God, I'm leaving Brazil, leaving behind my roots and my country. And for what? Why?

Argentina was right next door, but it might as well have been half a world away. In those days, telephoning Brazil from Buenos Aires could take hours. It is incredible to think this was barely four decades ago.

Simply finding someone with a telephone in their house was a massive ordeal. Then, to make a call, one had to take the phone off the hook, place the receiver on the table, and wait for a dial tone. Sometimes this took twenty minutes, usually longer. The connection was barely intelligible and cut off without warning. It should be noted, however, that Argentina was the height of modernity compared to Chile, where I ended up a month later—and where the only readily available communication with some family members in Brazil was via short-wave radio.

Information within Brazil was equally spotty, which gave the military carte blanche to do whatever it wanted. Under a virtual news blackout, the regime was under no obligation to commit one way or another by announcing what its ultimate intentions were. It had the luxury of opting for silence instead, and the vacuum was filled with rumor, lies, and fear. Against a background of rampant conjecture, the idea of a stable military order seemed even more attractive, so the armed forces were able to consolidate their rule. Everyone assumed, however, that the military would intervene only for a short while, as had happened on so many other occasions in Brazilian history, and then turn the country back over to democratically elected leaders as soon as the country stabilized. "As soon as . . ." turned into twenty years.

What happened in April 1964 was not just a coup; it was a profound clash in Brazilian society. The elite classes felt the experiment with democracy had failed. They believed that an ungrateful electorate had endangered the country—specifically, the privileges the elite had always enjoyed—by selecting incompetent leaders like Jânio and Goulart to lead Brazil. As the Harvard historian Kenneth Maxwell observed, "Democracy in Brazil has all too often been seen as the enemy of progress, the harbinger of anarchy, disunion and backwardness." And so, democracy itself was discarded.

The military was used as a tool to grab power on behalf of the business elite and a frustrated middle class. The ensuing "reorganization" did not destroy merely people, but entire segments of society. All the clout that Vargas, Kubitschek, and Goulart had given to urban workers in previous decades was taken away virtually overnight. In the next four years, the new military government issued more than 3,000 presidential decrees to reform the economy. Government spending was cut by a third, whereas income tax revenue quadrupled. The unions were stripped of their influence. Labor strikes, which had been almost a daily occurrence under Goulart, were outlawed. The regime set about remaking Brazil in its own image: authoritarian, secretive, and with precious little concern for the poor or for human rights.

It is an exaggeration to say that "Brazil couldn't even organize a dictatorship properly." But there was a kernel of truth to this, as the military showed itself prone to many of the same problems that affected the rest of the country, leading to a regime that was a very odd, very Brazilian hybrid. The result was not a classic, iron-fisted Latin American military government. It was, after all, composed of Brazilians, with the curiously improvised, consensus-based streak of character that has defined most of our rulers, military or civilian. Instead of having one iconoclastic dictator—as would soon happen in Augusto Pinochet's Chile—the presidency of Brazil still rotated every four years. Congress continued to meet, and it was even responsible for electing the executive every four years (although the regime's preferred candidate always won, of course). A single omnibus opposition party, called the Brazilian Democratic Movement, or MDB, was permitted to stand for state and congressional elections. A tentative freedom of the press was also reestablished. Kidnapping, torture, and murder did not become commonplace until a few years after the coup.

In retrospect, I believe I probably could have stayed behind in Brazil without my life being endangered, at least in the short term. If I had turned myself in on that first morning, I might have been detained for a day or two and then released. However, I would have been placed under severe restrictions in my academic work, and I would have been subject to the stifling intellectual climate and persecution of all suspected leftists. I would not have grown professionally. Plus, none of us knew what the military's intentions were upon taking power; we only knew that our friends were being jailed. Looking back, I think my decision to go into exile was correct, even though the consequences were dire.

Piece by piece, one tenuous phone conversation after another, I learned that my life in Brazil was being taken away from me. Investigative committees were formed at the university with the involvement of military officers; when they called on me to testify, and I didn't appear, the tribunal declared me a threat to national security and sentenced me in absentia to prison. I had left a letter with Ruth requesting formal leave from USP so that I wouldn't lose my job, but pressure from the political right eventually led to my outright termination.

This story repeated itself across Brazil, often under much more dire circumstances than my own. My mentor at USP, Florestan Fernandes, was briefly jailed after writing a manifesto denouncing the coup. Other professionals arrived at their offices to find their desks cleaned out and their belongings in a box. Some simply vanished. The era of mass political violence would not begin until several years later, but lives were being ruined nonetheless. Slowly, the people who had supported the coup—the middle class, principally—realized they were sinking into a long national nightmare. As usually happens with such tragedies, it was too late to turn back.

In Buenos Aires, I continued to work on my thesis, hoping the problems in Brazil would somehow disappear and life would return to normal. I spent most of my time in a friend's apartment—Jose Num, the current Argentinian minister of culture—reading whatever newspapers I could. I was hesitant to use the telephone too much because I feared the Argentine military was in cahoots with the Brazilians. I had a small group of Argentine friends I had met at previous academic conferences—among them Torcuato Di Tella, a well-known sociologist who many years later became Argentina's minister of culture. Most of my time, however, was spent waiting. For what, I didn't quite know.

Finally, a few weeks after leaving São Paulo, I was paid a visit by Nuno Fidelino Figueiredo, a former colleague of mine from USP. Nuno's father was the old man by the resort pool who, twenty years before, had encouraged me to enter USP and study sociology. Now, it was apparently time for another Figueiredo to give me a boost to the next stage in my life. Nuno worked at the United Nations Economic Commission for Latin America and the Caribbean, known by its Spanish acronym, CEPAL. CEPAL's influence went far beyond its official role as an advisory board for economic policy. It had gathered some of the finest intellectuals in the region, and its opinions on matters from trade to industrial development gained huge sway over Latin American governments looking for that elusive tonic called "progress." Nuno told me that José Medina Echevarria, a leading Spanish sociologist living in exile, wanted to offer me a job at CEPAL headquarters in Santiago, Chile. I jumped at the opportunity.

Exile has a way of driving you toward your own, and turning back the clock as well. When I arrived in Santiago, I rented a house with three colleagues from CEPAL: Celso Furtado, an eminent economist; Francisco Weffort, who was later my minister of culture; and another professor named Wilson Cantoni. We all started behaving like penniless bachelors again. My new job actually paid quite well, but we were so uncertain as to how long our stay would last that we all became absurdly, painfully stingy. We were such cheapskates that we refused to pay for heat in our house. This was ridiculous. Temperatures in Santiago often drop below freezing, and I remember that first winter as particularly gray and cold. There was no central heat in those days, so you had to buy a stove and then fill it with kerosene, which wasn't that expensive—but it didn't matter. We had massive fights over whether to get a stove; a majority of us ultimately voted not to. Needless to say, we nearly froze to death.

There were countless others for whom the suffering was more real.

There were exiled Brazilian lawyers who, of course, could not practice law in a foreign country. In economic terms, they fell very far, very fast. Other professionals, such as schoolteachers, simply did not have a strong enough grasp of the Spanish language to acclimate. Even the qualified sometimes had to wait months to find employment. A group of the more fortunate started a small cash fund for donations to help the recently arrived get on their feet. That fund later enjoyed quite an extraordinary evolution, as the original pot of money grew and was used to build a restaurant and then a Laundromat. All the profits were used to aid needy Brazilian exiles.

Despite the camaraderie, many people turned inward and became extraordinarily bitter. Not long after my arrival, I had lunch with Samuel Wainer, the famous Brazilian journalist who had supported Vargas during the 1950s and then contributed to his downfall by accepting questionable loans from the Bank of Brazil. A group of us went downtown to enjoy a long lunch of seafood casserole and wine.

After the second bottle of wine, Wainer burst into tears. "This is the second time in my life that I have been in exile!" he sobbed. "When will I ever be able to go home again?"

My friend Celso Furtado leaned across the table, trying to comfort him. "Don't worry," Celso said. "The dictatorship will last two years at most."

Wainer looked up at Celso, indignant. "There's no way the military would hold on to power *that* long!" he declared.

I nodded and energetically voiced the same opinion. We were all in error by nearly two decades.

For me, the tough times were never really that tough. Before long, Ruth and the kids came to Santiago. Our temporary stay turned into four years, and Chile became our second home. Life was quite marvelous despite our forced exit from Brazil, and looking back I have often compared my exile to "bitter caviar." I achieved a degree of international recognition with my job, and I was promoted. I received a handsome salary, and my diplomatic status allowed me to import a

Mercedes sedan, quite a status symbol back then. My young children learned how to speak Spanish and English, and for a time thereafter my daughter Luciana spoke Portuguese with a somewhat strange, foreign-sounding accent. We were becoming citizens of the world, acquiring a more global and open-minded point of view, something that would serve us well in the years ahead.

There is a certain camaraderie to exile, a certain stress that unites people from the same country, makes life seem slightly more vivid, as if there were a constant flow of adrenaline, stimulation tinged with sadness. Compatriots who might not otherwise become friends discover that they have a shared history—somehow, because of this, I often felt more Brazilian in Santiago than I had in São Paulo. Many of us gathered regularly for a traditional meal of *feijoada,* a hearty black bean stew that we had only rarely enjoyed in Brazil.

It was also in Santiago that I awakened to the concept of "Latin America." It seems quite intuitive now, but the concept of the region as a political and cultural bloc was still not popular back then. We just didn't believe that Brazil, with its Portuguese heritage and continental size, had much in common with Peru, Venezuela, or Mexico. Only when I lived in Paris during the early 1960s did it occur to me that it was easier for us to communicate with the Argentine or the Uruguayan expatriates than with the French—even though my French language skills in that era were far more developed than my Spanish. From that same era, I also remember a side trip to Amsterdam, where a group of Latin Americans gathered to listen to the radio for news of the Cuban missile crisis, and the only Dutch we understood was the phrase "Doctor Castro." All this camaraderie struck me as rather odd. It wasn't until I joined CEPAL in 1964, and worked with other expatriates from all around the region, that I realized that in fact Latin American countries were very similar.

What I remember most distinctly about Santiago is that there was a good smell, and there was a bad smell. The bad one came from that awful kerosene that at first, upon arrival, we had obstinately refused to buy—during winter, the smoke drifted onto the street and seeped into everything: our clothes, our hair. Santiago is nestled in a valley surrounded by the dramatic, snow-capped Andes Mountains—which are utterly invisible from the city during the winter due to the choking smog. The mountains are nothing more than a rumor for three months out of the year. Winters are cold and dry and gray and seemingly endless, especially for a Brazilian accustomed to the gentle warmth of the Atlantic coast.

Then, spring arrived, and with it the good smell. The good smell in Santiago comes from the flowers and the ritual explosion of life that takes place in the ample gardens and parks of the city. The air clears up somewhat in the summer months, and the mountains loom over the city like monsters, so close and imposing that you have to marvel at how anything so enormous could have disappeared for so long. The climate is dry and healthy, and the mountains' chapped golden slopes turn bright red at sundown—quite a fantastic sight for a Brazilian who grew up believing all mountains were only green. For most of the year, it is the good smell that wafts through the city, and it seemed to me like a tremendously well-cared for and civilized place.

Santiago shone as Latin America's foremost center of culture and intellectual thought, a distinction made all the more tragic by what came later. The city was tiny back then, making it feel like an intimate secret to which only a few lucky foreigners were privy. Chile was Latin America's oldest parliamentary democracy, and ideas flowed freely. There was a council of foreign relations in Santiago where government officials and intellectuals gathered to discuss ideas—such an organized forum would have been unthinkable in Brazil, and I remember being shocked by how refined and democratic Chilean society was. We entertained ourselves at museums, poetry readings, and academic conferences. We made friends with Chileans at work and in our neighborhood. Across the street from us lived the parents-in-law of Ricardo Lagos, who later became Chile's president in 2000. Ricardo and I remain good friends to this day, and he is part of a network of Chileans whom I hold close to my heart.

Then there were the parties. The Brazilian cultural attaché in those days was Thiago de Mello, a poet who had been appointed by Goulart and was allowed to continue in his post after the coup. Thiago was a very striking, charismatic man from the Amazon, with dark skin that made him look like an Indian. He and his Chilean wife rented their house from Pablo Neruda, the famous Chilean poet. The parties would stretch on into early morning, fueled by marvelous seafood, fine French cheeses, and no small amount of wine and pisco, the fine Chilean brandy. Celebrities from both Brazil and Chile streamed through, including Neruda himself.

Neruda was like a deity. Everyone at these parties practically fell over themselves to pay homage to him. On a personal level, I found him a bit dull, but as a poet he was unquestionably fantastic, deserving of all the credit he received and more. He always made grand entrances to these parties—it was his house, after all—and I remember one night when he barged through the front door loudly reciting one of his most famous poems, speaking with this very odd, breathy, high-pitched voice: *"Puedo escribir los versos mas tristes esta noche,"* or "I am going to write the saddest verses tonight." After that melancholy but powerful recitation, the party was irrevocably his.

Another fixture at these parties was Salvador Allende, the ill-fated leftist leader who became president years later and was then ousted by General Augusto Pinochet. I met Allende on several occasions. He reminded me of old-time Brazilian politicians: formal, elegant, a builder of alliances. He wore tailored navy blazers. Soft-spoken and refined, he liked to discuss poetry and literature, but only rarely politics.

Allende hardly seemed like a man who would soon be caught up in one of Latin America's most brutal and tragic revolts. Then again, nothing in Chile suggested the hell that lurked just around the corner. I am sad to admit that I never saw it coming.

There is a Brazilian word, *saudade,* which is said to be untranslatable. It roughly means "nostalgia," but it also implies feeling happy and sad at the same time. If there is a more Brazilian emotion, I am not aware of it.

For all our reputation as the world's greatest partiers, there is always a hint of underlying tragedy present in our revelry. And that is how I felt in Chile. As pleasant as that life was, it was not home. I felt great saudade for Brazil. I constantly thought about how I might return.

In the meantime, I went through the motions, struggling to do things and meet people that reminded me of Brazil. I tried to keep my teaching skills sharp by giving sociology classes at universities throughout Santiago. I didn't ask for any salary or even a title; I just wanted to maintain that bridge to the past. It was a kind of nostalgic indulgence that helped me as much as my students. One of my students was Salvador Allende's daughter, Isabel, who decades later would become an important politician in her own right. There was also another student who made an impact on me from the first second I saw him. I will always remember the image of him, sitting in the back of the classroom with these enormous, hawklike eyes, taking in every word. After that lecture ended, he bounded down the steps of the lecture hall and introduced himself as a young Brazilian exile named José Serra.

Politicians in Brazil tend to have exceptionally long careers, starting in their twenties and then continuing for another half century—provided they somehow manage to survive the stress and live that long. José Serra, who would become my minister of health and then my party's candidate to replace me as president in the 2002 elections, was already a veteran politician when we first met in that Chilean classroom in the 1960s. During the Goulart administration, Serra had been the head of the highly influential Brazilian Students Union, and he had been a main player in the pro-Goulart rally that precipitated the coup. Obviously, Serra was compelled to seek exile, and he arrived in Chile in 1965 somewhat adrift. Nevertheless, it didn't take long for his legendarily precocious, stubborn character to get him back in the political game. In Brazil, Serra had been an engineering student on the verge of receiving his degree, but in Chile he became hell-bent on reinventing himself as an economist. We all found out very quickly that when José Serra wants something, he gets it. He managed to earn a master's degree in economics without ever having received an undergraduate degree. Four decades later, I still marvel at his ambition.

Serra struck up a friendship with me and soon joined a seminar that we held in Chile, similar to the Marx Seminar back in São Paulo. This group was less famous, perhaps, but just as remarkable. One member was a filmmaker, Leon Hirszman, while another later became my government's leader in the Senate, Paulo Alberto Monteiro de Barros. Almino Affonso, who was Goulart's labor minister, and my old childhood friend Plinio de Arruda Sampaio also participated. This "Santiago Seminar" was much more overtly political than the Marx meetings—it became a think tank of diverse exiles. As the years passed, we began devising ways to try and influence politics back home. Pro-democracy leaders were always dropping by, and that was how we were graced one summer by a visit from the irascible former president Jânio Quadros.

After a long world tour, Jânio arrived in Chile by boat—the man was deathly afraid of planes, one of the few traits I am willing to admit that we had in common. His arrival coincided with a moment when it looked like the military's hold on power back in Brazil might be loosening. There was a broad front of leaders forming in favor of democracy, and Jânio was trying to drum up support for moderates within the military hierarchy who might restore democracy. So he came to gauge sentiment and support among the numerous Brazilian expatriates in Santiago. We went to a lunch organized by a friend of ours, and Jânio showed up fresh off the boat, dressed to the nines and with his mother in tow.

Jânio was still relatively young but already a man stuck in the past. He launched into a bizarre soliloquy about how the coffee economy needed to be revived at all costs. The rambling got worse as he downed whiskey after whiskey—the man would drink absolutely anything, but of course he favored the good stuff. Afternoon stretched into evening, and the men filed into a separate room from the women to discuss supposedly serious matters with a man who was, remember, a former Brazilian head of state. But Jânio was by now drunk beyond all reason, and he was totally flummoxed when the shrill screaming came from the other room.

"Jânio! My son! We have to leave!"

At first he opted to ignore his mother and uneasily tried to soldier on with his lecture about the fledgling democracy movement back home.

"My son! Jânio! Let's go back to the boat!"

We all stared at each other with a mix of embarrassment and bewilderment. Were they really going back to their boat that night? The nearest port was in Valparaíso, a couple of hours from Santiago.

"Jânio!"

Finally, he yelled back. "Moooooooooom!" he whined, like a small child. "Don't bother me, Mom, I'm trying to talk to my friends!"

"Jânio!" his mother said sternly, stomping into the room. "Let's go! There are earthquakes here!"

We learned that the Quadros family refused to sleep on land, terrified of the moderate earthquakes that rocked Santiago every so often. We protested, saying that staying on the boat was likely more perilous, since any major tremor could then unleash a tsunami—a far worse fate, we told our panicked guests. This scared them even more, and they briefly toyed with the idea of staying. But they would have none of it, and back to Valparaíso they went.

Unsurprisingly, with leaders like that, the front in favor of democracy fizzled out despite the efforts of many good people. The hard-line faction within the military retaliated, clamping down with increased vigor. The years to come were some of the most brutal in the history of Brazil.

I had just finished a tennis lesson one morning when Osvaldo Sunkel, an economist at CEPAL, showed up with an envelope for me. I knew right away that something was wrong because Osvaldo was uncharacteristically silent. He stood there with his head bowed as I opened it to find a telegram that read simply: "*Sapo morreu*"—"Sapo is dead."

I had no idea my father was even sick. Communications being what they were, I didn't find out until much later that he had suffered from heart problems. He hadn't been ill for very long. My grief transformed immediately into a cloudy, confused rage. What to do? Go back to Brazil? Grieve from afar? I had no idea if I could make it back in time for the funeral, or whether I could go at all—there was still a warrant out for my arrest. This was one of the worst possible things that could happen to someone in exile, and my heart filled with hatred for the regime that kept me from being at my father's side for his passing.

I needed to make a decision right away. Brazilian tradition dictates that someone be buried within twenty-four hours of death, so if I was going to make it to Rio for the funeral, I needed to leave Chile that same day. My diplomatic passport from the United Nations theoretically granted me a degree of immunity, but the Brazilian military tended to play by its own rules. Despite the great risk, however, it was obvious to me what my decision should be.

I bid a long goodbye to Ruth and the kids, left Santiago, and arrived in Rio around midnight. No one gave me any trouble at the airport. I took a taxi to my father's apartment, which was eerily empty, and got a few hours of sleep. The next morning, there was a private memorial service, where I saw my brother, my sister, and my mother for the first time in a long while. My mother wept inconsolably, overwhelmed by the loss of her husband of thirty-five years, and, I'm sure, by the sudden reappearance of her exiled son.

My father's casket sat in a corner of the room. I could see from a distance that it was open, which shocked me for some reason. I stared a good long while, speechless, before I turned to my brother and said: "Well, I guess we don't have much choice. Let's go take a look at the old man." I suppose I was trying to bring some levity to the situation, but then we walked over to the casket, saw him lying there, and grief washed over me. I remembered how I hadn't been there for the final years of this great man, whom I had always done my best to emulate. I allowed myself to shed some tears.

There was a formal public ceremony in the cemetery that was attended by perhaps 100 people. A great many of them were military, of course. They had come both to pay respects to my father, the general, and to keep an eye on his son, the rebel. They stood there, stern-faced and in full military uniform, watching the grave with one eye and me with the other. At one point, a senior officer walked over and began speaking in hushed tones to a cousin of mine. My cousin then approached me and put his hand on my shoulder.

"The general offered condolences on behalf of the Brazilian military for the passing of your father," my cousin whispered. "He also said that you will need to leave Brazil as soon as possible, after the seventh-day mass, or you will face arrest."

I stood there, dumbfounded, my head reeling just like it had the day I'd first gone into exile. I was overcome by a sense of alienation from my own country. My father had died, my history had been taken from me, and my life had been uprooted. Years would pass before I was able to recover from these injustices and reestablish a positive relationship with Brazil.

The arrest order against me was ultimately canceled in 1967, when my case made it to the military Supreme Court. There, a general named Peri Constant Bevilacqua—the grandson of Benjamin Constant, the famous professor of my grandfather's who had led the coup in 1889 against Dom Pedro II—launched a vitriolic diatribe against military oppression. As a result, the case against me was dropped. When the regime turned more hard-line a year later, Peri himself became the victim of persecution. The authorities forced him into early retirement and stripped him of his military decorations. Nearly three decades passed before, as president, I was finally able to return the medals to his family.

The death of my father infused me with a new drive. I wanted to make him proud. It was no coincidence that shortly thereafter, in 1967, I finished a book that is probably my best known academic work. It was a joint project with Enzo Faletto, a Chilean social scientist, called *Dependency and Development in Latin America*. Published in Spanish in 1969, Portuguese in 1970, Italian in 1971, German in 1977, and French in 1978, it launched my academic career on the world stage. By the time the English version came out in 1979, the Spanish version had been through sixteen printings.*

Why was the book so influential? Basically, it articulated a model that explained what was happening socially, politically, and economically in Latin America. In the early 1960s, with much of the region mired in economic stagnation, those on the ideological left were convinced that a terminal crisis of global capitalism was inevitable. They believed the existing system was broken. The rich countries, namely the United States and the nations of Western Europe, would subjugate the "Third World" in a helpless state of permanent poverty and backwardness until they broke free from their chains, so to speak. Many of my contemporaries believed this was true not just in Latin America, but in all of the developing world. They expected—and yearned for—a global revolution.

By the mid-1960s, however, something strange was happening: Many "Third World" countries, Brazil included, were experiencing quite robust economic growth. Particularly in South Korea and Taiwan, it was plainly obvious that poor countries that embraced foreign investment and developed a competitive export model were capable of prospering within the existing capitalist system. Meanwhile, countries that had actually undergone the dreamed-of socialist revolution—

---

*For further reading on my academic and political career, please see Ted Goertzel's fine book *Fernando Henrique Cardoso: Reinventing Democracy in Brazil* (Boulder: Lynne Rienner, 1999).

North Korea, Cuba, and East Germany, for example—suffered from sputtering economies and totalitarian regimes. To people who had embraced so-called Marxist dogma during their entire careers, the juxtaposition of these two realities was both puzzling and disturbing.

Faletto and I tried to address these truths not by formulating a new theory, but by coldly examining some key facts in several Latin American countries. We looked at the management of the economies in each country and saw that some governments and business communities had done a better job than others at attracting foreign capital and growing their economies. We also saw that some countries, particularly Argentina and Brazil, had been able to accommodate foreign companies without ceding control over their national interests. We postulated, then, that poor countries in a position of "dependency" on the rich ones could take certain steps toward progress in spite of the existing system. All of this sounds quite elementary and obvious now, but in Latin America in 1968, these thoughts were borderline heresy.

The book was widely interpreted as leftist because of its worldview—our delineation of the divisions between rich and poor nations, and our description of the *existing* relationship. However, the conclusions were not very leftist at all.

The primary message of *Dependency and Development* was that the people of Latin America had control over their own fate. Under certain circumstances, we could indeed operate within the existing system. Many alternatives were possible within that system, and the fatalism that dominated the region at that time was entirely pointless, we wrote. There would, of course, be certain restrictions, and we did not advocate blind free-market capitalism. In fact, we didn't advocate many specific initiatives at all. We simply described the changing world as we saw it, much as Marx would have. We pointed out that Latin American leaders were capable of making influential, self-determining decisions within that world. "The course of history depends largely on the daring of those who propose to act in terms of historically viable goals," we wrote. In other words: The problem faced by Latin America was political in nature rather than economic. Our backwardness was our own fault, not anybody else's. That stinging self-indictment was what made the book so controversial.

The book was read by academics, policymakers, and general public alike. In retrospect, I think it was so popular because it was a timely recognition of a new force that had just started to transform the world: What we were really writing about was the beginning of globalization. It didn't possess a catchy name back then. We saw that the globe was being linked by ever-better communications and that companies were emerging that had a foothold in several countries around the globe. Countries that harnessed those companies to their benefit would, in turn, prosper. Today, we would call these companies "multinationals," but this was a relatively new term then. Life has its ironies: As spotty as our understanding of this new phenomenon was in the 1960s, its titanic effect would probably be the most important, problematic, and perplexing force influencing my presidency thirty years later.

Dependency and Development opened a doorway to France. As the book grew ever more influential, my friend and former professor Alain Touraine, of the Industrial Sociology Laboratory at the University of Paris, with whom I had studied in 1961, invited me to teach at the university's new campus at Nanterre. As happy as I had been at CEPAL in Chile, I jumped at the opportunity. After years of turmoil in Latin America, I looked forward to a brief hiatus, fully expecting France to be a refreshing oasis of peace and "First World" prosperity. At first sight, the country seemed so placid. People joked that De Gaulle was like Louis XIV, only better, because there were no rebellions.

There was just one problem: This was 1968.

When Ruth and I first arrived, the façade was still in place. I suppose we should have recognized the first fissures, though. The university campus in Nanterre, a pleasant suburb near Paris's 16th arrondissement, was one of the city's wealthiest districts. Most of the students came from the upper middle class, and it was clear from the beginning that they possessed a kind of bourgeois angst. They resented the university's very traditional formality. For example, when a professor entered the classroom, he was preceded by a man who would declare *"Monsieur le Professeur!"* All the students were expected to stand, and they did so, but ever more slowly and with an occasional groan. Smoking was also prohibited. I remember when I saw the first cigarettes appear in my classroom, and the smug, rebellious faces of the students holding them. I didn't care one bit if they smoked, of course. But it did occur to me that a strange transformation might be under way.

The trigger for the "May Revolution" of 1968, and for the ensuing turmoil that spread across the planet, was of that same somewhat petty nature. The French sports minister came to our campus in Nanterre to inaugurate a new swimming pool. He was confronted by a large group of students angry over restrictions that forbade male students from visiting females in their dorm rooms. The minister jokingly replied that perhaps they should jump in the swimming pool to dampen their sexual desire. This prompted a student of mine, Daniel Cohn-Bendit, to accuse the minister of being a Nazi.

Pandemonium ensued. Cohn-Bendit, who had been born in France but was a German citizen, was called before a police investigative committee to explain his insult. Just before he was due to testify, he came to see me in my office. "Are you involved in politics in France?" he asked.

I told him I most certainly was not. Still, I offered to speak with Alain Touraine, who had gone to school with the French minister of education and might be able to intercede on his behalf.

Ultimately, it was of no use. The students at Nanterre organized a protest to support Cohn-Bendit, who became known around the globe as "Danny the Red," for his hair color as much as for his political sympathies. The protest ended in a brutal clash with riot police. This prompted the professors at Nanterre to close the university, saying conditions were too chaotic to hold classes. The students retaliated by breaking into the university and occupying it, sparking still more confrontations with the police. Within weeks, what had begun as a careless remark beside a swimming pool had been transformed into a general strike, a nationwide student and labor protest that shook France to its very core. De Gaulle ordered tanks into the streets, desperate to restore order.

In the eyes of a Latin American, the events in Paris that summer seemed, well, almost Brazilian in the combination of high emotion and political naïveté. The protesters adopted the language of traditional causes—Vietnam, imperialism, social inequality—but those matters usually had little to do with their struggle. I remember fat French women walking the streets with signs that said "No to world hunger!" Though they rarely admitted it, the students were far more concerned with matters of personal freedom and liberation; the girls already had the right to visit the boys' dorms—now the boys wanted to visit the girls'. During those days, it was prohibited to prohibit; sex, drugs, and rock 'n' roll ruled the day.

The motives ultimately proved irrelevant. People have since forgotten how unsure of itself the world was in 1968—every pillar of the global order was being called into question. It was a year of assassinations, revolutions, and turmoil. In that context, the mere sight of anarchy on the elegant boulevards of Paris, broadcast worldwide by the increasingly popular mass media of television, was enough to inspire copycat demonstrations from Prague to Berkeley. There, they acquired local—and perhaps more meaningful—significance. In Brazil, the May Revolution would have immeasurable repercussions that I wouldn't fully fathom until a few months later.

I was not interested in participating in the protests—this was not my battle. As a sociologist, however, I couldn't help finding them fascinating. They were an irresistible opportunity for research. There was a large group of Brazilian exiles working at the universities in Paris, and we frequently stopped by the demonstrations late at night after class. Touraine often came along as well. The students and workers had put up barricades, and they sat there on the street just talking with each other. Sometimes the leftover smell of tear gas still wafted through the spring night. We chatted amiably with the protesters, often staying up into the early hours of the morning discussing their personal problems and frustrations. Through these experiences, I learned how people could be mobilized in theory for one cause, when in fact they were most passionate about something entirely different.

Everyone has also forgotten that the whole affair wound down rather quickly. One of the French ministers, whose nephew was a friend of ours, invited us over to his house to listen to De Gaulle give a radio address. Everyone was terrified of what he was going to say, thinking maybe the old general was going to quit.

He did not. *"Assez de chienlit,"* De Gaulle told the nation. "That's enough bullshit."

Enough indeed. The protests began to fade by June, and though De Gaulle never properly recovered, everyone else turned their attention to other matters. The truth is that my head was never really in France—it was focused on how to get back to Brazil. I took advantage of the turmoil outside and practically locked myself in my house, writing my thesis and talking with friends back in Brazil, trying to gauge the mood back home. There was some talk of a thaw, of a relaxation of the dictatorship. Ruth and I were eager to get back after nearly five years abroad; our children barely spoke Portuguese anymore. We felt that if our connections to home frayed any further, we might never have an opportunity to return.

After sounding out some of my old contacts, I was informed that there might be a position available back at the University of São Paulo. The arrest order against me had just been canceled, and there seemed to be little danger of censorship. Ruth and I had a long chat and decided it was worth the risk.

We were going home.

CHAPTER

6

JEITINHO

J UST WEEKS AFTER I returned to Brazil, one stray bullet
ended any hopes I still harbored for a quiet life.

A little way down the street from the University of São
Paulo, where I had begun teaching again, was another, private university called Mackenzie. The two schools had always been different, but
now, all of a sudden, they despised each other. Students from our university declared that Mackenzie was a breeding ground for right-wing
shock troops. Mackenzie students, meanwhile, regarded USP as a nest
of radical leftist guerrillas. On October 3, 1968, more than 5,000 students from the two schools clashed in a massive street battle. They
threw eggs, crowbars, and Molotov cocktails. The police intervened.
Tear gas filled the street. Shots were fired. A twenty-year-old student
from a third school, who happened to be walking down the street and
then tried to take shelter toward the rear when the melee broke out,
was hit by a bullet and died on his way to the hospital.

I watched the whole charade, disgusted, from the second-story window of my office. My head spinning with disbelief, I drove to the Department of Public Safety, barged through the front door, and demanded to talk to the most senior official. I was told that he was busy and that I would have to wait. I sat there for hours until an officer finally consented to see me. "The university is in chaos!" I told him. "What will the police do to restore order and punish those responsible?"

"Perhaps," the officer hissed, a glint in his eye, "you should be more concerned about yourself."

Without saying another word, he briskly turned around and walked away.

I trudged back to my office, feeling defeated. When I opened the door, I saw that the files in my desk had been set on fire and destroyed. All my work was lost. I later found out that Mackenzie students had tossed a Molotov cocktail into my office.

I found myself thinking: Did I come back to Brazil for *this*?

I suppose I should have detected trouble from the moment I returned to São Paulo. I hardly recognized my country; it was like coming home to the moon. All the talk I had heard from Paris regarding a thaw within the military regime turned out to be utter nonsense. In reality, the opposite was taking place. After the clash that day between the two universities, I realized that I had in fact returned just in time to witness Brazil's worst era of political violence.

Inspired by the Cuban Revolution, Che Guevara, and, yes, the events of that spring in Paris, many university students had started scattered, hopelessly small guerrilla groups. They set off bombs, robbed banks, and kidnapped political and business leaders, believing their heroics would bring down the government. It was all hopelessly ineffectual. During bank robberies, for example, three or four guerrillas would take care of the messy business of handling the guns and stealing the money, while another group ran down the street, shouting revolutionary slogans and distributing flyers. When the authorities arrived shortly thereafter, policemen then ran down the street, hurriedly picking up the propaganda off the ground and stuffing it in their pockets so no one else would see it. Bystanders simply shrugged, bewildered.

In fact, when asked about the guerrilla movement, most Brazilians did exactly that—they shrugged. The young guerrillas were almost all students, largely from the middle class, and nominally Marxist in their rhetoric. By 1968, however, the public had little taste for Marxism, communism, or any "ism" that suggested a return to the mayhem of Jânio and Jango. The economy was growing at a healthy clip, inflation was relatively low, and at that point most Brazilians still believed the benefits would eventually trickle down to them, even if times were tough for the moment.

When the guerrillas recruited within poor communities in the remote Amazon jungle, they preached about V. I. Lenin and social justice to fervently Catholic peasants who had no contact with government at all, good or bad. Their actions were impeccably high-minded according to their own revolutionary convictions, but perfectly daft in practice. One strategy was to kidnap foreign ambassadors from the countries with the most foreign investment in Brazil—in order—starting with the United States, then Switzerland, and so on. Such actions failed to ignite sympathy among the poor, who didn't see the Swiss ambassador as a daily problem. The guerrillas were trying to lead a proletarian revolution without the proletariat.

The end result was tragedy. The guerrilla movement provided the dictatorship with a handy pretext to crack down on all forms of dissent. Between 1964 and 1985, the military killed about 325 suspected leftists, while more than 1,500 were tortured, according to later estimates by Amnesty International. The overwhelming majority of casualties occurred between 1969 and 1973, the period when guerrilla and military violence were at their peak. Both left and right became more extreme, and the center shrank quietly, not to be heard from for years. Perhaps nowhere was this battle played out more viciously or more dramatically than at the University of São Paulo, where teaching now seemed like an interlude between seismic upheavals.

I felt deeply conflicted. On one hand, I enthusiastically supported efforts to resist the military regime. I also appreciated the impact that civil resistance could have on an authoritarian state. But that was the key—it had to be *civil* resistance. In Brazil, where compromise is highly valued, a vast, coordinated campaign of peaceful demonstrations would have (and later did) put enormous, and positive, pressure on the dictatorship. It was obvious, however, that if the dictatorship's Achilles' heel was civil and political rights, the Brazilian public's sympathies on this subject would not be stirred by tiny bands of hooded bourgeois guerrillas throwing bombs, robbing banks, and abducting unknown diplomats. Above all, my passion was for democracy, while most of the guerrillas dreamed of installing a state that would be just as authoritarian as the one we had—but socialist. Ours was not a shared battle.

That said, civil resistance was no doubt a concept slightly out of place within the heavily polarized context of the times. That explains why a great many of my friends were connected in some way with the violent resistance. They weren't necessarily guerrillas per se; the lines were not that clearly drawn. Some people took up arms, but most others engaged in far less overt activities—offering a rebel on the run a room in their house to spend the night, for example. Social and political life tended to blend into one. On one occasion, I found myself in a car with a group of friends as we delivered a small shipment of machine guns to someone's house. This was done nonchalantly, as if it were one of several errands to be run that day. I don't even remember being particularly nervous. I am sure I would have protested if we had been robbing a bank or doing anything violent. At the time, however, driving around with a cache of illegal weapons did not feel especially momentous.

Perhaps I was desensitized because, from the moment I had stepped off the plane from Paris, the struggle against the dictatorship seemed to color every single aspect of my life. Since I was one of the first political exiles to return home, I became a bit of a symbol at USP. I often gave classes to standing-room-only audiences. This wasn't necessarily because my lectures were always fascinating, but because, in the minds of some students, to attend my class was a way to show opposition to the dictatorship. I found this distinction a bit exhausting, as I did not desire the attention. But, like it or not, I achieved a small bit of underground celebrity, and the students soon elected me as the head of the department of social sciences.

Unfortunately, this was an era of extremists, and their noise overshadowed all else. Some radical students were furious with me because I was bidding for a spot within the controversial *cátedra* system, which granted life tenure and other privileges to a small group of professors. I had also opposed this system before leaving for Chile, believing it was old-fashioned and concentrated power within too small a circle of people. Now these students were accusing me of selling out my beliefs for personal gain.

These accusations came to a head as I defended my thesis, the final step in the competition for the cátedra. This was a major public event before a panel of distinguished professors and other interested observers in the audience. As I spoke,* a group of students barged into the lecture hall and screamed at me to renounce my ties to the university. They held up signs and began chanting that I was a hypocrite.

As the bewildered crowd looked on, I tried to explain my motivation. "If I don't take this job, someone else will," I declared. "I think that it is better for this position to be occupied by a progressive who is capable of changing the system from within, and will try to transform this university."

It was of no use. I found myself pinned in on both sides. If the radical left merely disliked me, the extreme right was rigidly opposed. The minister of justice himself contacted the university dean and made it known that my candidacy for a senior professorship would not meet

---

*In addition to the written dissertation, a subject is chosen at random that the candidate must expound on in an oral exam. By a stroke of luck, my topic was the tenentes. Needless to say, I did quite well.

with official approval. In a direct snub to the regime's authority, the university panel named me to the post anyway—by a unanimous 5–0 vote.

At that point, we all knew that the status quo would not last. We waited breathlessly for the final provocation. I frequently thought of my experience in France, where Danny the Red's confrontation with the sports minister had been the match that started the fire. I suppose it came as no surprise that, in Brazil, the last spark was something equally trivial.

A young congressman from Rio named Márcio Moreira Alves suggested publicly that the general population boycott an Independence Day military parade to protest the dictatorship. Horrified by this show of disrespect, the hard line within the military ordered Congress, which was still operating with reasonable autonomy at that point, to expel Alves from the legislature. When it became clear that Congress would not bend to its will, the military leaders finally decided they had seen enough.

The regime retaliated on December 13, 1968, by issuing Institutional Act No. 5, an appropriately Orwellian-sounding edict that ended all remaining pretense of democracy in Brazil. The act, known as AI-5 for its Portuguese acronym, had an effect akin to a second, more severe coup; it purged Congress of dissident legislators, fired hundreds of judges and mayors, and imposed vigorous censorship on newspapers, including the foreign media. Military ranks were purged of "bland" officers sympathetic to democracy. USP was relatively untouched at first, but the writing was on the wall: They were coming for us too, and soon.

On a sunny morning in April 1969, as I was driving to work in my blue Volkswagen, I heard on the radio that I had been "retired" from the University of São Paulo. Seventy of us, including Florestan Fernandes, as well as José Arthur Giannotti, Octavio Ianni, Bento Prado, and others from the Marx Seminar, appeared on a list of so-called activist professors. Just as after the coup of 1964, this latest list was put together with the help of conservative professors who seized a golden opportunity to settle personal scores. The military dismissed us all from our posts, effective immediately.

The firings were handled in a peculiarly Brazilian way. On one hand, we were declared a threat to national security and forced from our jobs. However, we were also treated with an odd modicum of gentle respect. The military granted us a lifetime pension that was proportional to the number of years we had each taught. We would also be allowed to remain in the country with our families. This time, our exile would be professional.

During any dictatorship, though, respect is relative. When I arrived at the university that morning, I was still climbing out of the car when one of my students ran up to me, waving his arms.

"The police were already here to pick you up!" he declared, sweating and nervous. "They were angry when they didn't find you. They said you will have *problems* if you stay and try to give class."

I walked inside anyway. A group of about a hundred students and several professors gathered in the hallway, trying to make sense of what had happened. As we spoke, I heard police sirens in the distance. Before we could scatter, a dozen policemen with guns burst through the doors and instructed us to move to a big hall in USP's main building. They escorted us there and locked the doors. The students were terrified and began nervously exchanging stories they had heard about the horrors of prison, mentally preparing themselves for what was surely coming next.

My escape was a fluke. A guard stood at the door checking IDs and allowing people to leave if they were not on a handwritten list. I approached him, told him I had no ID, and flashed my checkbook at him, covering it so he could not see the name. He nodded solemnly and waved me through. I've never understood exactly why.

I was lucky; several students were taken away to prison that day. My heart pounding, I spent the rest of the afternoon taking a long walk through the city, contemplating my future. Suddenly, at the age of thirty-seven, I faced the very real possibility that the one career that I had sought to make my life's work was over just months after it had been resumed in my home country. In coming weeks, I received offers to teach at Yale and Nanterre. I had no shortage of opportunities to continue a prestigious academic career abroad. But I declined them all. I refused to exile myself for a second time—I had already been down that path and had no desire to repeat it. So I stayed in São Paulo and dedicated myself to bringing peace and democracy back to Brazil.

I knew several people who were murdered by the military regime. Among them was Rubens Paiva, a friend of mine who had been elected to the lower house prior to the coup of 1964. I had helped with his campaign. Years after that, Rubens fled for Chile, and we met on several occasions in Santiago. When Rubens returned to Brazil, he was said to have delivered a letter to a young lady—the daughter of a friend and a former congressman—who had participated in the guerrilla campaign. The police, somehow informed of the meeting, arrested him and took him to jail. Rubens was never seen again.

There was no such ambiguity regarding the fate of a journalist, Vladimir Herzog, a friend who was married to a former student of mine. When I was teaching in Paris, Vladimir, whom friends called Vlado, lived in London, and he would often come to visit us. He returned to Brazil and was invited in 1975 to work at a state-run television station in São Paulo. Shortly thereafter, he was summoned to the police station to "explain" a critical evening newscast. That was the last time he was seen alive. Days later, newspapers published photographs of Vlado dangling from a leather strap in a jail cell, supposedly proving that he had committed suicide. This outrageous lie was disproved when signs of torture were found on his body.

Vlado's wife came to see me. "They obviously killed him! They're lying!" she said. She was right, of course, and in Vlado's case this distinction was of colossal importance. He was Jewish, so if the official cause of death was found to be suicide, then his religion dictated that he would be buried in a separate corner of the cemetery as a reminder of his final sin. "Is there anything you can do to set the record straight?" his wife pleaded.

On her behalf, I went and saw my friend Cardinal Paulo Arns, the archbishop of São Paulo. A remarkably courageous man, Arns decided to hold an ecumenical ceremony on Vladimir's behalf. More than 10,000 people showed up. It was one of the first demonstrations of public opposition to the dictatorship. We later found out that surveillance photos were taken of nearly everyone present. The rabbi, Henry Sobel, of the Israeli congregation of São Paulo, and Cardinal Arns agreed that Vlado should be buried in the regular part of the cemetery—and so they openly challenged the verdict of suicide.

A great many friends suffered torture. Some disappeared for days, sometimes weeks, and emerged with hideous bruises and marks on their bodies. There were other cases, documented by human rights groups after the dictatorship ended, in which military police applied electric shocks to prisoners' genitals, or held their heads underwater for long periods of time, trying to coax a confession. Most of those who were abducted, of course, were innocent and had little to tell; their inability to "confess" anything of substance made their treatment even worse.

In this climate of fear, a nocturnal phone call could be terrifying. A doorbell could send people scurrying under their beds. It was no way to live.

The military's crackdown on the guerrillas was immoral and disproportionately violent. In a perverse way, it was also very effective. By the mid-1970s, the Brazilian guerrilla movement had been wiped out through a combination of repression and broad public disinterest. Armed resistance had been an abject failure. "The radical Left," wrote my friend Boris Fausto in his book *A Concise History of Brazil,* "had been totally mistaken when it thought it could turn Brazil into another Vietnam." Opposition would have to take a completely new and different form.

How to resist, then? In this climate of fear, everyone knew we couldn't do it directly and openly. So, instead, rebellion took other, less obvious forms. It became a game, a kind of intellectual exercise. Films, plays, and speeches became enormously important—anything that mentioned democracy, liberty, or merely *change* was an act of revolution. Everyone knew the stakes, including the regime. If a play or a concert went too far in its advocacy, troops smashed down the doors of the theaters and beat up the actors and musicians. Books of all kinds were banned, leading to a black market for academic materials—undercover messengers brought me forbidden texts in the middle of the night. In the end, no matter how threatening the consequences, people always found a way to express their opinions. The discontent was simply too massive to stomp out altogether.

I struggled at first, searching for my niche. I wanted to harness my energy and youth, but my forced retirement technically forbade me from doing research or teaching. However, I also knew that the dictatorship couldn't be everywhere at once. There is a peculiarly Brazilian way of breaking the rules in which, as long as you insist you are obeying the law, you can get away with pretty much anything. We have a unique, untranslatable word for this: *jeito* or *jeitinho.* It refers to the fact that there is always a way around the system, a certain tolerance of breaches of authority. Although the dictatorship had turned more violent, its focus had simultaneously become narrower; there was a very real possibility that we would be left alone. My colleagues and I believed that perhaps we could wear the regime out through one jeitinho after another—by breaking one little rule at a time.

With that in mind, we decided to start a new private think-tank called the Brazilian Center for Analysis and Planning, or CEBRAP. The foundation would produce sociological and economic studies, but the political goal was always to support democracy. The recent purge of the universities via the AI-5 allowed us to assemble a "dream team" of Brazil's finest academics. Five of the major figures in CEBRAP had been members of the famous Marx Seminar—José Arthur Giannotti,

Juarez Brandão Lopes, Paul Singer, Octavio Ianni, and myself. Cândido Procópio de Carvalho and Elza Berquó were also present from the beginning. All of us had been associated with the University of São Paulo. It was a sparkling group, all of us with a massive chip on our shoulders. Others joined this core group, among them Bolívar Lamounier, Carlos Martins, Vilmar Faria, Francisco Weffort, and Maria Hermínia Tavares de Almeida.

Ironically, by forcing us into retirement but continuing to pay us a salary, the military had liberated us to dedicate ourselves to undercutting them full-time. For CEBRAP to be viable and hire other intellectuals, however, we realized that we needed to obtain external funding. Through one of our friends, we sounded out the Ford Foundation about the possibility of a grant. This was like heresy to some of my friends and colleagues, who considered taking money from Americans akin to selling out to the enemy. In protest, Florestan Fernandes never joined CEBRAP, opting to teach in Canada instead, which broke my heart.

The Ford Foundation was hardly a proxy for the U.S. government, though. The top officials at its Latin American program were liberal academics, many of whom had served in the John F. Kennedy administration. They were wholeheartedly anti-Communist, but they were not bound by the knee-jerk rejection of progressive ideas that had led Richard Nixon to support dictatorships in Brazil and elsewhere in Latin America. They were looking to fund groups such as CEBRAP that would explore a democratic, capitalist solution to the region's problems, a kind of "third way," before such a phrase existed. We represented an opportunity for them as well. On an early trip to Brazil, a team of Ford officials wrote that Brazil was "ready for transformation . . . to the condition of a 'real nation,' instead of a coastal strip, semi-dependent on Europe and the United States."

What the Ford Foundation representatives may have lacked in diplomacy, they more than made up for in generosity. Peter Bell and William D. Carmichael, the foundation's representatives in Brazil, were of immense value in helping us. The foundation awarded us a $100,000 grant to get CEBRAP on its feet. Contrary to Florestan's fears, it was the finest benefactor we could have imagined. The representatives gave no preconditions for the foundation's support, and they largely left us alone. Some years later, the Ford Foundation gave us an additional $1 million. We would receive additional support, over the years, from the Catholic Church in France as well as from Swedish, Dutch, and Canadian institutions devoted to supporting such causes in developing countries. We also obtained several contracts with private-sector businesses to do economic research.

CEBRAP's influence came from its ability to provide information that no one else could. With the military firmly controlling newspapers and other media, there was a general ignorance of what was going on in Brazil. Polls showed that nearly 80 percent of Brazilians favored the dictatorship. But we believed that if people knew what was *really* happening, especially with regard to the economy, we could undermine the dictatorship's monopoly on power.

I used to compare CEBRAP to a monastery. We were isolated from the turbulence of society at large and, inside our walls, free to do whatever we liked. There was nothing else quite like it in Brazil. We offered the only reliable venue for mature, intellectually rigorous political discussion. Every week we had a *mesão,* or a roundtable, where we invited other political actors and thinkers to come and brainstorm with us on the crucial issues facing the country. Many of the people who, decades later, would be running Brazil—Pedro Malan, Celso Lafer, and Celso Furtado, to name a few—dropped in to debate with us. No matter what the topic, we never lost sight of our main goal of supporting democracy.

CEBRAP hired several people who had been in jail, such as Vinicius Caldeira Brant and Francisco Oliveira. It also hired people like Lucio Kowarick, an independent social scientist. Those who, like myself, had been "retired" by the regime via the AI-5 were given top priority for positions. As time went by, we hired bigger names and took bigger risks.

In a speech in the south of the country, I publicly accused the regime of torture. This was an open provocation of the military, but nothing happened to me. We realized that if the Brazilian public was to begin supporting a return to democracy, we had to win the battle of ideas. The best way to fight the regime was to take the moral high ground, to assume a broad position that was unassailable and then stick to it.

No subject was more provocative, or potentially controversial, than Brazil's economy. By the early 1970s, the economy was growing at an average rate of over 11 percent per year, a torrid pace that had some speaking of a "Brazilian economic miracle." Industrial production and foreign investment soared. However, the high growth was severely skewed—between 1960 and 1978, 80 percent of Brazil's population suffered a *decline* in income. This was because the military government conducted economic policy to benefit its power base—the rich elite—at the expense of the poor majority. The government controlled the unions, so workers were not allowed to seek pay increases, meaning that their wages fell relative to inflation. Also, despite the growth in gross domestic product (GDP), sectors such as health care and education were neglected; quality-of-life indicators—infant mortality, for example—hardly improved at all during those years.

Many Brazilians cited the economic "miracle" as evidence that the dictatorship was a success. For us, the truth was exactly the opposite. The statistics only strengthened our conviction that only democracy could bring broad prosperity to all the citizens of Brazil.

Determined to bring attention to these economic trends, CEBRAP published a book entitled *São Paulo: Growth and Poverty.* It was a critical and commercial success. Only 128 pages long, it was illustrated with scenes of squalid, ever-expanding favelas and the miserable working conditions in factories. The pictures were especially important because they reinforced our written conclusions in a way that could not be denied. The book was a collaborative effort by a panel of authors, including myself. It reflected a wide range of opinion among its authors, and though some of the conclusions may not have been correct, the overall message was right on target: The military was neglecting the needs of Brazil's majority.

The book's credibility was boosted by the courageous participation of the Catholic Church, which commissioned the work. The church in Brazil was influenced by the growing prevalence in Latin America of "liberation theology," which encouraged bishops at the local level to push actively—sometimes violently—for the rights of the poor. The prologue of *São Paulo: Growth and Poverty* was written by my friend Cardinal Arns. He set the tone for the book, denouncing the "evil" of a "pattern of economic growth based on the destruction of the lives of workers obliged to labor excessive hours to compensate for the reduced purchasing power of their wages." The rest of the book pulled no punches, openly declaring that "the entire organization of the Brazilian state is designed to prevent and, when necessary, repress organized forms of opposition."

These were brave, charged words, telling the truth when no one else would. Our provocation did not go unanswered. Just after the book was published, a bomb exploded at CEBRAP headquarters. The intention behind it was to frighten rather than kill—the bomb went off at night—but many books and personal files were ruined. The secretary of public security in the state of São Paulo, Colonel Erasmo Dias, had the audacity to publicly accuse us of planting the bomb ourselves as a publicity stunt. He told the media that our book was "essentially Marxist." "This is my bible," he said, furiously waving around a copy. "I read this book every day in order to get angry."

Dias had forgotten the cardinal rule of publishing: Any publicity is good publicity. His declarations helped us sell thousands more copies of our book. As we became ever more popular and well known, the regime lashed out again and decreed that CEBRAP was a "subversive organization." The authorities sent a letter demanding that all CE-BRAP researchers, myself included, report to military police headquarters to testify on an assigned day.

I appeared at headquarters as scheduled, accompanied by my friend

Roberto Gusmão. At the back door, a hood was placed over my head. Darkness descended and I fought for my breath. Then I felt a giant hand on my back pushing me inside the building.

Once I was inside, the officials removed my hood and took a police photograph of me, attaching a sticker with a number on it to my suit as if I were a common prisoner. Then they escorted me to a cramped, filthy room where they pushed me down into a wooden chair. A stack of papers that I had written, mainly newspaper and magazine articles, sat ominously in the corner. Two burly men entered the room and stalked like zoo animals from one end to the other, silent.

They began asking me questions so absurd that I didn't know how to answer them. When I hesitated, they screamed in my ears. They shoved fingers into my chest. When I could not answer to their satisfaction, the two thugs, who were barely capable of speaking correct Portuguese, disappeared into another room, where others were obviously formulating the questions. Then they barreled back into the room, louder than ever, yelling and spitting on my face. "You know that we can put you into the *pau de arara* if you don't cooperate!" the guards yelled.

The "parrot's perch" was a primitive but widely feared instrument of torture used during the dictatorship. The victim was suspended from a bar by the back of his knees, with his hands tied to his ankles. Once on the perch, the victim, often stripped naked, was subjected to beatings, electric shocks, and near-drowning.

"What if I confess to you what I don't know?" I yelled, indignant.

They interrogated me about Argentina and Uruguay, where the guerrilla movements were stronger than in Brazil, asking me if I had "subversive contacts" there. They also asked about the governor of the state of São Paulo, Paulo Egydio Martins, who had helped us organize CEBRAP. "That motherfucker," one of the thugs said. "One day he'll be with us here. Then he'll see what happens to him!"

My interrogators seemed particularly obsessed with Ernest Mendel, a Belgian intellectual who was a major figure in the international Trotskyist movement. A few months before, I had met him during a sociology conference in Oaxaca, Mexico. Ironically, I had spent the entire seminar loudly disagreeing with Mendel, who had a far more radical vision of the world than I did. After the conference ended, I ran into him and his wife at the airport in Mexico City. Trying to be polite, I offered to carry his wife's suitcases into the terminal. And that was, apparently, how surveillance photos came to be taken of Mendel and me together, photos that my interrogators now furiously waved in front of me under a bright lamp, evidence that I was part of a worldwide Trotskyist conspiracy.

"You have big problems, mister professor," one of the thugs said in a taunting, sing-song voice. "Big problems."

My thoughts turned to my father, and the advice he had given me as a child about making casual conversation with one's jailer. I tried this, but I must admit it was difficult. Frustrated and tired, I could think of only one way to defuse the tension: I asked if I could get up and use the restroom.

I walked through a dark hallway where I passed several small cells. Through the bars, I could see defeated souls slumped on the floor, leaning against the wall. They did not make a sound, and their resigned silence echoed in my ears. These were interrogation rooms, one person per cell, where prisoners were beaten and then taken elsewhere to be detained for a longer period—or executed. I did not see torture with my own eyes that night, but it was obvious what was happening. Many people, some of them friends of mine, were severely beaten in that same building. Others, like Vlado, died.

Looking back, I have sometimes felt guilty for having survived the struggle against the dictatorship. Many people who fought for democracy far more bravely than I did lose their lives. Others bear psychological and physical scars from torture to this day. Although I never explicitly used my family's connections to get me out of danger, it is probable that my social status and my degree of professional renown spared me greater trauma. That is a fact, though it was the furthest thing from my mind that night at midnight, when I was released unharmed. I had no room for any emotion other than relief. The jail, deep within a police precinct headquarters otherwise like any other, still stands in São Paulo. I've never had the stomach to go back.

This endless battle between left and right was like a virus, methodically spreading to every country in Latin America. By 1973, it had even infected the one place that I had always believed would be immune: my beloved Chile.

That year, I returned to Santiago with my family for a couple of months to do consulting work for CEPAL. The enviably calm, mature oasis of democracy that I had known during my exile a decade before was now utterly unrecognizable. Salvador Allende, whom I had met at the glamorous parties at Pablo Neruda's house, had been elected president, vowing to lead a socialist transformation in Chile. In line with the paranoia of the times, the Chilean elite and the U.S. government heard "socialist" and thought "communist." Henry Kissinger, in particular, was convinced that Allende was hell-bent on turning Chile into another Cuba.

I always questioned this analysis; the Salvador Allende that I knew hardly resembled Fidel Castro. In fact, during Allende's visits to Havana in the 1960s, he had reportedly been mocked behind his back by Castro's entourage for his aristocratic tastes: fine wines, European suits, and expensive art. When I knew him, Allende had been more of a social democrat, and it seemed to me that his radical turn as president derived more from a political alliance with the Communists and Castro supporters within Chile than from deeply held ideological convictions.

In the end, however, this point was only academic. Nixon ordered Kissinger to "make the Chilean economy scream," so the United States instituted a choking trade and investment embargo. As a result, Santiago suffered widespread food and fuel shortages. Cars were so impossible to obtain that, to move about the city, I had to rent an auto from Hertz, the

U.S. car rental agency. Mysteriously, Hertz never seemed to suffer from the same gasoline shortages that everyone else did.

In a strange way, Chile's stable past became its biggest curse. With no experience of political upheaval, the country reacted a bit like a confused child, lashing out in a much more bizarre and severe fashion than any of its Latin American neighbors, which were more seasoned in the ways of political and economic chaos, would have responded under similar circumstances. Everyday life became ever more surreal. One night, I had dinner at the home of José Serra, my old Brazilian student and colleague from CEPAL. Having never returned to Brazil, Serra had now been in Santiago for nine years and was advising Allende's finance minister, Fernando Flores. We were joined by an English statistician who was building a Cold War–style "situation room," of all things, in the finance ministry, presumably so the economists could watch in safety while their country was going to hell.

Suddenly, there was a phone call for Flores. "I'm sorry, I have to leave," he told us coolly, and politely excused himself from dinner. We later found out that he had been informed that a leading right-wing terrorist was having dinner in a restaurant downtown; Flores had joined a group of officials to go make the arrest. The finance minister making an arrest! It was preposterous.

By August, bombings and assassinations had become common. Fearing for my family's safety, I sent Ruth and the kids back to São Paulo. I didn't plan on staying much longer myself. As rumors of a coup swirled, Allende appointed my friend Ricardo Lagos as his ambassador to the Soviet Union. Before leaving for his post, Lagos invited Francisco Weffort and me to dine at his house, where we were joined by Clodomiro Almeyda, Allende's foreign minister. This was no ordinary dinner party; it felt like a house under siege.

Almeyda had just been on a visit to Moscow with Carlos Prats, the head of Chile's armed forces. I asked him how Prats's demeanor had been on the trip.

"I don't know," Almeyda sighed. "He and I barely spoke."

"I see," I said.

There was a long silence.

"How much longer are you going to be in Chile?"

"Maybe a month," I responded.

"Well," Almeyda mused, his voice barely a whisper. "You may get to see the page of history turn."

His sense of timing was impeccable. Shortly after I departed Chile, Allende sacked Prats and replaced him with a general who was reputed to be more moderate and pro-democratic: Augusto Pinochet. The final betrayal was now at hand. On history's second-most famous September 11, Pinochet led a spectacularly brutal coup. As air force jets shelled La Moneda presidential palace, Allende retreated to his quarters and, much like Getúlio Vargas, shot himself.

Determined to restore Chile to its God-given status as an oasis of peace, Pinochet then immediately set about murdering all the troublemakers. A death squad departed Santiago by helicopter and made several stops in villages in the interior, gunning down dozens of victims in a massacre famously known as the "Caravan of Death." Thousands of other suspected agitators were shepherded into the national soccer stadium in Santiago, including a Brazilian who had stayed behind: José Serra.

When he ran for president decades later, Serra rarely spoke about what happened to him next. I suppose that he did not want to appear to be exploiting his experiences for political gain. But it would not be an exaggeration to say that Serra may have cheated death that day. Many of the prisoners, in fact, were taken into the stairwells underneath the soccer stadium and executed by Pinochet's henchmen. In the ultimate testimony to his legendary stubbornness and ability to persuade, Serra managed to convince his guard that his United Nations passport granted him immunity from arrest.

When Serra walked out of the stadium that day, he had been failed by both his own country and his adopted home. Had he gone to the Brazilian embassy, they likely would have handed him over to the

Chileans. So Serra sought refuge in the only place he had left: the embassy of Italy, the country in which his parents had been born. He spent months stranded there.

Chile would never be the same. Pinochet's dictatorship left a death toll of more than 3,000 people; only Argentina's *junta* was more murderous. In the years thereafter, I made several return visits to Santiago, usually to do consulting for CEPAL. Much of my time was spent visiting the families of old friends who were in jail. I would stay at their houses until dusk and then take long walks through the empty streets of downtown back to my hotel. Inevitably, gunshots would crackle in the distance, police cars would speed by with their sirens blaring, and I would have to cut my walk short and jump, dismayed, into a taxi.

Every once in a while, I noticed the familiar good smell that I associated with Santiago: the flowers, the sweetness of spring wafting through a city that had once been so civilized and enlightened.

It made me absolutely furious.

Those were the darkest of days, not just for us, but for all of Latin America. Like dominoes, democracies were collapsing everywhere: Uruguay, Chile, Argentina. Back in Brazil, no one knew how or when the dictatorship would end. Or *if,* for that matter. As long as the Cold War raged on, the military would always have a pretext to hold on to power. No one imagined in those years that the Berlin Wall would ever fall; for all we knew, the Brazilian dictatorship would endure for the rest of our lives. Still, some of us were convinced that, if the right arguments were made, and the right *compromises* were struck, we could eventually create an opportunity for democracy in Brazil. If that was our hope, the reality was pure hell. Every time I tried to find such an opportunity for change, a door was slammed in my face.

Looking for a mass audience, I began writing columns for an opposition magazine named *Opinião,* whose publisher, Fernando Gasparian, is one of my closest friends. We wrote about such bland topics as the sociology of economics, but our work was always, in essence, a protest of the regime. It became tremendously popular. Some people purchased the magazine and kept it on their coffee table, not necessarily because they wanted to read it, but because they wanted to show they were against the military. At our peak, the circulation topped 40,000, an enormous number back then—nearly half of what Brazil's premier newsmagazine, *Veja,* sold on a weekly basis.

Once again, our success attracted scrutiny. The military assigned us censors who edited out even the most minuscule references to politics. Before long, the magazine's crossword puzzle was being censored. We started preparing two versions of each issue of *Opinião:* one for the censors, and one for ourselves. By the twenty-fifth edition, the magazine was so hacked to pieces by our minders that the final product was illegible to the point of absurdity. Our circulation declined by half. Soon thereafter, *Opinião* was shut down. We attempted to regroup and start a new magazine called *Argumento,* which was to be more literary and far less political in nature, but by then they were on to us; the fourth edition was prohibited outright.

I had been pushed to my option of last resort. For the first time in my life, I attempted to use my family connections to keep *Argumento* afloat. I decided to pay a visit to Oswaldo Cordeiro de Farias, a retired general who still wielded influence within the military hierarchy as a godfather type of figure. He had been among the most respected of the tenentes, the young lieutenants who had helped bring down the Old Republic during the 1920s. In fact, along with my father, Cordeiro de Farias was one of the men who appeared in the now-famous photo of the tenentes in prison, gathered around a piano. This was the man who could help me regain a bit of normalcy in my intellectual life.

The general received me in his office with a handsome but oddly fatigued smile. I was accompanied by Antonio Candido, a renowned intellectual, USP professor, and literary critic. "Everything I know, I learned from your grandfather," the general declared warmly. But when all the niceties had been said, Cordeiro de Farias quickly grew serious and pulled out a note from his desk. "Someone left this in my office," he said gravely.

The message read: YOUR TELEPHONE IS BEING TAPPED.

My jaw must have dropped.

"I'm afraid I can't help you much, young man," Cordeiro de Farias said. The look on his face revealed that he shared my astonishment. The dictatorship had become so extreme that even relatively moderate sectors of the military itself were being ostracized. He sighed mightily. "This madness cannot go on."

If such a man could not help me, then who could?

I felt lost. I had been banned from academic life and censored when I wrote in public. In the coming months, many other people from CE-BRAP would be thrown in jail, sometimes for days at a time. Simultaneously, the military was conducting a secret trial against me because of a new book I had just published, *Democracy and Authoritarianism,* which rather overtly expounded on the benefits of the former while belittling the latter. Certain ideologues within the regime were pushing for the book to be banned and for me to be arrested again—and imprisoned, perhaps for a long while. I knew nothing about this trial until two decades later, when I became president, but I did not find out by poring over government records; instead, I read about it in the newspaper.

The old general was right. The madness could not go on. After all the doors that had been slammed in my face, I took a long look at my life and realized there was just one way to go forward.

CHAPTER

7

CHANGE, NOW!

A T A BIZARRE academic conference in Brasília during the mid-1970s, my determination to enter politics crystallized as never before. We spent more time worriedly watching the door than listening to the dissertations. Rumors flew that the police were going to burst in, arrest Florestan Fernandes and myself, and take us both to jail. All of this intrigue over something as staid as a meeting of the Brazilian Society for the Progress of Science (SBPC). I was accompanied by my friend Albert Hirschman, the legendary Princeton professor and development economist, who was understandably bewildered by the atmosphere. Each time the door swung open, people jumped in their seats and gasped. Inevitably, just another professor in an ugly suit walked through the door with a cup of coffee, and you could hear the whole room exhale in relief.

Between speeches, Albert leaned over to me and whispered: "This might be the strangest conference I've ever attended!"

That night, things got even more strange. We attended a dinner held by Severo Gomes, the military government's minister of commerce and industry. Severo was a prominent dove within the regime, and the dinner was an overt expression of support for our cause. The logic was that as long as we were dining with Severo, we couldn't be arrested. I remember thinking that Albert lingered over his dessert a bit longer than usual.

When we woke up the next morning and realized that we were still free people, Ruth and I decided to drive from Brasília to Goiás, the old provincial capital where my ancestors had lived. We took Albert and his wife, Sarah, and showed them the governor's palace, the Palácio dos Remédios, where a portrait of my great-grandfather still hung in the hallway. Goiás is a Baroque city of sheer white buildings rising out of a brown, arid, treeless plain. Coming straight from Brasília, with its spaceshiplike structures and futuristic design, Albert must have thought that he had just returned to the eighteenth century.

From there, we proceeded straight to the seventeenth century, setting out for my cousins' ranch near Jaraguá to have lunch. Our tiny sedan lurched over bumpy dirt roads, flying at improbable speeds through the dusty expanse of nothingness that is the Brazilian *cerrado,* or high plateau. I have a terrible sense of direction—I am notorious for once getting lost while driving from my office to my apartment—and for a few tense hours I had no idea if we would actually find my cousins. We rode in nervous silence. By some miracle, however, we arrived in time for lunch.

The ranch house was a simple, wooden, one-room structure with a thatched palm roof. The tiny kitchen was outside. The house was packed full of my distant cousins, lounging about on a Sunday afternoon. As for the ranch itself, it was little more than an endless fence, a handful of wiry cattle, and some very, very lonely trees. Professor Hirschman was always unfailingly polite, but I knew him well enough to decipher the expression on his face: We're eating lunch *here?* I thought we might just have to turn around and speed back to

Brasília for a hot meal when I heard Albert shriek: "My God, what is this?"

There, on a crooked old wooden table in the middle of the room, sat a gleaming copy of the very latest edition of the *New York Review of Books*. Albert picked it up and gingerly leafed through it with the care and utter astonishment of a man who has just discovered water in the middle of a desert.

One of my cousins, dressed like a common ranch hand just like all the others, stood up, vigorously shook Albert's hand, and smiled. "I just returned from the Soviet Union, and I picked that up at the airport in New York. It is most decidedly *not* their most compelling edition of late," he told Albert, speaking a casual, confident English. My cousin explained that he was a diplomat on a short visit back home to Brazil, and then he immediately struck up a conversation with Albert's wife—in fluent Russian.

Albert looked like he was going to faint.

My cousin's grin broadened. "Can I get you something to eat?"

"That," Albert sighed, a smile spreading across his face, "would be lovely."

That afternoon, I sat in a corner by myself, eating and watching as Albert bounded around the room like a young child, drinking in the joys of life in Brazil. There he was, on a primitive ranch in the middle of nowhere, dining on a succulent steak and discussing French literature with a group of overeducated ranch hands. It was refreshing to see my country through the eyes of an enthusiastic foreigner, and it set me thinking. I had forgotten how diverse Brazil could be—How many centuries had we traveled through in the previous forty-eight hours? Three, at least. During the many years that I had maintained such a problematic and distant relationship with my country, I had, perhaps, been unable to see that Brazil was more than just a simple military dictatorship. It was, in reality, vibrant, diverse, and full of complicated potential.

If the country was so varied, I mused, so must be the leadership—

even within the military itself. I sat there, contemplating our dinner with Severo the night before, reexamining what it had meant. We had dined with a *minister* who supported us and openly opposed the government's "security" policies. Ernesto Geisel, the military's newly nominated president of Brazil, was also proving to be surprisingly moderate, in relative terms. He had a policy of *distensão,* "an easing of tensions" aimed at dismantling the police state, slowly but surely. Soon thereafter, he would go as far as to revoke the dreaded AI-5, the act that had canceled civil liberties back in 1968. Even if Geisel was not fully able to control the hard line within the armed forces, it was undeniable that times were changing. The guerrilla movement was now gone, and with it any weak pretext that had previously existed for crackdowns on academic conferences, literary magazines, and the like.

I began to wonder for the first time in many years if it might be possible to accelerate the process and change things from *within* the government. Would it not be better to seize on the thaw and take the fight for democracy inside the regime? After all the censorship of previous years, after all the arrests of my friends, I was growing tired of the idleness of academia.

That night, I drove back to Brasília with a renewed sense of purpose. Our stomachs full, Albert and I chattered happily about the marvels of Brazil and mused about the chances for democracy and change. This time, on the road home, I didn't even get lost.

Shortly thereafter, the opportunity I had been waiting for presented itself. Much to my surprise, my good friend Ulysses Guimarães asked me to be a candidate for the Brazilian Senate in the 1978 elections. CE-BRAP had helped Ulysses formulate a platform for the opposition party in previous elections, and now he was looking for a candidate to help capture the middle-class vote in São Paulo.

There was just one small problem: Running for office would almost certainly be illegal. When I was forcibly "retired" from the University of São Paulo a decade before, my political rights had been suspended for an indefinite period. Under the most strict (and likely) interpretation of the law, I therefore could not be a candidate. Ultimately, however, we decided to use this to our advantage. Ulysses and I decided that I would mount a protest candidacy—if I was later banned from running, so much the better. Such an event would probably generate more favorable publicity than the campaign itself.

Besides, under no circumstances did I expect to actually *win* the election. I would merely be one of two candidates from São Paulo running for the Senate within the Brazilian Democratic Movement (MDB), the omnibus opposition party, of which Ulysses was the president. Under Brazil's two-party system of that era, three candidates could run from each party. The biggest vote-getter went to Congress, as long as his party had secured a majority of the vote. There was already a strong candidate, Franco Montoro, who was widely expected to finish first in the race for the MDB. I was just a former university professor, well known in intellectual circles, perhaps, but hardly likely to garner massive popular support. My only reason for running was to have a bigger platform from which to give rousing speeches in favor of democracy in and around São Paulo.

I assured my family that there was no chance that I would actually become a senator. "That," I promised Ruth, "is too ridiculous a possibility to contemplate."

At the beginning, my campaign was a comedy of errors. My first few speeches literally put the audience to sleep because I lectured like a sociology professor. Because I had lived in Europe, people saw me as a snooty intellectual who was disconnected from Brazil. It didn't help that I spoke French and frequently quoted French and English authors in my speeches. At one particularly disastrous campaign stop, when asked what I thought about Brazil's landless movement, I responded with a lecture about the distribution of land in England in the sixteenth century. One of my friends who was present later told an interviewer: "I can guarantee you that no one knew what the hell he was talking about."

Those same friends knew that certain aspects of politics did not come naturally to me. "The first time I saw him raise his arms and make the same gestures that all politicians do, I felt a bit disturbed," my friend José Giannotti later recalled. "He was a good speaker, but he still retained a little bit of that intellectual arrogance. Later, I suppose we got used to it."

I got used to it as well. Campaigning in Brazil, as elsewhere, is all about routine; perhaps the only distinguishing characteristic here is that, in my country, it also involves unthinkably massive amounts of coffee. Coffee is the elixir that drives all social contact in Brazil, and every single political meeting requires at least one cup. Most of that first campaign was spent between *cafezinhos,* literally "little coffees." Usually, I woke up at five in the morning, while it was still dark, and had my first cup with Ruth. Then I traveled, often by city bus or train, to the industrial suburbs outside São Paulo, where I spent my mornings in meetings with city councilmen or union leaders—for every group, a separate cup of coffee. With lunch, another cup, perhaps two. Then it was on to a full afternoon of stump speeches, after which strangers would often invite me into their homes for a chat, which was usually the last straw that pushed me over the brink into clinical over-caffeination. At dinner I gathered with either my aides or party officials, and we ended our meal with yet another cup. Afterward, it was not unusual for me to then join another group for a *second dinner,* which could last until one or two in the morning. And of course no dinner was ever complete without still more. . . . Well, you get the idea.

Over those nine or ten cups a day, I was slowly being trained in the art of politics. I slowly realized that the most important skills are very simple: listening to people's problems, and speaking in a language they could understand. Ever since my days as a young assistant professor exploring the favelas of the Brazilian south, clipboard in hand, I have had no problems relating to people from all walks of life. I can hold a conversation with anyone. But I had to learn to incorporate a straightforward political message: that only democracy could solve the problems of Brazil. In those intimate, one-on-one meetings over an espresso, I could easily see if my message was getting through just by looking at the expression on someone's face. From that close, you can see whether someone's eyes are sparkling. So coffee taught me two critical lessons of campaigning that I would always hold dear: to keep my message brief and simple, and to always, *always,* accept if someone offered to let me use their restroom.

I was surprised by how receptive people were. Factory workers, street cleaners, and bankers alike would take my campaign leaflets, fold them with great care, and put them into a pocket to take home and share with their families. At rallies, the public clapped and cheered raucously when we spoke about how the dictatorship wasn't doing enough to improve their lives. It might seem odd that we were able to say such things without facing persecution, given what had happened in the recent past. But this was the key to the system; since we were participating in the "legitimate" world of electoral politics as defined by the military, it was much harder for them to accuse us of subversion. We were playing by their rules, even if we were bending them a bit. Because of this, some of my friends on the ideological left accused me of legitimizing the dictatorship by running for office. I responded that, with each stump speech on a muddy street corner to dozens of workers, I became ever more convinced that participating within the system, and using it to our advantage, was the surest path to democratic change.

Besides, as I told my still-skeptical friends, this campaign was utterly *romantic.* I had just turned forty-seven years old, but I felt invigorated by the support of the young artists, professors, and musicians who all rallied to our cause. Under the military's so-called Falcão Law, candidates could appear on television only in the form of a tiny picture and a curriculum vitae; all other campaigning on TV was forbidden. This, obviously, made personal contact paramount—hence all the coffee and dinners. Meanwhile, since we had no corporate or party financing to speak of, almost all of our expenditures were financed through the sale of about 2,000 engravings donated by Brazilian artists. We held many campaign rallies in theaters. One of Brazil's best-known musicians, Chico Buarque, came up with the campaign jingle.

The most touching—and conspicuous—campaign gift came from Severo Gomes, the rebellious government minister who had hosted the dinner for Albert Hirschman and me back in Brasília. Severo's beloved son Pedro had recently died in an accident, and Severo gave me his car. It became the only vehicle we had for our campaign. Besides its usefulness, the gift was also a meaningful show of support from someone within the regime.

As the campaign drew to a close, I received another electoral gift—this time, from the dictatorship. Government prosecutors declared my campaign illegal and sought to ban me from appearing on the ballot. This was a huge tactical error. The Brazilian media, becoming bolder by the day, ran a series of scathing stories about the professor who preached for democracy and was banned from being a candidate. All of a sudden, people across all of Brazil knew who I was. More important, they were outraged about what had happened to me. My example laid bare the unpalatable fact that people were still living under a hard-line, authoritarian regime fourteen full years after a coup that was originally supposed to be temporary.

My friends and I decided that with our newfound national celebrity, we had achieved our goal. We had run a successful protest candidacy, talked to thousands of people about the benefits of democracy, and attracted national attention in the process. I believed that I would return to CEBRAP and continue my work as before, though perhaps with a higher profile.

And then—an accident.

Just two weeks before the election, the Supreme Court ruled that I could in fact be a candidate. In a strongly worded decision, the court declared that neither I nor any other Brazilian could be deprived of political rights indefinitely. I was stunned. It was a monumental ruling, the most daring institutional challenge to the military's authority in years. As a result, the story of Fernando Henrique Cardoso made another round in the national media. Through no real merit of my own, I became more than just a candidate—I was suddenly a powerful symbol against the dictatorship. The court decision made it inevitable that my name would indeed appear on the ballot, synonymous with a vote for change.

I received 1.2 million votes, more than the candidate running under the government ticket. It was a shocking outcome for a previously unknown university professor. Only Montoro, my colleague within the MDB, garnered more support. He became the new senator from São Paulo, while I was named his alternate.

Being the alternate had no significance that I was aware of, but it was a victory nonetheless. My first foray into politics had successfully introduced me to Brazil, and I had become a national player in the fight for democracy. The achievement was its own reward—and so, having avoided the family business for forty-seven years, I suddenly found myself hooked.

※

During the 1978 Senate race, I counted on the support of a man who would later become one of the most important figures in my public life. There are grainy photos from the era showing the two of us campaigning side by side, which many Brazilians now find humorous because of all that happened between us in the years thereafter (and also, probably, because we both looked so much younger!). This man has, through the last quarter century, been both a key ally and, at times, my biggest political adversary. Our relationship continues to be very complex, but we have tried not to lose our respect for each other. He was my opponent in the presidential campaigns of 1994 and 1998, and then he ultimately replaced me as president in 2003. He has now achieved a good deal of celebrity around the globe, where he is known by just one name: Lula.

I first met Luiz Inácio Lula da Silva in the mid-1970s, when I was doing research for CEBRAP. Even then, I had heard bits and pieces of his remarkable life story, the kind of rise from dire poverty to political prominence that was, regrettably, uncommon in Brazil back then. The sixth of twenty-three children born to a farmer in the impoverished northeastern state of Pernambuco, Lula had it rough from the very beginning. He was the only one of his siblings to finish primary school. As a young child, he sold peanuts, tapioca, and oranges on the streets after his family moved to the industrial suburbs of São Paulo to seek work. The family lived in a tiny apartment in the back of a bar, and they had to share a bathroom with the tavern's customers. It was then, Lula later recalled, that he first realized that his family was poor.

As a teenager, Lula found a job in a factory producing screws. Working the late shift one night, he was replacing a nut on a machine while a colleague held down the brake. His colleague nodded off, and the blade on the machine slipped forward, cutting off the little finger on Lula's left hand. By the time Lula turned eighteen, he was already a grizzled member of the country's emerging working class. Up until that point, Lula's life, with its mix of hardship and misfortune, had been entirely typical of Brazil's neglected masses—but there was little to suggest the path that awaited him.

We all had our reasons for entering politics. Lula never told me his, but I do know that he was exposed as a young man to the darkest, most hideous side of Brazilian poverty. In 1971, his wife, Lourdes, was several months pregnant with their first child when she started vomiting. Lula took her to the hospital. Her doctors initially shrugged. They told her that nausea was normal for a pregnant woman, advised her to eat more Jell-O, and sent her home. Days later, Lourdes collapsed. She was rushed back to the hospital, where doctors found what they had missed the first time: hepatitis. By then it was too late. The next day, when Lula showed up at the hospital with new baby clothes in hand, he was told that both his wife and child had died.

After that, Lula seemed to experience a political awakening. He engineered a rapid rise to power within the metalworkers' union in the industrial suburbs of São Paulo. The union included assembly-line workers at giant foreign automakers such as Volkswagen, Ford, and Mercedes-Benz, and thus had the capacity to exert tremendous influence over the national economy. To the surprise of everyone, Lula then reinvented the union as one of the most unlikely protagonists in the fight against the dictatorship in Brazil.

Prior to the late 1970s, the military exerted stifling control over relations between unions and companies. When disputes broke out over working conditions or salaries, the government's union federation decided in favor of the corporate interests with infallible consistency. Under Lula, however, the metalworkers' union was audacious enough to bypass the federation and start taking their grievances directly to labor courts that had a different, more nuanced approach and were not entirely controlled by government stooges. The threat of intervention by the court compelled the auto companies to start granting considerable concessions. Suddenly, for the first time in years, the deck was not stacked against the working class. And that was when Lula's union began to develop a taste for power.

Lula's greatest skill, then as now, was his ability to relate to people. He never, ever forgot his roots. As a carefree youth, he had possessed no interest in politics, preferring sports instead. Remembering that now, Lula organized soccer tournaments within the union as a way to get workers to come together. Before the games, Lula would give a five-minute speech. Afterward, there was beer and barbecue for all. Slowly, a new generation of workers became politicized, one soccer match at a time.

It was in that context that I first met Lula, in an attempt to learn more about the unions' emerging influence for a CEBRAP study. I interviewed Lula as I would have any other subject, treating him almost like the subject of a science experiment, while he seemed to regard me as a slightly out-of-place curiosity. So I was somewhat surprised when, years later, during my 1978 Senate campaign, Lula quite literally summoned me to meet him in his union office.

Unions in Brazil have long been a rather mystifying world unto themselves. They often have their own lawyers and doctors, multiple cars at their disposal, even their own newspaper. This top-down structure engendered a rigid hierarchy and behavior that was, ironically, quite military in nature. As I entered the enormous headquarters of Lula's union, I saw that the workers hung about like soldiers on holiday. I was escorted to a waiting room, where these men addressed each other forcefully, by their first names, according to their "rank."

"Give me water!" a senior officer barked to an underling.

"Paulo, ashtray!" bellowed another.

I sat there quietly, a bit bewildered, wondering what these people really wanted from me. Finally, I was escorted to a small, smoky office where Lula sat, squinting, behind a wooden desk. Several burly men stood menacingly behind him, their arms folded. Lula regarded me for a long moment and then got right down to business.

"It is good to see you, Professor," he began, using the name he continued calling me for years thereafter. "I have made the decision to support your campaign. I confess that I cannot do many things for you. But I am going to try and help you."

I was shocked. I asked him what I had done to deserve his endorsement.

"You never pretended to be the candidate of the workers," Lula responded. "You never talked down to us or demanded our support. You never made promises to the workers that we know you cannot keep. That is a sign you are an honest man."

At that moment, I knew that Lula was going to be a formidable politician. I would have never guessed just *how* formidable, of course, but it was apparent then that he possessed natural drive and instinctive political intelligence. I realized that the fuzzy, flattering reason Lula gave for supporting me had nothing to do with his real calculus. Rather, it was realpolitik in the purest sense. Montoro, my companion on the ballot who eventually won the election for the MDB, was campaigning as "the workers' senator." At campaign rallies, he gave out a pamphlet listing what he had accomplished during his career on the behalf of the working class. And it was true; Montoro had done a lot. But Lula, in 1978, was already on his way to becoming a political leader. In his mind, he was competing with Montoro. So my candidacy offered Lula the benefit of a broadly sympathetic political agenda, without actually posing a personal threat to him.

Whatever his motivations may have been, Lula kept to his word. He gave several speeches on my behalf and was a fixture by my side during the campaign. We walked the streets of the factory town of São Bernardo do Campo, handing out pamphlets one by one. We shared numerous long lunches, late-night *cachaças*—the Brazilian sugar cane alcohol—and no small amount of coffee. We became friends.

Lula was raw in those early years. His grammar was atrocious. Through no fault of his own, he lacked the formal schooling that most of my colleagues possessed, and he was visibly uncomfortable around the artists, professors, and other intellectuals who collaborated with my campaign. Lula compensated for these shortcomings, however, with straight talk and an honest soul. He was unfailingly good-natured, spontaneous, unassuming, and kind. Conversely, because of his outsider status, Lula could say audacious things, true things, that no one else could. At a time when censorship and oppression still existed, this mix of gifts amounted to political dynamite. He was clearly a star on the rise.

Indeed, as my campaign drew to a close, Lula's was only just beginning. That same year, Brazilian unions dared to go on strike en masse for the first time under the dictatorship. Realizing that such a challenge would be difficult and drawn out, Lula resolved to do everything he could to keep morale high. Almost every day during the strike, the union held a massive rally in a soccer stadium. As many as 90,000 workers crammed inside for each meeting to listen to Lula's speeches. Often, there was no sound system, not even a platform for him to stand on. He would simply speak as loud as he could. People within earshot would turn around and repeat Lula's words to the people behind them, and so on, until everybody got the message.

The strike hit a chord with Brazilian society. Lula received an enormous amount of publicity, and virtually overnight it seemed as if every evening newscast and every magazine cover was graced by his bearded face. It is interesting to examine why. On one hand, Lula possessed immense appeal to the working class as a daring, rebellious symbol of their resurgent power. On the other, Lula was also relatively *safe* in the eyes of the military and the ruling elite. Here, after all, was a charismatic labor leader who was not a Communist. A devout Catholic, Lula was young and fresh and unencumbered by the bitter battles of years past. At union events, he refused to allow sympathetic university students to participate, saying they should not get involved in a workers' struggle. He went out of his way to discourage guerrilla tactics. Ideology was far less important to him than practical questions such as salaries and health care. In this sense, Lula was a post–Cold War figure even before the war officially ended. So, when the media transformed Lula into the darling of the Brazilian opposition, the military did nothing about it. One can imagine that officials might even have been relieved.

If anyone believed the military was going to tolerate a direct challenge to its authority, however, they were mistaken. Lula found this out the hard way when what should have been his greatest victory turned into one of his worst defeats.

By late 1978, more than 3 million Brazilian workers had joined the strike. Lula continued to hold fervent rallies in the soccer stadiums until, unexpectedly, a labor court ruled in the unions' favor. It was a miracle, the biggest victory the working class had enjoyed in years. The business owners would have to comply with their demands. There was only one catch: The strike would have to end. Since the dispute was now resolved, Brazilian law mandated that the union workers go back to work.

A friend of mine, a lawyer and state congressman named Almir Pazzianotto who represented the metalworkers' union in court, invited me to attend the announcement of the court's ruling. Afterward, Pazzianotto and I rushed to the stadium to give Lula the news.

We entered the stadium through the back entrance so we could more easily walk through the crowd and savor a little bit of the youthful energy. After slowly pushing our way through, we found Lula backstage and told him of the court's decision.

"What are you going to do, Lula?" I asked.

His broad shoulders heaved a weary shrug. "Well," he said hesitantly, as if not quite believing what had happened, "we have been victorious, so we have to stop the strike. I guess that's it."

We murmured our approval, and Lula climbed up on the stage. The crowd went crazy with applause. True to his word, he began his speech by telling the crowd that the strike was over. The workers had won, he said, and it was time to go back to work.

An eerie hush fell over the audience. Many of the workers present had known only dictatorship during their adult lives, and they seemed stunned by the notion that it could ever really lose a battle. Pazzianotto and I noted that the crowd almost seemed disappointed—they had been prepared for, perhaps even looking forward to, a much longer fight. Now, it was as if a referee had called off a heavyweight title fight during the very first round.

People started trudging out of the stadium, their shoulders slumped, before Lula even finished speaking. Lula surveyed the scene and suddenly seemed perplexed and a bit angry. Perceptive, as always, he understood the situation. And then, he quite simply changed his mind.

"Let's continue the strike!" Lula blurted out. "Those among you in agreement with me, raise your hands!"

Pazzianotto and I looked at each other and gasped. What had he just done?

As Lula had known they would, the entire crowd punched their hands into the air, wild with unconfined cheering.

Lula concluded his speech, brashly vowed the strike would continue, and strutted off the stage with a triumphant swagger. Once he was out of public view, however, he staggered and slumped down into a chair, his head in his hands. His face had gone completely pale. The thousands of workers happily filed out, buzzing with anticipation, and soon the stadium was empty.

The three of us climbed into Pazzianotto's car and rode back together to the union headquarters. Lula rode in the back seat in sullen silence before he finally erupted: "We have to stop that strike!"

Pazzianotto turned around and gaped at him. "But what can be done now?" he asked incredulously. "Lula, you know this is against the law! Have you lost your mind?"

Lula shifted around in his seat, panicked. "Professor," he said to me, "perhaps you can try to influence your friends among the big industrialist businessmen. Perhaps you could help make all of this okay?"

I had no idea what he meant. "I don't know what I can do now, Lula. I think it's too late."

The humor of the situation, if there was any to begin with, quickly faded. As the now-illegal strike continued, the military lost patience with the rebel they had previously seemed willing to tolerate. A few days later, I was back in São Bernardo do Campo, sitting with Lula at a small bar. On the radio, we heard that the military had used its powers to intervene in the union and expel Lula from its ranks. Shortly thereafter, he was thrown in jail.

The military probably did not plan on locking Lula up for very long. The authorities merely hoped to scare him and then let him go. But tragedy does not respect such clumsy intentions; while Lula was still languishing in jail, his mother passed away. He was permitted to go to the funeral, although a police escort accompanied him. I also attended, along with several of our friends and colleagues. Lula was kept isolated from the rest of us, surrounded by a phalanx of policemen, and he looked utterly numb and defeated. It was as if this was one tragedy too much. He couldn't cry anymore.

I stood and watched him, transfixed, reflecting about how, despite our very different backgrounds, Lula and I were also quite similar. For on this occasion, I knew *exactly* how he must have felt. A decade before, I had attended my father's funeral under eerily similar circumstances: stung by personal loss, estranged from my country, in trouble with the law, and, most of all, determined to bring that rotten dictatorship to an end. This was no way to live. As the police shoved Lula into a squad car and whisked him back to jail, I felt the same pang of outrage and helplessness that had haunted me for the past fourteen years. At least now, I thought, I had a powerful companion fighting alongside me.

Few of us recognized it at the time, but the world was slowly changing in ways that would have a profound impact on Brazil. In the early 1980s, I made a trip to Poland to attend a conference organized by the International Sociology Association, of which I had been elected vice president. The meeting was held at an old palace outside Warsaw, where we were supposed to debate the latest research on social change.

There was no point in looking at dull research, however, when social change was taking place in real life, right there outside the palace doors. Poland was swept up in the height of the Solidarity movement. The selection of Karol Wojtyla as Pope John Paul II had emboldened the church as an agent for democratic change in Poland. Enraptured, we watched on television as the Polish cardinal addressed the nation. We didn't understand what he was saying, of course, but we understood the symbolism. This was the first time that the Polish government had ever dared to allow the cardinal such a large forum. Our Polish hosts were terrified that a Soviet invasion was imminent.

Just as in Brazil, the Catholic Church in Poland had formed an alliance with labor unions to oppose an authoritarian regime. I was intrigued by the similarities. The thick atmosphere of tension also seemed a bit like Paris in 1968, except this was a political struggle with an ideological and military superpower. Despite the anguished pleas of our hosts that it was too dangerous, four of us decided to make a trip to Gdansk so we could witness the Solidarity movement firsthand. We rented a small Volkswagen and drove there ourselves.

When we arrived in the drab port city, I was shocked. In every window, there was a lit candle and a picture of the pope. The old papal banner hung from rooftops. Despite all these symbols of protest, however, Gdansk was surprisingly quiet. We parked the car and walked down to the Lenin Shipyard, where Lech Walesa was inside speaking. The area was so densely packed with people that we couldn't enter, but loudspeakers were set up outside, so we could listen anyway. We could not understand Walesa's individual words, but, again, there was no escaping their greater significance. We knew we were witnessing something monumental.

Although the Polish government eventually tried to crack down on Solidarity, it was unable to destroy it. Something deeper had already irrevocably changed. Therein resided the beauty of the movement in Poland: It illustrated that there could be no going back for the countries of the Soviet bloc. It was plainly obvious that communism had failed. The so-called great social experiment had yielded only suffering, oppression, and economic stagnation.

A few years earlier, I had made a road trip across Eastern Europe with my friend Manuel Castells, a distinguished Spanish sociologist. We started in Bulgaria, drove through Romania, and stopped at a beach resort on the Black Sea. Even the beach made me sad, though. Everywhere we went, it was dark. There were no people on the streets. There was no nightlife. As we wove through the mountains and on through East Germany, Castells and I spent countless hours waiting at police checkpoints. I thought to myself: How do these people live like this?

Suddenly, when we crossed the Austrian border and arrived in Vienna, it was as if someone had turned on all the lights. Here, finally, was a bright, happy, Western city. Relief and happiness washed over me. When I saw the two realities so vividly, side by side, there could be no doubt who was winning the battle between capitalism and communism, between democracy and authoritarianism.

Most historians talked about the end of the Cold War in terms of Ronald Reagan's military buildup and the ensuing economic collapse of the Soviet Union. I am convinced, however, that this simple truth of visual contrast was just as important. Television, in particular, was crucial in illustrating the reality for the vast majority of people who could not travel. Thanks to TV, people behind the Iron Curtain could finally appreciate with their own eyes just how good life was on the other side of the Wall. Even the Soviets could behold simple pleasures of Western life, such as the nightlife, the department stores, the refrigerators, and say to themselves: They're way better off than we are! By the 1980s, with the spread of broadcast media, this kind of subversive information was practically impossible to suppress. Television bestowed the United States with more power to change the world than a million nuclear warheads ever could have.

My work with the International Sociology Association, of which I became president in 1982, led me to make several fascinating trips to the Soviet Union. The Soviet regime had become particularly rigid and paranoid, and I was eager to meet Russian students to talk to them about their country and hear whether they had a plan to change it. Setting up such a meeting was understandably a delicate matter. Finally, on a trip that I took when Leonid Brezhnev was still in power, I met an old Armenian professor, a fascinating man whose brother had long ago been executed by Stalin. He promised to arrange a meeting for me with some students from the University of Moscow. An aide of his agreed to accompany me and translate.

At ten o'clock at night, we departed my hotel for University City in Moscow. We went to the apartment of a young Russian woman named Ekaterina—I will never forget her name. She had enormous pigtails and was a bit overweight. She led us into her cramped, overheated living room, where three male students sat slumped in chairs, regarding me with intense suspicion. As well they might have.

The conversation was difficult at first. But in the end, as night stretched into dawn, vodka soothed our nerves and the young men stopped watching the door. A ferocious rainstorm raged outside as the students told me about life in Russia. They never said outright that they opposed Brezhnev, or the Politburo, or communism in general. Such a direct confession would have been dangerous for them, no matter how many vodkas we shared. Instead, they talked enthusiastically about American music and movies. It was tantamount to saying they wanted to start a revolution. Bob Dylan, *Raiders of the Lost Ark,* Luke Skywalker, and *Saturday Night Fever*—that was the language of the first rebels in the Soviet Union.

Inevitably, the people became bolder and more direct. They started challenging the repression itself, declaring that they wanted to be free. I returned to the Soviet Union years later, when Mikhail Gorbachev was in power. I met with Lenina Pomerantz, an old Brazilian-Russian classmate of mine from the University of São Paulo. "Things here are changing. This is a different country now," she told me excitedly. "There's going to be a meeting tonight, and it will be worth it for you to attend."

The meeting was in the cultural center of a lamp factory on the outskirts of Moscow. Both the venue and the atmosphere were weird. Some people stood guard at the doors, while another group stood inside, playing violins. Pasted all over the walls were letters from people who had been inside the Gulag, the Soviet concentration camps. There were also sketches of what the camps looked like. The theater was packed, and the tension reminded me of the plays and concerts in Brazil during the 1960s and 1970s, when the police used to barge in and start beating up the actors. Maybe, I thought to myself, it wasn't such a smart idea to be there.

My translator that night was João Prestes, the young son of Luís

Carlos Prestes, the Communist leader who, half a century before, had famously clashed with Getúlio Vargas. We settled into our seats. The lights went off and a white screen dropped from the ceiling. Projected on the screen was a grainy photograph of the Politburo, with a superimposed caption in Russian.

I turned to my translator. "Um, what does that caption say?"

The young man winced as he read it back to me. "It says, 'These are the enemies of Russia.'"

"João," I said, laughing, "I think it's about time we got out of here."

Somehow, he talked me into staying. We heard rousing speeches against the regime by several intellectuals, including one of Nikita Khrushchev's sons. The police never showed up. At the end of the night, there was a vote, and the assembly decided to pool resources and build a monument to those who had died in the Gulag.

As elsewhere, the protests in the Soviet Union were often about highly specific local issues but spoke to a greater national struggle. Building a monument to the Gulag was, in that sense, a sublime act of revolution. Individual acts like that have a way of gathering critical mass and producing sudden, sweeping social change. Back in the 1980s, I made several speeches at academic conferences where I referred to this kind of historical phenomenon as a "short circuit." Nowadays, it might be described as a "tipping point." The idea is essentially the same.

The events in Eastern Europe and the Soviet Union had a profound, if not immediately visible, effect on Brazil. As the Cold War showed signs of fading, so did the excuse that had been used to justify two decades of military rule. Of course, none of us could have predicted the fall of the Berlin Wall. But communism clearly no longer posed a threat to conquer the world. It was as if a bomb had been defused. While some isolated battles still raged on due to either local factors or U.S. paranoia, namely in Nicaragua and El Salvador, the rest of Latin America began accepting by the early 1980s that democracy was inevitable.

Thanks in part to the developments in Eastern Europe, as well as in

Portugal and Spain, we now sensed in Brazil that our own autocratic regime was nearing its end. We were on the verge of our own "short circuit." With the promise of the 1978 campaign still buzzing in my ears, I wondered what could deliver that one final blow that would bring the dictatorship tumbling down. But, as usual, the action would find me first.

By 1982, I still had one foot in academia and one foot in politics. I spent a stimulating semester that year as a visiting professor at the University of California at Berkeley. The intellectual life was rich, and I was happy. At the end of the semester, the head of the sociology department, Robert Bellah, invited me over for tea. To my surprise, he offered me a tenured professorship to replace the esteemed sociologist Jürgen Habermas, who was returning to Germany. Bellah insisted that Berkeley needed me and promised me a pleasant, quiet life by the sea in Northern California.

I smiled and told him: "Professor Bellah, I'm flattered. But I can only accept your offer if you can also guarantee me a seat in the U.S. Senate. Otherwise, I'm going to have to turn you down, because I'm about to become a senator in Brazil."

Bellah looked only slightly more stunned by my response than I felt. My life was changing yet again because of fortuitous events that I could not possibly have engineered on my own. Back in Brazil, Franco Montoro, who had finished first in the Senate campaign in 1978, was now on the verge of being elected governor of São Paulo. Since I had finished second in the 1978 elections, I was Montoro's alternate. If he became governor, I would automatically take his place in the Senate.

Sure enough, when Montoro won the November election, I became a member of the Senate, effective as of March 1983. Through pure accident, I suddenly had my first job in politics. My life would never be the same.

I received yet another deluge of criticism from my friends on the left. They argued that Congress was just a farcical theater that the military tolerated in order to pretend Brazil was still a democracy. "How can you participate in this fraud?" they asked again, just as incredulous as they had been in 1978.

I told my friends that, yes, to some extent, they were right: The Senate had little real power. Nevertheless, it was abundantly clear that the opposition, as watered down and restricted as it may have been, was now in a position to exert unprecedented influence. Momentum was on our side, due in part to a pronounced downturn in the economy. Inflation was running at over 200 percent per year. Among the working-age population, a stunning 40 percent were either unemployed or working part-time at marginal, unskilled jobs. Owing to volatile world oil prices, a regional debt crisis had shaken all of Latin America. Brazil's foreign debt exploded from $43 billion in 1978 to $91 billion in 1984. Many wealthy and middle-class Brazilians, who had been willing to ignore the dictatorship's uglier side as long as the economy was good, suddenly became indignant about the human rights record. Better late than never, I suppose. As a result, the military's popularity hit all-time lows. Many officers stopped wearing their uniforms in public for fear of ridicule.

All we lacked was a prominent opportunity for the public to voice its opposition to the dictatorship. Whatever we did, we knew that we would have to be careful. The public opposition would have to be on a massive scale, and it would have to be visible. Yet it would also have to be nonconfrontational and nonviolent. If the gesture was *too* strong, then the military would feel threatened and lash out. There was the risk of a repeat of 1968, when clumsy opposition merely provided an excuse for the hard-line officers to consolidate their power. Yet, if our protest was too weak, then there was simply no point. Franco Montoro determined the final plan, deciding that we should organize a large street demonstration in São Paulo on January 25, 1984, which would coincide with the anniversary of the city's founding. Thus, the event would have the requisite patriotic tint to defuse the inevitable accusations from the right that, by protesting, we were being "anti-Brazilian."

Every protest needs a rallying cry. We decided on *"Diretas já!"*— "Direct elections, now!" If the slogan sounds a bit dull, in retrospect it reveals a lot about our strategy and the politics of the times. Presidential elections were scheduled for early the following year, 1985. The military had continued to stage these so-called elections every four years throughout the dictatorship, but up to this point they had been little more than window dressing. The military had absolute power over the selection of the candidates, and Congress ultimately voted to determine the winner. It was a kind of Electoral College that, naturally, always picked the candidate preferred by the small group of officers who ran Brazil. In contrast, "direct elections," as we envisioned them, would give the Brazilian public the vote and permit any candidate, even a civilian, to run. So *"Diretas já"* was an indirect way of demanding full democracy.

The deeper meaning wasn't lost on anyone, much less the military. As the date of the demonstration drew nearer, President João Baptista Figueiredo appeared on television and thundered that *"Diretas já* is the same as subversion."* Just a few years earlier, such a pronouncement might have scared everyone into submission; the whole protest might have been called off. But times had clearly changed, and Figueiredo's words had the opposite effect. Word of the protest spread like wildfire. Several newspapers began loudly publicizing the event. With the notable exception of the *O Globo* media empire, which maintained a cozy relationship with the military much longer than nearly every other media outlet, Brazilian journalists were remarkably courageous in their coverage. Without their work, the movement might never have caught on.

We did everything we could to raise the stakes. I gave the opposition party's keynote speech in the Senate in favor of *"Diretas já."* We handed out flyers and invited political leaders of every hue, including Lula, whose recently founded workers' party, PT, had already staged a small demonstration. For all our efforts, we expected perhaps 10,000 people to ultimately show up. That, we mused, would have been enough.

On January 25, 1984, in the Praça da Sé in São Paulo, more than 300,000 people gathered to chant *"Diretas já!"* There wasn't even enough room in the plaza to hold all of them. We were shocked. Not even a torrential rainstorm could drive the crowd away or dampen their enthusiasm. The demonstrators were largely middle class and hugely enthusiastic. The atmosphere was more like a party than a political confrontation. People danced, sang, and formed human chains. I gave a speech, as did Ulysses Guimarães, Franco Montoro, and Lula. The words were unimportant, however. In fact, the sound system was so bad that about half the crowd couldn't hear a thing. Luckily, the symbolism of the event transcended anything we could have ever said. At the end, all of us joined hands and sang the national anthem. It was a profound show of unity and national willpower.

Lula and I smiled at each other as we surveyed the vast, singing crowd before us. The gauntlet had been thrown down. The only question now was how the military would react. "We did it!" Lula yelled, euphoric, as the crowd's chanting echoed through the city. "We did it!"

Two months later, I was summoned to a one-on-one meeting with the president.

Despite the military's best efforts, *"Diretas já"* was blossoming into a nationwide movement. *O Globo* television had originally tried to pass off the demonstration in São Paulo as a spontaneous celebration of the city's anniversary rather than a mass protest for democracy—but the Brazilian public was, by now, too savvy for such lies. People everywhere had started wearing T-shirts that said, with almost comical bluntness: "I want to vote for president!" Copycat street demonstrations, led by Ulysses Guimarães, took place over the ensuing weeks. In Rio, 800,000 people gathered. In another demonstration in São Paulo, over a million. At that point, even *O Globo* had no choice but to get on board. The phenomenon was not about to go away.

President Figueiredo was an unlikely but strangely fitting candidate to lead Brazil to democracy. During the late 1960s, he was the head of the SNI, the national intelligence service, during the crackdown on the guerrillas. Now, like the regime itself, he was old, tired, and burned out. His health was failing, and he had undergone heart surgery in the United States. Figueiredo asked for me to come to see him shortly before a state dinner in tribute to Miguel de la Madrid, the visiting president of Mexico. I expected that the president would probably want to talk to me about simple matters of protocol rather than politics.

I was escorted to a private room, where Figueiredo had been for a while, biding his time and waiting before he was to enter the spacious banquet room at the Itamaraty Palace, the foreign affairs ministry in Brasília. He was on his own, dressed in civilian clothes. He smiled warmly and shook my hand.

"My father was a very good friend of your father's," he said.

Indeed, Figueiredo's father had briefly gone into exile in Buenos Aires on account of his participation in a 1932 revolt against Getúlio Vargas. Typically, however, his sins were soon forgiven, and the elder Figueiredo had gone on to a distinguished political career. By an odd coincidence, my house in São Paulo was on a street named after him. Years earlier, the street sign on our block had fallen down, and I had taken it upon myself to replace it. I had painted the sign myself and nailed it to a wall on the street corner.

This story made the president laugh. "That is very, very strange," he said, smiling. "Thank you for doing your best to preserve the dignity of my family name!"

The ice was broken. We proceeded to chat for a long while about Getúlio and the tenentes and other episodes in Brazilian history. It was classic small talk. I started to wonder why he had really wanted to see me.

"One time," Figueiredo began, suddenly choosing his words with great care, "someone told me they thought direct elections would solve the problem of corruption." He shifted around uneasily in his seat. "But look at the case of Adhemar de Barros," he continued, naming an ex-governor of São Paulo who had been found guilty of fraud. "He was elected by the people. That didn't stop corruption at all!"

This was a subtle yet tremendously important thing for the president to say. Although he was being combative, the mere mention of *diretas* meant that he was at least considering the possibility of direct elections. That he would broach the topic with a leader of the opposition like me was, indeed, a monumental step forward.

I hesitated a moment and then responded: "But if people believe that *diretas* would solve the problem, Mister President, then we have one more reason to do it!"

Figueiredo smiled, nodded, and stared blankly at me for a moment. Then, he deftly changed the subject, and we never discussed it again. But I suppose that what Figueiredo heard from me and other opposition leaders was enough to convince him that he should not interfere with the liberalization process. Soon thereafter, the legislature began making plans to vote on whether to institute direct elections for president in the coming year. The military would not interfere with the result. Essentially, Congress would decide whether Brazil would return to democracy with a simple vote.

The country buzzed with anticipation, believing victory was now a certainty. But, looking back, I can see that the warning signs were there from the very beginning. The vote was set for April 25, 1984. A week earlier, President Figueiredo had decreed a state of emergency in Brasília, which meant that television could not broadcast the vote—thus pulling a mysterious veil of secrecy over the proceedings. On the day of the special session, 6,000 soldiers were stationed throughout the capital. When the voting started, thousands of people drove their cars around outside of Congress, honking their horns to show their support for democracy, and the soldiers desperately tried to stop them. The ensuing confrontation produced one of the most truly absurd scenes in Brazilian history: Mounted on a white stallion, the military commander of Brasília, Newton Cruz, galloped around the jam-packed streets of the city, beating cars with his riding whip to try and make them shut up.

Cruz's whip couldn't stop the honking, of course, but it did show us that the military might not cede power as quietly as we had previously thought. As the moment of the vote approached, I realized we were in trouble.

On the floor of Congress, 298 deputies voted in favor of direct elections, with 65 against and three abstaining. But the absence of 112 congressmen left the result 22 votes short of the two-thirds majority we needed to change the constitution.

The movement for *diretas* had failed.

We were livid. How could this have happened? With Brazil united in favor of democracy, how could Congress have so flagrantly violated the people's will? Unfortunately, the answer was simple: Congress was still controlled by the ARENA Party, the military's political wing. Most legislators therefore had a vested interest in preventing full-fledged democracy. The legislature did not reflect the people's will at all. So the real question became: What now? With Congress discredited and hostile to reform, the next step was unclear. Some members of the opposition deliberated quitting Congress altogether. We were on a road to crisis.

Just three days later, I gave on the Senate floor what I consider to be one of the most important speeches of my life. It was certainly among the most controversial. The theme of my speech was *"Mudança já!"*— "Change, now!" I argued that the opposition should continue to press for change in the spirit of *"Diretas já!"* but with a new objective. I said that we had to be realistic: Direct elections in 1984 were not going to happen. That vote, albeit on a technicality, had been lost. Yet there was no time to be bitter, and the stakes were too high to just walk away in anger. Instead, I said, the opposition should try to win the presidency within the existing Electoral College system. We could nominate a civilian candidate and then pressure the military to allow Congress to elect him. Such a plan would allow the military some say over who the next president would be, permitting democracy without the military authorities having to worry about a radical taking power. I believed this was the surest path to *mudança,* to democratic change. We just had to accept our previous defeat and do what was possible, rather than what was ideal, or else a historic opportunity might slip away. We had to do what was possible.

After the speech, I was instantly labeled a hypocrite. The left, in particular, accused me of having no principles. Some said that I was a stooge of the military regime, sent to derail the opposition and ruin the quest for democracy.

Nonetheless, a broad opposition coalition nominated Tancredo Neves, a seventy-five-year-old elder statesman, as its candidate for president in 1985. Tancredo was a discreet, charming, nonthreatening career politician who appealed to us without frightening the military. He had been Getúlio Vargas's minister of justice during the 1950s, and he had agreed to serve as prime minister in 1961 when the military wanted to keep power away from President Goulart. He retained cordial contacts within the military regime and had been negotiating behind the scenes to assure them that the armed forces would be well treated if he became president. Tancredo was no puppet, however; he promised that, if elected, he would rewrite the constitution and strip away all vestiges of military rule. Even though the Electoral College system was still in place, electing Tancredo would unequivocally mean that the dictatorship was over.

On January 15, 1985, the Electoral College elected Tancredo Neves as the next president of Brazil. After more than twenty years, an imperfect democracy had returned. Some of us had never believed we would see the day when the military handed over power. The process had been agonizingly long, and it had culminated in a classic Brazilian compromise. All over the country, people celebrated, dancing and setting off firecrackers in the street. A billboard in Brasília blared, "Good morning, democracy!"

As Tancredo prepared to take office in 1985, we mused that we had found the perfect man to lead Brazil into a new era. As it turned out, we were absolutely right—except for one horrible, tragic problem.

CHAPTER

8

KINGS OF THE JUNGLE

ISTURBING RUMORS about Tancredo Neves's health
were already circulating by the time I went to see him, just
days before he was to be inaugurated as the president of a
newly democratic Brazil. Perhaps he had throat cancer, people whispered. Other speculation centered on various awful digestive ailments.
Maybe, at seventy-five years old, his whole body was just breaking
down. I nervously contemplated all of this, and what it would mean
for Brazil, as I sat in the living room of his country house outside
Brasília, waiting in vain for Tancredo to appear. As an hour went by
with no sign of him, I had a sinking feeling that something sinister was
indeed afoot.

Nevertheless, when Tancredo finally emerged, he was as jovial and
charismatic as ever. He enveloped me in one of his trademark bear hugs
and gregariously slapped me on the back. Tancredo and I deeply respected each other. Our political styles were similar—he was popularly

known as "The Great Conciliator"—and our easygoing personalities clicked as well. We chatted amicably for a while, reflecting on the times of heady change in which we were living and the unique opportunity that Brazil now enjoyed.

Over coffee, Tancredo confirmed what I had already been told: He wanted me to be his government's main representative in both houses of Congress, a position that would be enormously difficult, given the volatility that would certainly accompany this new era of democracy. I accepted his offer.

"I want you to be my man of confidence in the Congress," he boomed, putting his arm around my shoulder. Then, he dissolved into hearty laughter and added: "I'll see if I can get some walls knocked down in the Senate so you can have a bigger office!"

I laughed along with him, but my suspicions were still not allayed. I decided to stay for lunch. We sat down at a long table with his family and a handful of his friends, including Governor Miguel Arraes from Pernambuco, a legendary leader of the Socialist Party. Before Tancredo entered the room, his wife pleaded with us: "Please don't offer any wine to the president." She seemed on the verge of tears. I hurriedly switched his glass of wine with my own cup, which was still empty.

Clearly, something *was* horribly wrong.

We waited for an awkward eternity, during which an awkward hush fell over the table. Finally, Tancredo stomped into the room and sat down.

Very concerned by now, I decided to get right to the point.

"How is your health, Tancredo?"

His head snapped up, and I saw a brief but unmistakable look of alarm flash across his face. It vanished just as quickly, replaced by a toothy smile. "I've never been better!" he exclaimed. "Really, Fernando Henrique, I feel fine."

I took a sip of my—his—wine. "That's good to hear," I said. "Because you know that, in São Paulo, there are . . . rumors."

"Ridiculous!" Tancredo blurted, waving his hand at me dismissively.

"I'm in perfect shape. You know, I don't even need to exercise anymore."

"Why not?"

"There's no point. Everyone knows that lions don't go to the gym—and they're the kings of the jungle!"

It was a strange and forced joke, but everyone was so relieved that we joined him in a chorus of raucous laughter anyway. After that, Tancredo deftly managed to change the subject to his upcoming agenda as president.

When I left, Tancredo accompanied me outside. He swung open my car door and I protested: "I'm honored that the president of Brazil is opening doors for me," I teased him, "but protocol does not permit such gestures."

Tancredo doubled over with laughter and waved good-naturedly as I drove off.

History has never clarified precisely what happened to Tancredo. Because of the lingering mystery, and the high drama of the times, some Brazilian conspiracy theorists have inevitably claimed that he was poisoned. However, at that sadly memorable lunch, it was apparent that Tancredo's health was already in conspicuous decline. He gave a great performance that day, but he could not disguise that something was wrong.

Days later, on the night before Tancredo's inauguration, a group of us were having dinner in Brasília with the president of Portugal, Mário Soares, when the phone at the embassy rang with the news that Tancredo had been hospitalized, reportedly with appendicitis. We all jumped into our cars and sped to the hospital.

I rushed into the waiting room and spoke with Tancredo's nephew, Francisco Dornelles, who said he would need emergency surgery. Minutes later, doctors ran—literally ran—past us, wheeling Tancredo away on a stretcher into the operating room. I caught a glimpse of the president-elect's face, pallid, sweating, and wracked with pain, before he disappeared behind the hospital's swinging doors.

I slumped into a chair and stared blankly at those gleaming white doors, wondering if any lingering hope for democracy had just vanished behind them. It is difficult to put into words the despair that I felt at that moment. I feared for my friend, and I feared for my country. In Tancredo, we thought we had found the perfect man to lead us out of dictatorship. He was truly one of a kind, a miracle, a statesman acceptable both to the military and the opposition. Now, on the very eve of what was supposed to be a new era, he had been struck down by a mysterious ailment. I wondered, not for the first time in my life, if Brazil suffered from some kind of terrible curse.

I trudged upstairs to the waiting room. Some of the most important figures in Brazilian politics were sitting there, on an eerie sort of death watch. José Fragelli, the president of the Senate, talked in hushed tones with my friend Ulysses Guimarães, who was now head of the lower house. General Leônidas Pires Gonçalves, who had just been named minister of the army, sat in a corner cradling his head in his hands. Off by himself, spread out on a couch and utterly depressed, was Jose Sarney, who was scheduled to be inaugurated the next day as Tancredo's vice president.

Sarney was an odd case. During the dictatorship, he had been a member of political parties that supported the military. He had only recently split from the party, and his pairing with Tancredo in the 1984 elections had been quite controversial; it was, more than anything, designed to add a conservative balance to the ticket and to collect more votes at the Electoral College. We accepted this at the time through gritted teeth because the vice president of Brazil, by tradition, had no institutional importance. No one ever imagined that Sarney would be anything more than a symbol. But now?

A large crowd was gathering outside the hospital in an impromptu vigil, and their melancholy singing echoed through the waiting room. Sarney sat up for a moment, listened, and shook his head in despair.

"I have no intention of taking office as president. I have no such intention," Sarney mumbled, almost to himself. "Does anyone here even know how the succession is supposed to work if Tancredo becomes incapacitated?"

We all looked at each other and shrugged.

We chewed over the question for a while, but we could not agree on what the constitution said. Since Sarney had not yet been sworn in as vice president, some of us thought that the head of the lower house—Ulysses—was legally next in line to be president. This might have posed a serious problem, however, because Ulysses had long been a severe critic of the dictatorship. There was a possibility that the military would not accept him as president. We were stumped. Finally, we gave up and decided to seek a definitive ruling from the people whose opinion likely mattered most anyway.

Leaving Sarney to await news of Tancredo, Ulysses, Senator Fragelli, and the general and I slipped out the back door of the hospital, taking care to avoid the hordes of media outside. Then, we jumped into the general's cramped sedan and sped away across Brasília. After running our share of red stoplights, we arrived at the home of João Leitão de Abreu, the chief of staff for Figueiredo, the outgoing military president. Leitão de Abreu was the government's lead lawyer and political coordinator, and we believed he was the man who could best advise us as to both the legal specifics of the situation and the political reality—that is, what the military would or would not be willing to accept.

Leitão de Abreu answered the door in a formal black suit, rubbing his eyes. He glared wearily at us as if we were a group of noisy children who had just woken him up. "What do you want?"

There was just one lonely copy of the constitution in the house, a tattered little book with print so small it was barely legible. As the night stretched on, each of us read and reread the document in painstaking detail, our eyes tearing up from the fatigue and stress. General Gonçalves, Senator Fragelli, and I were not trained in constitutional law, so we mostly listened in silence while Ulysses and Leitão de Abreu discussed the matter.

To our surprise, Ulysses passionately argued that the job fell to the vice president–elect, Sarney. This was the reverse of what I had expected, because Ulysses had never made any secret of his desire to lead Brazil. But the crucial assumption was that Tancredo would recover; none of us could imagine anything but an interim presidency for Sarney. Ulysses believed that there was no point in jeopardizing democracy by putting himself in the presidency for such a short time. As the hours dragged on, we became convinced that it was the right thing to do.

"So we're in agreement, then?" Leitão de Abreu asked, satisfied.

We nodded, said goodbye, and trudged out of his house at three in the morning. We didn't know it at the time, but we had just decided the future of Brazil.

The next day, we attended the most joyless inauguration one can possibly imagine. Sarney looked exhausted, understandable given that he had received a phone call at four in the morning informing him he would be sworn in that very day as the new leader of Brazil. It was a difficult job that he had never asked for and did not know how long he would possess.

Tancredo, bless his soul, clung to life through seven excruciating surgeries in thirty-eight days. Every time they fixed one problem, something else would go wrong. During the initial operation, so many of Tancredo's aides and party leaders crowded into the operating room that sterile conditions were impossible; later, possibly as a result, an insidious, wasting infection set in. The doctors rushed to repair his heart, then his abdomen, but nothing ever seemed to improve. "Tancredo Neves is still alive," the hospital's chief surgeon said with awe and frustration, "only because of his sheer determination to live."

Meanwhile, hundreds of Brazilians gathered outside the hospital day and night, weeping and waiting for the next medical bulletin on television. One man dragged a large wooden cross along the hospital sidewalk; another followed, flagellating himself with a whip. "It wasn't just Tancredo in intensive care," one reporter observed. "It was the whole country." In Tancredo's home state of Minas Gerais, the archbishop prayed for a miraculous recovery at a mass attended by 10,000 people.

To no avail. On April 21, 1985, Tancredo Neves passed away without ever being sworn in as the president of Brazil. Our young democracy was left with a gaping leadership vacuum, the magnitude of which became immediately and tragically apparent. Following a solemn state funeral in Brasília, and a procession attended by 2 million people in São Paulo, Tancredo's body was returned to Minas Gerais. As a crowd of thousands pressed frantically on the doors of the palace where Tancredo's body was to lie in state, someone started screaming. The mourners panicked. The ensuing stampede killed five people and left more than two hundred injured. Yet again for Brazil, a moment of great hope had turned into a national nightmare.

The tone for the first few years of democracy had been set.

Brazilians are capable of extravagant acts of forgiveness, especially in politics. Never was this more true than in 1985, when every last politician from our checkered past seemed to emerge from the woodwork, claiming to be the heir to a new era of democracy. As if to remind us just how unpredictable a country we lived in, Jânio Quadros, the eccentric former president, decided to stage the most improbable of comebacks. He was now sixty-eight years old, but the intervening years had only made him more jumpy and unpredictable, if such a thing were possible. Jânio announced that he was running for mayor of São Paulo, the same job he had once held three decades before. He even brought back his famous broom, gleefully promising yet again to sweep away corruption and his filthy, thieving, unworthy opponent.

That opponent was me.

I'll be honest: I never thought Jânio had a chance. I didn't see how Brazilians could possibly vote for him again, given the way he had abandoned us before. This proved to be an arrogant mindset for starting a campaign, and I never quite recovered from it. To make matters worse, I didn't really want the job. The idea to run for mayor of São

Paulo came from my party. I was quite content with my growing leadership role in the Senate, but I let myself be talked into running anyway. Most important, though, Jânio was a wily old fool who wasn't about to let scruples—or the truth, for that matter—interfere with his cutthroat brand of politics.

I belatedly realized that I was in dire trouble following a speech one afternoon in Cidade Tiradentes, a poor neighborhood outside the city. A tiny elderly woman approached me, trembling and near tears. I'll never forget the look of abject terror on her face as she tugged on my shirtsleeve, looked up, and asked, "Is it true that you are going to put marijuana in kids' school lunches?"

I just stood there, dumbfounded. "Is it . . . *excuse me?*"

"I heard that Fernando Henrique is going to make all of Brazil's children smoke pot every day. Is that true?"

"Where did you hear such a ridiculous thing?"

"From Jânio's followers."

And then I knew. Years before, during a magazine interview, a reporter had asked me if I had ever tried marijuana. I had been hounded on this issue before, especially after my semester teaching at Berkeley, where it was apparently assumed that the whole world sat around smoking joints all day (the truth, now that I think about it, was not that far off). I told my interviewer that, yes, I had tried marijuana once in my life, but I hadn't particularly enjoyed it. I perceived it as an honest and rather bland answer and proceeded to forget about the whole affair.

It was a foolish mistake, providing Jânio's army of propagandists with the kind of ammunition they needed to, improbably, run a campaign on moral values. At speeches all over São Paulo, they referred to me only as "the pot smoker." I laughed off the accusations, believing that no one would take them seriously, especially coming from a man like Jânio. It was another misjudgment. For all its worldwide fame as the anything-goes land of Carnival, the real Brazil has a strangely conservative streak that tends to show itself at the most unexpected moments. Many Brazilians will forgive their politicians for graft and incompetence—or, apparently, for having once resigned the presidency after just seven months—but politicians are often held to the highest of standards in their personal lives.

Indeed, just days before the end of the campaign, I made yet another faux pas. In a live, televised debate with all the other candidates but Jânio, the moderator asked me if I believed in God. Shocked and somewhat indignant, I responded that I honestly didn't see why my religious convictions were relevant to how I would perform as mayor of São Paulo.

By dawn the next day, Jânio's posters were already plastered all over the city: "FERNANDO HENRIQUE IS A POT-SMOKING ATHEIST."

I'm not an atheist, nor am I particularly superstitious, but I *have* seen in my life that disasters tend to come in threes. The final blow was delivered the night before the election, when I conducted an ill-advised interview with a local newsmagazine. The photographer asked me if he could take a picture of me sitting in the mayor's chair at city hall. It was for a weekly publication, and the photographer promised me the photo would only be published if I won the election. Assuming no harm could be done, I consented. But as I sat there with a cheesy grin, posing in that chair for a job that was not yet mine, a photographer from a daily newspaper just happened to wander by the office and snap his own picture of me. That most smug of photos was then plastered across newspapers the following day—election day. As a man who has always been accused of arrogance, this made me look like I was taking victory for granted in a tight race.

Jânio ended up beating me by 2 percent. After the result was announced on television that night, a parade of Jânio's supporters circled the block around my apartment, blaring on their horns well past midnight in ecstatic celebration. The noise was so incessant that Ruth and I fled São Paulo for the refuge of our country home in Ibiúna. When I turned on the television the next day, there was Jânio, as big a caricature as ever, frowning as he sprayed disinfectant on the now-famous mayor's chair that I had sat in.

No one likes to lose. I spent most of that weekend in Ibiúna moping around, reading my books, and generally feeling sorry for myself. However, I quickly reemerged, eager to apply the lessons I had learned. I would never again underestimate an opponent in a campaign. I would also, for the rest of my political career, refuse to discuss certain aspects of my personal life. As I discovered in that campaign, there are private matters that are simply irrelevant to one's life as a politician. Out of respect for my family, I have endeavored to protect our privacy ever since.

In the end, everyone is capable of learning from their mistakes—even Jânio. His time as mayor of São Paulo was blessedly uneventful. This time around, he served out all four years of his term, without so much as threatening to quit. Jânio passed away shortly after leaving office, in 1992, having achieved a tiny degree of redemption. I think it is safe to say that Brazil will never see another public figure quite like him.

I remember learning once in a psychology class how, in many species, males will clash when they are put together in a shared space. Lions will do this—maybe that's what Tancredo was really joking about at that ill-fated lunch. Roosters are another prime example. Put ten of them in a cage and they will scratch the others' eyes out, sometimes fighting to the death until a pecking order is finally established. Only then can a degree of calm be restored. I think it would be only a slight exaggeration to compare that process with what happened in Brazilian politics in 1985.

During the previous twenty years, the military had monopolized political power in Brazil. True, some responsibilities were doled out to the civilian Congress and municipal governments, but make no mistake: Final authority on all important matters had *always* rested with the generals. Now, virtually overnight, politics was a real power game again, and all kinds of people—Jânio was only one example—rushed to fill the void. They came from exile, they came from the elite, and they came from nothing. Democracy would not be possible until every player had a role. But establishing the roles turned out to be a tricky process because, even if the faces weren't new, the roles were. Brazilian politics was roiled by innumerable turf wars as all these kings of the jungle struggled to find their own niche. Meanwhile, the feathers flew.

Through it all, I think I usually managed to stay somewhat above the fray. I know that might sound naive or self-aggrandizing, but it's true. Because I had essentially arrived in Congress by accident, I never felt like I had to compete in order to succeed. I had the luxury of acting more like a mediator, a role that came naturally to me because of my upbringing and my personality. Of course, I did have ambitions, just like any other man. But I never felt the need to push others out of the way to achieve them.

Politics and social life overlap everywhere in the world, but especially in Brazil. The smallness of Brasília, with its interlocking web of family and friends, could sometimes be shocking, even to me. My son, Paulo Henrique, ended up marrying the daughter of José Magalhães Pinto— who had been one of the chief ideologues of the 1964 coup and later a foreign minister under the dictatorship. I had known him for years, and in fact had gone to his house in Belo Horizonte back in 1961 when Jânio Quadros resigned as president. Since then, however, politics had driven us apart. During the 1980s, when our children began seeing each other, Magalhães Pinto was a deputy in the lower house of Congress. One day, I entered the chamber and sat next to him.

He whispered out of the corner of his mouth, "You know about our children, don't you?"

I grinned. "Yes, I do."

"Well," Magalhães Pinto said, smiling too. "If that becomes public, politically it could be a little awkward. I think we'd better keep it a secret, don't you?"

Of course, when our children eventually did get married, it wasn't awkward at all. Family took precedence over politics. But there were many other cases when the association of the two worlds had its dark side.

During those years, democracy became an excuse for politicians to fill the ranks of government with their close friends, relatives, and benefactors. The federal government's spending on personnel nearly doubled, jumping from 2.5 percent of gross domestic product in 1986 to 4.5 percent by 1989. Many Brazilians had believed that democracy alone was enough to solve our problems—in fact, it was creating new ones. As politicians jockeyed for favor, a new rule began to operate in Brazil: Never say "no" to anyone.

At no time was this more apparent than when Congress sat down in 1987 to write Brazil's seventh constitution since independence. Every Brazilian interest group imaginable emerged with demands—some legitimate, others less so. No matter how ridiculous the request, Congress was never able to turn it down. It reminded me of 1968 in Paris, when it was "prohibited to prohibit." I saw this firsthand. Ulysses Guimarães was selected to lead the constitutional convention, and he put me in charge of drafting the rules for how the convention was to proceed. Meanwhile, another congressman, Bernardo Cabral, was charged with processing the 1,947 constitutional amendments that had been proposed by lawmakers all over Brazil. Through no small feat, he managed to edit them down to "just" 697.

No amount of editing could save the day, of course. While the Constitution of 1988 did help redemocratize the country and provide a framework for a new era, the final document was more of a completely unrealistic wish list. It guaranteed outlandish "rights" that Brazil simply could not afford, creating laws and expectations that would haunt the country's politicians for years thereafter. Government workers received life tenure after only two years of employment. Petrobrás, the state oil company, was guaranteed a permanent monopoly. Workers received a cut in the work week to forty-four hours.

These privileges were absurd, especially in a country where the minimum wage was $25 a month and half the population suffered from malnutrition. Even if we could have afforded these privileges, we had chosen the wrong time to implement them. Brazil was trying to create a welfare state at the precise moment in history when the welfare states of Europe were collapsing.

Meanwhile, a pecking order was slowly, chaotically, taking shape. The dictatorship had tolerated only two political parties: the pro-government ARENA and the opposition omnibus party, the PMDB (it had recently added the "P" to its name). This forced arrangement had produced innumerable political marriages of convenience. Now that we enjoyed sudden and total freedom to associate with whomever we pleased, the "divorce" rate soared through the roof. By 1985, there were eleven parties represented in Congress. By 1991, the total was nineteen. One of the new parties, in fact, was my own. I had stuck with the PMDB during the final years of dictatorship when a great, united opposition movement made practical sense. Later, I had stayed out of sheer admiration for Ulysses Guimarães. Now, however, the PMDB had lost its raison d'être, and the unwieldy group of holdovers included too many people whose politics were too far to the left or to the right of my own.

In 1988, along with Mário Covas, José Serra, Franco Montoro, and a hundred other disaffected PMDB members, I helped to found the Brazilian Social Democracy Party, or the PSDB. We firmly established ourselves as a center-left coalition of committed democrats. While most of the other new parties focused on appealing to narrow niches of Brazilian society—the labor unions, for example, or government workers—we aimed to build as broad a consensus as possible. We advocated a blend of free-market reform and social responsibility, much like leaders such as Felipe González, the successful prime minister of Spain. Our party symbol was the toucan, the colorful Brazilian parrotlike bird with a giant beak, and we became popularly known as the *tucanos*. Indeed, I was thrilled with everything but the name—"Social Democratic

Party" seemed too European, especially for the unjust class structure of Brazil. Something like "Popular Democratic Party" would have better reflected our philosophy.

There was no time to argue about such academic questions, however, while the country was falling to pieces. Even though President Sarney did his best to defend democracy and reestablish friendly relations with our Latin American neighbors, his government still ran into one disaster after another. In 1988, after his plan to introduce a new currency failed, inflation soared to a mind-boggling 1,038 percent. Brazil went through three different currencies in five years. As each currency lost its value, the government had to stop payment on its foreign debt, the vast majority of which had been accumulated under the military regime. Investment plummeted, the real economy floundered, and the poverty rate grew. By January 1989, a poll in Rio and São Paulo showed that 70 percent of the population had "no confidence" in their government. And who could blame them?

It would be glib to chalk all of this up to the inevitable growing pains of democracy. There was, in fact, no excuse for the chaos. Some transitional problems may have been inevitable, but this was beyond acceptability. People began whispering that, yet again, Brazil had proven itself unfit for democracy. About the only positive aspect was that they were just that: whispers. Most Brazilians, including myself, remained firmly committed to the belief that only democracy could solve our problems in the long term. Unfortunately, the next few years would test that faith like never before.

In times of crisis, beware of the white knight in shining armor. That was the difficult lesson Brazil would learn from the 1989 presidential elections, when the country had to choose between two such men. They were both self-styled rebels who had turned their back on the traditional political establishment, no surprise given the disorder of the previous few years. Apart from that, however, it is difficult to imagine two more vastly different candidates.

In one corner was Fernando Collor de Melo, a tall, handsome, forty-year-old governor from the northeast who claimed to be the Brazilian answer to John F. Kennedy. Certainly, he could claim similar dynastic ties: His grandfather had been labor minister under Getúlio Vargas in the 1930s. His father, Arnon, a senator, had earned a somewhat less reputable place in history in 1963 when he shot dead a fellow legislator on the Senate floor (he was later acquitted on self-defense). And whereas the Kennedys had touch football at the beach, the Collors embraced adventure sports with an equally public zeal. Somehow, a camera always seemed to be nearby when Fernando was riding a motorcycle at 100 miles per hour without a helmet; the reporters were certainly there later when, as president, he piloted a jet fighter at the speed of sound. Such exploits, in retrospect, should have alerted us to certain aspects of his personality. However, at the time, the stunts successfully distracted attention from his planned agenda, or lack of it. No one really knew what the man stood for. I imagine that Collor probably wanted it that way.

The other rebel, in contrast, made no secret of his desire to lead a radical leftist transformation in Brazil. In the years since our shared fight against the dictatorship in the 1970s, Lula had skillfully parlayed his union fame into a national role in politics. But along the way he had reduced himself to little more than a symbol, perhaps a cliché: the angry worker. The labor unions of the previous decade now formed the backbone of his new party, the Workers Party, or PT, which also included Trotskyites and other radicals. In the first of what would be three failed campaigns for president, Lula seethed with a red rage that was almost adolescent. Instead of mellowing with age, he had become much more radical than he had been during his union days. The gentle, sweet man I had once known now screamed and sobbed on the podium during rambling speeches about the injustices of Brazil.

Of course, there was a lot to be furious about in our country, especially then, but Lula's prescriptions to fix things were horribly misguided and out of date. If elected, Lula said, he would spearhead a wholesale re-distribution of wealth. He wanted to start by nationalizing all the banks. He proposed a moratorium on the foreign debt as well as a sweeping land reform that would be run by his old friends in the agrarian move-ments. The press would be controlled by a government-selected commit-tee of journalists and editors. His rhetoric was hostile to foreign investors and private enterprise in general.

In a meeting with Lula's advisers that year, I asked them, incredu-lous, "Why don't you just go ahead and abolish private property?"

Lula had no answer for that question, or for many others. At a time when the Berlin Wall had just fallen and the last Communist outposts of Eastern Europe were embracing capitalism one by one, Lula's ideas seemed surreally anachronistic. Although his up-from-nothing biogra-phy was inspiring, 1989 was just not Lula's time. The country's power-ful business interests were absolutely terrified of him, and so was most of the middle class. It is difficult to blame them. Lula wasn't ready for Brazil, and Brazil wasn't ready for him. Both he and the country would have to go through a long, twisting evolution over the next decade be-fore Lula's time would come.

In a runoff, Collor took 43 percent of the vote to Lula's 38 percent, becoming the first Brazilian president elected by a popular vote since Jânio Quadros in 1960.

In the interim, Brazil was much changed. The overall population had jumped from 65 million to 145 million. The percentage of people living in cities had soared from 45 percent to 75 percent; households with a television had increased from 2 percent to nearly 80 percent. Brazil had gone from being a rural and isolated backwater to an urban country where most people were connected not just with each other, but with the world.

When Collor took office, he immediately began a series of reforms ostensibly aimed at "modernizing" the economy. He announced plans to privatize state enterprises, cut taxes, and reduce the bloated state bu-reaucracy. He declared war on the "*marajás.*" This is a Hindu word meaning "king" and is used in Brazil to describe privileged public workers who earn a fat paycheck for doing nothing. At first, it seemed exactly like the sort of modern agenda that many of us, including myself, had been advocating to help end the fiscal crisis and integrate Brazil into the global economy. I was sufficiently seduced by Collor's initial plans that I nearly accepted an invitation to become his foreign minister. After four decades of intense change, it seemed, briefly, as if Brazil might finally be on a new path.

Yet, as the old cliché goes, the more things change, the more they stay the same. No amount of reform could have saved Collor's government, because capitalism, in Brazil as elsewhere, will always be incompatible with endemic corruption.

At first, the stories seemed unlikely. I heard whispers from friends in business and politics: Collor's friends were demanding bribes and funneling huge amounts of cash into offshore accounts. This seemed impossible to me. Graft was an age-old Brazilian problem, permeating the entire political system, but it had rarely occurred at the very top. There was precious little history of presidents using their power to get rich. Getúlio had died relatively poor, as had Dutra. Most of the military rulers—men such as Geisel or Figueiredo—had left office quietly and led similarly austere lives. The Brazilian presidency seemed like too high-profile a position for ostentatious corruption, I thought, because society would inevitably find out about it. The spotlight was too bright. I just didn't think it was possible.

I was wrong. Collor's friends and associates set up a kickback scheme of superlative proportions, reportedly demanding that a huge fee be paid for many government contracts. It was later said, but never proved, that Collor's campaign manager and fund-raiser, Paulo César Farias, held a massive party to celebrate what was said to be his first billion dollars in graft. Farias had already amassed millions of dollars and several mansions, and he flew about in a private jet known as "the black bat." A magazine published pictures of the work that had been done on Collor's home in Brasília. The project was said to have cost about $2 million, and it included a vast landscaped lawn, fountains, and a lake filled with Japanese carp. Right next to a sauna was a swimming pool. Pedro Collor, the president's estranged brother, detailed in a magazine article in *Veja* just how far-reaching the corruption was. By then, it was undeniable that Fernando Collor was running a true klepto-presidency.

To our credit as a nation, once Collor's true nature came to light, the Brazilian public would not tolerate him. By August 1992, Collor had a disapproval rating of 84 percent. Demonstrators were painting their faces the colors of the flag as a symbol of support for removing him from office. I was unsure about the wisdom of impeaching him at first—in a speech to the Senate, I compared impeachment to "an atomic bomb; it's useful as a deterrent, but it should never actually be used." But the magazine interview with Pedro Collor changed my mind. I decided to nuke him after all.

First, the House of Representatives voted 441 to 38 to suspend Collor from office. His case then went to the Senate, which would have the final word under the constitution. Twenty minutes into the Senate's deliberations, Collor delivered a note to the legislature saying that he had resigned as the president of Brazil, hoping to avoid the indignity of being forced out. The next day, Congress voted to impeach Collor anyway.

The first popularly elected president of our new, much-ballyhooed era of democracy left in disgrace, and Brazil, yet again, suffered worldwide derision. In a strange way, however, the nation derived a certain confidence out of the incident. Brazil's institutions had proven to be stronger than any one man. We had handled a severe crisis by the book, and without the intervention of the military. After the vote, a crowd of 100,000 Brazilians, many of them young, danced and sang in front of Congress. "For the first time," said Aristides Junqueira, Brazil's chief federal prosecutor, "we have a chance to resolve a political crisis in line with the constitution, and without armed soldiers."

Ulysses Guimarães, who had led the impeachment proceedings in Congress with unflinching determination, professed a similarly bittersweet outlook. "I thank God for having allowed me to live as I lived and for allowing me to reach this point of my life to observe an event like this," Ulysses told the nation. "The triumph of the citizenry, democracy and my country. It is an example for all of Latin America."

In private, however, I know that the impeachment ate at Ulysses's soul. Among his friends, he confessed to being crushed that democracy had not done more to solve Brazilians' problems. Saying he needed a break, Ulysses took a well-deserved weekend vacation on a verdant island off the coast of Rio de Janeiro. On the way back, his helicopter crashed into the sea. The greatest hero of Brazilian democracy died just two weeks after its biggest disappointment had taken place. The crash also killed Ulysses' wife, as well as Severo Gomes—the same man who had donated his son's car to my first campaign in 1978—and his wife, Maria Henriqueta.

At that moment, Brazilian democracy hit rock bottom.

The man suddenly left behind to run Brazil was a quick learner: Prior to taking office, he presented Congress with a list of all his personal assets. Unfortunately, that was about all we knew about Itamar Franco. With typical savvy, Collor had sought a running mate whose respectability would make up for his own shortcomings. Itamar was a senator like myself, an unassuming and essentially good man whose only prior administrative experience had been two terms as mayor of a mid-sized town in his home state of Minas Gerais. He could plausibly claim to have known nothing about Collor's corruption network, although some Brazilians remained cynical. We were left with another weakened vice president in charge of Brazil.

Itamar was keenly aware of what people were saying about him. As he prepared to take the presidential oath, he summoned me to his office. He looked worried as he folded his hands and asked me, "Do you think I'm stupid?"

"Of course not," I said. "But you *are* stubborn. Very much so."

Itamar stared at me for a long moment, seemingly unsure whether to be offended or not. Then, he broke into a giant smile and declared, "You and I are going to be friends!"

And he was right. From that point on, Itamar and I were always close. As with Lula, our relationship would have some very pronounced ups and downs in coming years. But at that moment and many others, he and I needed each other. One day over coffee in my kitchen, Itamar asked me if I would be his foreign minister. I said that wasn't really necessary, but if he wanted me to have the job, I would accept. My responsibility in his government was not really limited to that area, though. The president sometimes called me five times a day, frequently regarding day-to-day matters outside the realm of foreign affairs.

Being foreign minister was not quite the ideal job that I had expected. On one hand, I did get to travel the world representing Brazil, which was a privilege and an honor. I met men like Mikhail Gorbachev and Bill Clinton for the first time. But I also found that I spent the overwhelming majority of my time apologizing.

There was a lot to be sorry about, but there was one issue that trumped all others: inflation. Prices in Brazil rose an astonishing 2,500 percent in 1993. This kind of "hyperinflation" is difficult to imagine for someone who has never lived through it. It dominates business and daily life. On pay day, people lined up outside supermarkets, desperate to spend their money before it lost its value. Prices on basic goods such as rice—the Brazilian staple—could double in just a day. All contracts—bank accounts, tax bills, and salaries—had to be adjusted to inflation, a process that was imprecise and allowed for tremendous corruption. It was, in other words, economic hell.

Regrettably, this was nothing new. Precise calculations were tough to come by, but one estimate put the accumulated Brazilian inflation rate from 1968 to 1993 at a mind-boggling 1,825,059,944,843 percent. This reflected nothing less than the total failure of the Brazilian government to administer monetary policy. In fact, we had seen seven currencies in the previous eight years.

By the time Itamar took office, many economists believed that Brazil's inflation problem could not be solved. Attributing it to inherent structural issues within our economy, they simply threw up their hands in defeat. The causes of inflation were so complicated and ingrained in Brazil's economy—and its culture—that it *was* tempting to just give up. However, Itamar did not have that luxury. Prices were climbing so fast that he justifiably feared that, one day, Brazilian money might lose its value entirely. All of us had nightmares about people running around with suitcases full of worthless cash. This would cause unimaginable riots and social unrest.

Motivated by this very real worst-case scenario, Itamar was obsessed with trying to solve—or at least control—the inflation problem. His only difficulty was that his fuse was a bit short. Itamar blazed through three different finance ministers in seven months, never really giving them time to come up with a credible plan. Being named finance minister became a kiss of death within his administration. If you were fired, your political career was over. Understandably, nobody wanted the job. I watched this game of career Russian roulette with a certain degree of consternation because it affected *my* job. I had to travel the world and explain to foreign investors and diplomats why Brazil couldn't seem to pick a course and stay with it. There were even rumors that Itamar himself might resign out of frustration. Everywhere I went, I received angry stares and very undiplomatic recriminations. Why, they asked, can't you people stop being such screw-ups?

On the evening of May 19, 1993, I had just finished such a trip to Japan, where I was berated by impassioned businessmen who had lost enormous amounts of money in Brazil. Jet-lagged, hungry, and a bit depressed, I sat down for dinner in New York with a dozen friends at the home of Ronaldo Sardenberg, Brazil's ambassador to the United Nations. The mood was subdued, as was typical in those days. We had started trying to enliven things with a toast when the phone rang. I walked into a cramped room and picked up the receiver.

"Are you sitting down or standing up?"

The voice belonged to Itamar.

"Well, I'm sitting now," I said.

"I was thinking of naming you finance minister," he said.

A shiver ran down my spine.

"Look, Itamar," I intoned, desperately trying to reason with him. "We've already talked about this. I told you what I think. I'm perfectly happy in the foreign ministry."

"I know," Itamar said. "But it's not me that needs you. It's Brazil."

I sighed at the obvious manipulation. "Itamar, I do not want this job. I think it would be better for the current minister to stay. I have run out of words to explain to people abroad why we keep making changes. But I am not there in Brazil, so I can't judge the circumstances. You're the president, and the final decision is yours."

"Well, I'll think about it," Itamar said begrudgingly. "I'll see what I can do. If I have anything else to say to you tonight, I'll call you."

He didn't seem very convinced, but it was the best I could do from 4,000 miles away. I hung up the phone and moped back to the dinner table, seriously concerned. Everyone was staring at me. I tried to disguise my feelings, but I must have done a terrible job.

"You're going to be finance minister, aren't you?" someone at the table inquired, with the same tone of voice you'd use to ask someone if he had cancer.

"No, no, no," I insisted, probably a bit too strongly. "I would never accept that job. Don't be ridiculous!"

After a dinner that seemed to drag on forever, the ambassador's wife strolled back into the room and told me the president's aide-de-camp had called with a message. "He said the president will not need to speak to you again tonight," she declared.

I sighed and muttered under my breath, "Thank God."

That night, I went back to my hotel, where I settled into a relieved, almost euphoric state of deep sleep. But I had committed a classic error: I had forgotten that in Brazil, the land of improvisation, nothing ever goes quite as planned. And sure enough, just after midnight, the phone started ringing. Reporters from Brasília, reporters from New

York, all of them in a frenzy, all with the same question: "What are your plans now that you are the finance minister of Brazil?"

I told them they had gone mad, implored them to let me sleep, and hung up.

Very early in the morning, Ruth called. She had heard the news on the radio. "Fernando Henrique, I *cannot* believe that you didn't tell me first," she said, hurt. "Why did you keep this from me?"

"It's not true!" I protested. "They've all lost their minds!"

"Well, I don't know what you told Itamar on the phone," Ruth said. "But whatever you told him, he thought you said yes."

"But that's impossible!"

To this day, Ruth still doesn't believe it all happened like this.

Finally, at the first light of dawn, there could no longer be any doubt. My closest collaborator in the foreign ministry, Luiz Felipe Lampreia, called and said, "*Ministro,* you've been named the new finance minister of Brazil."

"No . . ."

"What do you mean, no?" he asked. He had a copy of that morning's *Diario Oficial,* the official government bulletin. "It says here that it's true!"

"Oh my God," I muttered. "I'm ruined."

I picked up the phone and dialed Itamar's residence, but his maid said he was in the bathroom. I waited for an eternity, chatting nervously with the maid, before the president finally picked up the phone. His voice sounded eerily jolly and content.

"I took the liberty of naming you finance minister!" Itamar boomed, as if everything was suddenly right in the world. "Your appointment has gone over very well here. The public response has been excellent!"

"But, Itamar, what am I supposed to do now?"

"Oh, do what you want," the president said breezily. "Hire who you want, and fire who you want. But remember that I need this inflation problem solved. I'm sure you'll do fine. Best of luck!"

Click.

CHAPTER

9

A *REAL* PRESIDENT

Before I departed for the crucible of Brazil, I went back to the ambassador's residence in New York for a final meal— a kind of last supper, I suppose. Now that I was officially the new finance minister, everyone there treated me like a condemned man. As the ambassador's wife served me my plate, she smiled and asked, "Is it really true, Fernando Henrique, that you don't believe in God?"

I laughed. "Even on my last trip to Tokyo," I responded, "I still went to church."

"That's not a real answer," she said, "but it's good enough." She told me that she had a religious pin she had brought home with her from a trip to Salvador, in Brazil's northeast. "Can I pin this on you for good luck?"

I could hardly refuse. "I think I can use all the help I can get."

I still have that pin. But I also realized that neither luck nor mysticism would get me very far. My success as finance minister would be measured by just one thing: whether I could beat inflation. Not just any inflation—2,500 percent inflation! Once I got over the initial shock of being named to the job, I realized that I had an opportunity to solve Brazil's biggest policy problem. If I failed, my political career would be over. I would become a footnote. But if I pulled it off, it would be a historic achievement and, most important, a great help for my country.

So, I thought, what the hell. I might as well go down swinging. On the nine-hour overnight flight back to Brasília, I didn't read or sleep; I just stared at the back of the chair in front of me, playing the possible scenarios in my head. If this was going to work, I needed a clear diagnosis of the problem, a plan to end it, and then the political support to carry such a plan through.

I was not an economist. So, in thinking about how to solve the problem, I decided to start with the big picture. The root cause of inflation in Brazil was really very simple: The government spent more than it earned. When the budget turned up a big deficit every year, as it inevitably did, the government printed more money to cover the difference. Any grade-school student knows, however, that you can't just print endless amounts of cash without having something tangible to back it up. Otherwise, the money loses its value. That, at the most basic level, was precisely what was happening in Brazil.

So the obvious solution—which I hardly needed a Ph.D. to understand—was for the government to stop spending so much money. In fact, the International Monetary Fund, and our foreign creditors, had been telling us to do exactly that for years. This prescription had a flaw, however: It didn't take into account the sheer magnitude of our problem. Inflation at an annual rate of near 2,500 percent indicated a whale of a budget deficit. In fact, the estimated deficit for the coming year, 1994, was $20 billion—out of a total budget of roughly $90 billion. Such a massive shortfall simply could not be solved overnight. Even if Brazil's Congress had been willing to tolerate enormous spending cuts (and it most decidedly was not), we couldn't slash a fourth of the budget without having the government fall apart the very next day. So, while we knew that serious spending cuts would be needed, we couldn't rely *exclusively* on them to solve the inflation problem.

Itamar had made this clear very early on. Not long after I returned from New York, he invited the entire Cabinet to attend an impromptu late-night meeting at the presidential palace. A bit mystified, all of us filed into a room, where Itamar showed us a glowing documentary about Franklin D. Roosevelt and the New Deal. I squirmed in my seat as black and white images of Hoover Dam flashed across the projection screen. The implied message was that Itamar wanted an economic plan that would shrink government as little as possible (if at all) and build the nation's confidence rather than tear it down.

The moment the lights went up, I stood and addressed the room. "Roosevelt did the right thing," I said, my eyes flickering toward Itamar, "but that was the United States in the 1930s, when the private sector was a disaster, and the government was in relatively good financial condition.

"In Brazil today," I continued, "our situation is exactly the opposite. We have an insolvent state, while our businesses are in relatively good shape. We must therefore act to shrink government, not expand it, so the economy can recover."

Itamar murmured approval, but some other ministers in the room exchanged disturbed glances—a sign of trouble to come.

I also informed Itamar that *some* sacrifice would be needed. Recent Brazilian history was a graveyard of inflation plans that had failed because the government didn't have the stomach or the skill to see them through. Most of the plans had frozen prices and wages; others had slashed government budgets; still others had frozen people's bank accounts. On paper, many of these plans looked perfect. Some had been designed by the most brilliant minds to be found; Brazil had long been a cause célèbre among the world's best economists. And, very often, inflation did halt for a short time. Inevitably, however, these plans cracked under the demands from society: Workers wanted a raise, or businesses wanted to raise prices, or people wanted their savings back. Inflation roared back with a vengeance, usually worse than before.

A foreign traveler once wrote: "Upon landing at Rio and making your first purchase, you are amazed at being told that some trifle you have selected will cost so many hundreds of this or even thousands of that; and you are no less astounded when the bill of an ordinary account is presented you which contains five or six figures. The Brazilian currency is probably, at least in theory, the most infinitesimal of any in the world."* This observation was made in 1890, but it could have been true in 1994. While the circumstances and causes had varied over the years, inflation seemed just to be part of Brazilian life.

Over time, people had learned to live with these failures. Inflation was built into virtually every contract in Brazil with a monetary value: rent, taxes, bank loans, utility rates, and so on. This "indexation" of future costs was meant to shield people from a spurt in prices. As long as prices and wages rose broadly in sync, Brazil could avoid an experience like Germany's epic hyperinflation after World War I, when money became essentially worthless. Ironically, however, this indexation system also ended up causing much higher inflation over the long term. It guaranteed a floor; the more people expected prices to rise, the more they would. Thus, indexation became almost as important a cause of inflation in Brazil as the original sin of budget deficits. At times of high political or economic drama, a handful of people would panic and boost their future estimates of price rises—which then became a self-fulfilling prophecy as other contracts across the economy raced to keep pace. Those who panicked first were usually rewarded with an easy profit.

There were two dirty little secrets of Brazilian inflation, and this was one of them: It benefited a great many people. Among the biggest winners, in fact, were the politicians. As long as there was inflation, they never had to say no to anybody. No spending request was ever too large; just print more money! It was a diabolically efficient way to solve disputes. Even though inflation would eventually take away any gains, at least everybody felt good in the short term. For a shaky democratic government or a military dictatorship of questionable legitimacy, dol-

*Frank Vincent, *Around and About South America* (New York: D. Appleton, 1890).

ing out money was the most obvious way to stay in power. The modern era of runaway inflation had begun in earnest in the 1950s, when President Juscelino Kubitschek, having decided to advance "50 years in 5," ordered an ambitious public works plan, including the construction of Brasília. The result was hailed as a modern miracle: a modernistic new capital built from scratch in just three years. However, there are few real miracles in life or politics; cynics joked that Juscelino's term was marred by "50 years of inflation in 5."

The politicians weren't alone in their sins, however. Banks turned a lucrative profit from a process known as "floating," which could not have existed without inflation. Then as now, many Brazilian customers went to banks to pay their bills for utilities such as water and electricity. The banks then had to transfer that money to the utility companies, but they could wait up to three days to do so. In a stable country, such a delay would be insignificant, but in Brazil, with inflation running as high as 80 percent per month, it was an absolute scandal. At that rate, a bank could pocket an easy 8 percent profit in real terms by waiting just three days to make the transfer, since the money was losing its value at such a rapid pace. If this sounds like pocket change at first, consider that up to a *quarter* of Brazilian banks' profits came from "floating" back then. Billions of dollars a year were made this way. As a result, many of the banks had an enormous stake in seeing that inflation continued.

Inflation also made corruption much easier. Nobody paid much attention to balance sheets back then, since they were so unreliable. So a little missing cash was hardly ever noticed. This was true in both the public and private sectors. Such petty corruption was in a way more corrosive to society than big scandals; it was as if inflation had caused Brazilians to become more tolerant toward "small" crimes, which in turn led to "big" ones. Money lost its value so quickly that the act of theft never seemed so outrageous in retrospect. For example, if someone stole 100 *cruzados,* such an amount would be practically worthless in a matter of weeks. How could you get angry about that?

The list goes on and on. Corporations were happy because they could always massage their profit statements. Government and private-sector workers were happy because they would always receive a paycheck, no matter what. Their demands for salary increases were always met one way or another, without ever seeming to reduce corporate profits. Inflation allowed for a delicate balance; everybody felt like they were winning, even when they really weren't. Over time, a zillion little maneuvers were invented so that Brazilians with money—the same people who always win in Brazil—were shielded from the problem. Indexation spread to every corner of the economy. Inflation even developed its own little cult: Many Brazilians loudly insisted that inflation was *good* for Brazil, because it made economic growth easier. This theory probably had a kernel of truth at one point in history, akin to arguments that running a small budget deficit can be healthy. By the 1990s, however, chatter over the bright side of inflation was an urban legend of the highest order, equaled in our history only by the insistence that Brazil was a racial democracy. I don't make that comparison lightly. In fact, the two myths had more in common than one might think.

For the second dirty little secret was that the poor in Brazil were the ones most punished by inflation. For decades, no one in Brazil wanted to acknowledge this. It was said that inflation allowed the government to stimulate economic growth, and thus to generate jobs for the working class. But this was a myopic, cynical view; the real truth was there for everyone to see. In practice, the poor were the only ones who ended up with fistfuls of worthless cash. They had no access to the indexed bank accounts or the numerous other tools that the middle and upper classes used to shield themselves. Congress made a cottage industry out of mandating pay raises, ostensibly to protect the poor; but adjustments to salaries *never* rose as fast as prices did. As a result, the buying power of workers' wages had been slowly eroding for nearly thirty years. Inflation acted like a regressive tax that made poor people poorer.

Meanwhile, the world was leaving us behind. Inflation kept Brazil isolated, an island unto ourselves, at a time when the new buzzword was "globalization." After the collapse of the Berlin Wall, euphoric investors from New York to Tokyo were eager to pour vast amounts of money into developing countries. Brazil's economy was bigger than Russia's, and we had numerous successful companies. But these foreigners demanded a certain degree of security for their money. In Brazil, there could simply be no viable long-term contracts as long as there was rampant hyperinflation. How could anyone make a deal when they didn't know the value of something as basic as money? A further consequence was a general breakdown of trust in civic institutions. If the currency could not be trusted, why should Brazilians have faith in the power of government or in the rule of law? For decades, inflation had helped produce the sensation in our society that nothing, absolutely nothing, was written in stone.

By 1993, however, these weren't secrets anymore. More than at any other point in our history, the Brazilian public now demanded that the problem be solved. I believe this was another logical step in the evolution that had been occurring in Brazil for a half century: As people migrated to the cities, they were making their voices heard. The poor would not tolerate inflation any longer, and the wealthy were tired of seeing their business plans and investments distorted by rising prices. Other countries, such as Israel and Argentina, had recently solved their hyperinflation problems. The country cried out for its politicians to do something. After so many failures, this was democracy in action, working like it was supposed to.

We needed more than just an inflation plan. We needed to reinvent Brazil.

Untold gallons of coffee went into the making of the *Plano Real,* the Real Plan. We spent countless nights poring over economics textbooks, scribbling equations on chalkboards, and arguing until four in the morning. I assembled a powerful economic team, including men such as Edmar Bacha, André Lara Resende, Persio Arida, Gustavo Franco,

Pedro Malan, Winston Fritsch, and many others. They were brilliant. My main responsibility was to make them keep things simple. I kept telling them, "I'm the poor guy who's going to have to sell this plan on television, so if I don't understand what you're talking about, then something is definitely wrong."

For months, we met secretly in people's homes and back offices. We were terrified that the press would get wind of our plans and then stir fear in the public. "One leak and this whole thing is over," I warned them. In the beginning, we even kept many of our deliberations secret from Itamar. Meanwhile, as we debated all the different ideas, prices continued to rise at vertiginous rates; the clock was ticking. Finally, by December 1993, we took a collective deep breath and announced a course of action.

The Real Plan had three main elements.

First, and most important, there would be a new currency, called the *real.* The name has several meanings in Portuguese, all of which conveniently reflected the intentions of our plan. It meant "royal," and it harkened back to a currency used in the colonial era, giving the name an air of historic permanence. It also meant "real"—implying that the currency did, indeed, have real value and was here to stay. But beyond having a pretty name, this new money would also have solid fundamental support. The central bank would act to maintain the real within a broadly steady range of value against the dollar. This would be done by buying and selling Brazil's foreign currency reserves in a system similar to a currency board. From the beginning, we knew that the real would have to be an exceptionally strong currency in order to gain credibility among the Brazilian populace. In practice, the real ended up trading at a value even greater than the dollar, and then slowly devalued as time went by.

Second, there would be a round of steep budget cuts. This would be administered through a mechanism we called the "Social Emergency Fund." In retrospect, I find the name a bit strange: There was nothing "social" about it, and it was not a "fund"; the only accurate part was that we were in an "emergency." I suppose, however, that a little bit of creative nomenclature was necessary to convince Congress to support the idea. It is not hard to understand why. Through the fund, Congress essentially ceded control of about $15 billion of earmarked government spending, which was now at the discretion of the finance ministry. This meant that I now had direct control over roughly a fifth of the money in the entire government budget. Put another way: I could slash spending as I pleased, thus addressing the most basic cause of inflation.

The third and final aspect of the Real Plan involved a somewhat complex sleight of hand. At its simplest level, we needed a mechanism to gradually slow us down from 3,000 percent inflation to 3 percent; it couldn't be done from one day to the next. The public had to see that prices were leveling out over time before they would believe in any new currency. So, prior to the actual launch of the real, we would ask stores to list two prices for items: the price in the old currency, the *cruzeiro real*, and the price in the soon-to-be new currency. For about six months prior to putting the real into circulation, the public would be able to see its value. This would also help cure the ills of indexation— we would replace all inflationary contracts with this new unit, and then very gradually slow the pace of price rises. It would be like jumping into a runaway train and applying the brakes. The bottom line was rather simple: By the time the real came out in bills and coins on the streets of Brazil, people would already be familiar with its steady value.

If much of this sounds like a combination of half-measures and wishful thinking, well, it was. The Real Plan left many questions open; it was a kind of permanent work in progress. The new currency would have a limited period to gain acceptance, and that period was our main focus. For it to succeed over time, however, Brazil would have to ad-dress the structural issues behind inflation—namely, our budget imbal-ances and our inefficient government—in a more meaningful way. We would need to build a more modern, competitive economy. Other-wise, the real would be just another link in a long chain of failures.

But I was pleased with the proposal. It was not perfect, but I thought it had a better chance of success than any other option out there. That was the most important aspect of the plan. Through my entire political career, I've always focused on finding the best way *possible* to reach an ideal goal. I believed that the Real Plan was the best we could do under the circumstances. Now, the only thing left to do was to present our ideas to the country.

Naturally, almost everybody hated it.

From the left and the right, from inside and outside Brazil, there was a hailstorm of criticism and mockery. "Our nice, charming, and intelligent minister can't resist the impulse to make everyone like him," teased Roberto Campos, a conservative senator. Lula was outraged, declaring that the plan would "only cause more misery." Celso Martone, an orthodox economist, called the Real Plan "one more melancholy example of the weakness and lack of imagination that have characterized finance ministers." Antônio Carlos Magalhães, a powerful right-wing governor from the northeast, urged me to be "more aggressive and less conciliatory." A January 1994 headline from the newspaper *Folha de S. Paulo* read, "The IMF and the World Bank see little chance of success for the plan."

Even Itamar had his doubts. There were constant rumors that he might fire me, or perhaps resign himself. "The president is disappointed with the result of the plan," *Folha* reported in January 1994. In one-on-one conversations with me, he was always supportive, of course. But I had my doubts about his inner feelings. At one point, Itamar reportedly told his closest friends: "You know, I wasn't born glued to this chair. I can leave any time I get a notion."

As we anticipated, the members of the old-time Brazilian establishment reached into their deep bag of tricks to protect their interests. Numerous attempts were made to sabotage the bills before Congress that were needed to convert the Real Plan into reality. I threatened to resign on several occasions, but Itamar and Congress always seemed to back off at the very last moment.

In the meantime, I soldiered on the best I could, virtually alone except for my loyal aides in the finance ministry. I became a kind of traveling salesman. I appeared on countless TV talk shows, at city council meetings, and at business conventions. I also relied heavily on my invaluable experience as a senator, and my now-legendary tolerance for caffeine, to push our proposals through Congress. I spent so much time there, in fact, that people apparently started getting weary of my incessant lobbying. "Cardoso's style is disliked by Congressmen," *Folha* reported, quoting the legislator and former finance minister during the military regime, Delfim Netto: "Cardoso is resorting to terrorism when he says that his plan is the only solution for the country."

Still, none of these congressmen had any better ideas of their own. It dawned on them that they would lose their jobs unless they met society's demands to end inflation. That was the power of democracy: an accountability that was new to Brazil. One by one, via whispered messages and midnight phone calls, they confided to me that the Real Plan would have their support, even if they couldn't say so in public. Good enough, I said. By February, it looked as if the initiative might get the support it needed to pass.

At the last moment, the whole plan was nearly ruined by the most bizarre, and quintessentially Brazilian, trick of all.

The Carnival of 1994 was unusually insane, which is saying something. I suppose that Brazilians were overcompensating for the rotten year that had just passed. Topless models danced the night away on the elaborately decorated floats, the spectators chugged down the beer and *caipirinhas,* and by nightfall the whole country was stumbling about in a blurry mess.

In the middle of it all was Itamar, who wanted to show an uncharacteristically downtrodden and cynical country that he too knew how to have a good time. As a sixty-three-year-old divorcé, Itamar, I suppose, was within his rights. He thus became the first Brazilian president to watch Carnival from the Sambódromo, the giant complex in Rio that houses the famous, glittery parade at the center of the world's greatest party. Itamar watched the whole show from a special presidential balcony high above the action, waving serenely at the crowd.

It is not entirely clear how she got up on the balcony, but a twenty-seven-year-old model named Lilian Ramos made her way to Itamar's side. She was one of the participants in the parade, a scantily clad "Persian Princess." Someone had thought to cover her up, at least partially, with an oversized T-shirt when she came to meet the president. But each time she clapped her hands, her shirt rode up just a bit—and it soon became quite apparent that the young woman was wearing no underwear. Apparent to everyone, including the Brazilian press, which gathered underneath the balcony and began furiously snapping pictures from below.

Itamar and Ms. Ramos were bathed in a flurry of white flashbulbs, but they were not fully aware why until they saw the newspapers the next morning. A photo montage of the Brazilian president cozying up to a nearly nude model circulated not just in our country, but across the whole world.

It was one of those seminal stories, the kind that shows up in newspapers in far-flung places like Memphis or Fort Lauderdale that run one story about Brazil every decade. "Naked Ambition," blared the normally staid *Financial Times*. "In Brazil, a Kiss Is Not Just a Kiss," teased the *Dallas Morning News*. There is nothing Brazilians hate more than being portrayed as a banana republic, but we were somehow, yet again, in the world spotlight as little more than a band of good-natured but hopeless revelers.

The scandal came swiftly and with a dead-serious overtone. The military was outraged at this latest affront to Brazil's image, and the Catholic Church loudly urged Itamar to "be an example to families." Much of the public was exasperated as well with the latest stumble of democracy. In fact, no one could have anticipated the severity of the scandal—except, possibly, the people who had engineered it.

To this day, I strongly suspect that Lilian Ramos was being used by the opposition to intentionally embarrass the president, perhaps in an effort to derail the Real Plan. At what point they co-opted her, I do not know, but the timing and exposure were too complicated for her to have possibly orchestrated it all by herself. When she called him by phone the next day, a camera crew from *O Globo* television just happened to be there—in her home—to record the whole conversation.

"I can't deny it. Itamar is free and uncommitted," the model cooed before the cameras. "He's a sweetie, a gentleman, an interesting person. I'm pleased we started this friendship. That is how big love affairs are born."

Shortly thereafter, Ms. Ramos declared that she wanted to run for office.

Already well-schooled in the perils that Carnival could represent for politicians, I had fortunately decided to watch that year's festivities on television. The year before, a passing drag queen had spontaneously planted a big, wet kiss on my cheek, and the whole episode had been caught on camera. I suppose I must have appeared suitably embarrassed in the photo, and no scandal ensued. But now, I was horrified that "Carnival-gate" might force Itamar to resign and ruin everything we had worked for.

I have never told Itamar this, but a representative of the military approached me and asked how I would react if Congress impeached him and handed over power to the president of the lower house, who was next in line for succession. The Brazilian military was still close to power in those days—through informal social ties, if not direct political ones—and retained the ability to marshal considerable support in both chambers. The democracy we had all fought for would not have survived another impeachment. I told them, politely but firmly, that I would not support such a thinly disguised intervention. "Those days," I said, "are over."

Thankfully, with time, the scandal blew over. After this most Brazilian of political crises, everything returned to where it was before, more or less, as is our tradition. Congress soon passed all the laws we needed to launch the Real Plan. Itamar's popularity rating inched back up. The Catholic Church launched a campaign promoting family values. Lilian Ramos renounced her plans for a career in Brazilian politics and instead happily married a member of the old Italian nobility.

And I . . . well, I started thinking about running for president.

Until then, 1994 seemed destined to be the year of Lula. Since losing the previous presidential election to Fernando Collor de Melo, Lula had never really stopped campaigning. He had spent five years tirelessly driving from town to town in a van. Mounted on top were speakers that blared Brazilian rap music while a recorded voice urged, "Come meet the first worker president in the history of Brazil!"

Under torrential rain or torrid sun, Lula drew hundreds at a time, people eager to hear him speak of the injustices of Brazil, in their own lives, and how he wanted to fix them. In these matters, Lula wielded a credibility that no other politician in Brazil could dream of matching, because he had lived their misery. He had lost by a whisker to Collor; now, vindicated by the way *that* experience had ended, Lula seemed like the only logical choice for president in the election of 1994. In polls early that year, Lula enjoyed support of around 40 percent; no other candidate managed double digits.

But what was good for Lula was not necessarily good for Brazil. The election posed a terrible dilemma. By March 1994, we were phasing in the first steps of the Real Plan. The real was scheduled to enter circulation sometime in the middle of the year. The election would follow on October 3. The currency would be launched amid the frenzy of a political campaign and would therefore be seen as a political tactic, not a national imperative. The timing was rotten, but, in truth, our biggest problem was the man himself.

If Lula were elected president, the Real Plan would have certainly been in danger. I was sure of this. The year before, when we were honing the last details of the plan, I had invited Lula and his top aide, José Dirceu, over to my apartment in Brasília to try and gain their support. I hoped that such an intimate meeting would tone down the thunder and lightning that Lula spoke with in those days. No such luck. Lula was less interested in economic consequences of the success of my plan for his voters than that it might bring political defeat to him.

I was deeply disappointed with Lula, for I believed that he was placing his own interests above those of the country. He knew that if the economy was in bad shape, the instability would bolster his campaign. Five years would pass before I had another significant, face-to-face conversation with Lula.

I should have known better. Lula was still little changed from the man who had lost to Collor and who had advocated extreme leftist measures, such as default on the foreign debt and nationalization of the banking sector. Lula harbored wild delusions about creating a sweeping, FDR-style public works plan that would employ millions of Brazilians, although, of course, he had no idea how to pay for it. Like most politicians in Brazil, Lula did not worry about such trivial details. This was exactly the sort of philosophy that fed inflation. What was the point of working so hard on the Real Plan if it was just going to be dismantled three months after its launch?

That fear alone motivated me to become a candidate. Otherwise, it would have been a preposterous idea. How was an "elitist," "uncharismatic," "arrogant" former sociology professor from São Paulo going to beat a man like Lula? I firmly believed Lula's agenda was wrong for Brazil, but he had once been a close ally, and I didn't particularly relish the idea of campaigning against him. I had never run a national campaign before, and it would mean a great strain on me personally. My family was also against the idea.

In the unlikely event that I won, Brazil's presidency would be a particularly thorny crown. Democracy had been a disaster so far. The government was in tatters. In sum, I viewed running for president as exactly the sort of accident one crosses the street to avoid. I'm still not certain exactly why I did it.

❦

At first, I had my share of awkward moments.

I was on my way to a political meeting in a small city in Alagoas when a group of thirty or forty locals rode by on horses. They tipped their hats to greet me and said they were on their way to the same meeting. "I'll go with you!" I declared. They had an extra horse with them, and they lent me a worn leather hat to protect me from the sun, so off we went. I'm a decent horseman at best—certainly not as good as my grandfather, but good enough to ride at a slow pace for some time. We rode to the meeting site as the sun went down, triumphant, like cowboys in an old American western movie.

The men laughed good-naturedly and said I looked pretty good on a horse. Most important, they guaranteed that I would have their vote. I was delighted with the whole experience—until the next day, when the newspapers in São Paulo and Rio published photos of the bespectacled former sociology professor who suddenly thought he was John Wayne. I was widely ridiculed.

I could never seem to convince the media that I had any sympathy for ordinary people. On a trip to Pernambuco state, where Lula had grown up, I was taken to a rural area, where I gave a speech and then sat down for a meal typical of the region featuring *buchada,* a gritty Brazilian tripe.

When the plate arrived, the reporters who had come from São Paulo looked at each other with a suspicious smirk.

I knew exactly what was coming.

"Do you *really* like this kind of food, Fernando Henrique?" one of the reporters asked with a roll of his eyes.

"Oh yes," I answered, digging in enthusiastically. "My mother used to make buchada all the time."

This was true—my mother's family was from Alagoas, and she had prepared this dish from time to time when I was a child. In retrospect, however, I really should have just left it at that and moved on to another subject. Instead, as I chewed, I added: "Plus, I used to enjoy something very similar when I lived in Paris! They made it with fine French white wine. It was truly delicious."

The media had their fun with that one.

The "elitist" tag followed me for my entire political career, and I was never sure what to do about it. On one hand, it would be silly for me to pretend that I did not come from a certain degree of privilege, both economic and social, being from the upper middle class. And, yes, I had spent many years of my life living abroad. But I have never, ever thought of myself as a snob, or even as a common product of the Brazilian elite. Still, Brazil is a country where deep class divisions are perhaps *the* central fact of life. So it was logical that my class background would be an issue, especially when my opponent was Lula.

Campaigns in Brazil are just as slick and media-oriented as those in Europe or the United States, and there was a good deal of hand-wringing about how to market me to a skeptical public. We consulted with numerous friends and public relations firms; we even briefly brought in the American political consultant James Carville, who was fresh from helping transform Bill Clinton into the "Comeback Kid." I also had a top-notch Brazilian consultant named Nizan Guanaes. It was decided that, for me to mount my own comeback, I should appear more often in shirtsleeves and try to be funnier. There was also some discussion that maybe I needed a nickname. Someone suggested "FHC," but we decided that sounded too much like DDT. Ultimately, we just stuck with "Fernando Henrique."

By May, I was seriously contemplating quitting the race. I had made precious little headway in the polls, and I still trailed Lula badly, garnering only 19 percent of the projected vote compared to his 41 percent. Meanwhile, I had been compelled to resign my position as finance minister, as required by Brazilian laws regulating presidential candidates, and I felt a bit isolated. Day-to-day preparations for the launch of the real, which had been ultimately scheduled for July, were now in the hands of Rubens Ricupero, my very capable replacement. But it had become apparent that my campaign might be dead by then. In May, we organized a fund-raiser, and only a handful of people showed up. One night over dinner, I told Ruth and our children that I thought I might have to withdraw from the campaign.

At that point, I realized that no amount of slick marketing, or fund-raisers, or acting like a cowboy, was ever going to get me elected president. My fate depended exclusively on the success of the real. And, in that respect, I was about to be aided by yet another fortuitous accident.

As most of the world knows, *futebol* is not merely a sport for us; it is an obsession. It is said in Brazil that every youth is born with a soccer ball attached to his foot. However, I am living testimony that this is an outright lie. I am woefully incapable of kicking much of anything. That is probably why I never watched much soccer on television; I always preferred reading a good book instead. In truth, I am a Brazilian who doesn't much like soccer.

In 1994, however, I became an absolute, over-the-top soccer fanatic.

As fate would have it, the July 1 launch of the real coincided with the beginning of the World Cup, which Brazil entered as a favorite to win. This represented an intriguing opportunity. I knew, of course, that no success on the soccer field would make up for technical shortcomings in the Real Plan. A well-placed penalty kick was not going to magically end inflation. But there was something to be said about the mood of the country and how that might impact the real. So much of economics is linked to expectations; if people expect a new business or a new policy to fail, it usually does. The opposite is also true. If Brazil did reasonably well in the World Cup, we thought maybe the country would relax a little bit and start believing in itself again. Maybe a bit of the optimism would rub off on the real and give it a better chance at success.

So my campaign team decided to take a risk. Not only did I start watching the games, but I invited the media over to my campaign headquarters. They snapped pictures of me cheering in front of my television set during the games, and then the next day the newspapers published the photos after the Brazilian team won. Was it a slightly hammy bit of political theater? Yes, of course. But it was also quite dangerous. If I was to be identified publicly with the team, what would happen to me if Brazil lost?

Ironically, Lula, who is a *much* bigger soccer fan (not to mention better player) than I am, wasn't willing to take that chance. He watched the games quietly in his home, with no reporters watching him.

By the time the new currency entered circulation on July 1, Brazil had already breezed undefeated through the opening round. On July 4, we managed a close win over the host, the U.S. team, followed by a 3–2 victory over the Netherlands on July 9 that put us into the semifinals. By this point, I could barely watch the games because I was staying up all night plotting out strategy for the campaign. But, of course, I still found time to tune in on July 13, when a thrilling goal with just 9 minutes left against Sweden put Brazil into the championship final against Italy.

On July 17, before 85,000 fans in the Rose Bowl and another 175 million Brazilians dancing, singing, and chanting in near unison back home, the two teams battled to a tie. When the extra time was over, the game went to penalty kicks. Brazil prevailed 3–2, and, to the surprise of everyone, we won the World Cup.

In a country that had been depressed for so long, people grasped at this proof that Brazil was still capable of greatness. People confidently predicted that the win would carry over to all walks of life. "The victory inaugurates a new phase in Brazil's history: the return of national self-esteem," wrote one newspaper columnist, Teodomiro Braga. "The best in soccer can also win the battle against misery and backwardness." Márcio Moreira Alves, the congressman whose speech had provided the military with the excuse to close down the Congress, now a journalist, added, "There is now a relaxed feeling that things aren't so bad after all." Even Itamar joined the fray, declaring, "This dignity that the players have achieved should be transferred to Brazil itself."

As all this was happening, our data indicated that the new currency might be working, but we couldn't quite be sure. Brazil was so caught up with soccer fever that it was difficult to talk to people about anything else. Business had ground to a total halt. When the team won the Cup, the entire country went on a binge for several days, and we could barely get any information at all. I could see that the wave of nationalism and hope would help us, but I couldn't yet gauge how people really felt about the real.

A few days after the World Cup finals, when the initial euphoria had been replaced by a more settled aura of quiet confidence, I made a campaign trip to an impoverished city in the northeast. The towns there are bathed in a brilliant, cleansing white light, and as I squinted through the car window, I was surprised to see that hundreds of people had gathered along the side of the unpaved road to watch my motorcade pass. They stood there under a brutal midday sun, waving Brazilian flags and smiling. When I rolled down the window to wave back, I heard people screaming: "Look, there's the man who made the real!"

When I got out of the car, I was mobbed. People hugged me, kissed me, and posed for photographs with me. I thought, Who am I now, Elvis? A man approached me holding a fresh one-real bill, flashed a toothless smile, and asked, "Would you please autograph the real for me?"

I nodded and asked one of my aides for a pen.

The aide frowned. "I think it might be against the law for you to deface the currency by putting your autograph on it," he warned.

"No, no," I laughed. "It's not illegal, because my signature is already on it!" I took the pen, signed the bill, and bounded up to the podium to give my speech.

When I started talking, the crowd lifted the new real bills up and waved them happily in the air. Their cheers almost drowned out what I had to say, but I knew my words didn't matter. The real was the star of the show. "It's worth more than a dollar!" people yelled—people who had never seen a U.S. dollar before in their life, but they were proud nonetheless. Our currency was now something positive, no longer that old piece of junk, that worthless thing you threw in the trash.

That same week, a poll showed that I was tied with Lula for the first time. And I began to wonder if there was a chance we might win this thing after all.

We never expected inflation to fall so far, so fast.

Following monthly rates of 45 percent in March and April, inflation slowed to only 2 percent in July, the month the real was launched. The consequences of this were revolutionary. Since money no longer lost its value, the buying power of an average wage in Brazil would increase by an astonishing 30 percent before the year was over. As expected, the poor benefited most. They could suddenly afford items that had heretofore been beyond their reach, basic items like chicken or yogurt. Meanwhile, the middle class indulged in an outright buying spree, snapping up refrigerators, televisions, and property. The hallmarks of Brazil's culture of inflation—the long lines at supermarkets, the fistfuls of worthless bills—disappeared almost overnight. It was like living in a different country.

Lula was bewildered by all this. He continued to disparage the new currency despite all the visible evidence. "The real is not a dream," he declared. "It is a nightmare! It is based on massive propaganda that says the workers are going to be in heaven if inflation falls. That's just not going to happen. This plan will only freeze the misery in Brazil!"

In September, the month before the election, prices rose just 1.51

percent. The economy had entered a full-fledged boom, and I kept rising like a hot air balloon in the polls. Lula got desperate. At one rally, his vice presidential candidate, José Paulo Bisol, said that "when the state is not prepared to defend the poor, violence justifies violence." This fed many of the old fears about the radical leftist elements in Lula's party. At a rally in the Amazon, Lula himself declared: "Imagine if Christ came back to earth today. What would he have been called? A communist, a communist. It was for this reason that they crucified him. If he were among us today, those who call me a communist would have said the same about him."

Meanwhile, I had the first solid currency in decades in my favor. I promised a modern policy agenda to bring the stability of the real to all sectors of our economy. Everything I did later as president came directly from what I outlined during my campaign. I promised to help create a Brazil that was part of the world economy as well as stable at home.

On October 3, 1994, I was elected the new president of Brazil with 54 percent of the vote. Lula received 27 percent, with the rest of the electorate divided among other candidates. It was an exceedingly rare first-round victory; no runoff was necessary. I carried every state except Rio Grande do Sul and the Federal District of Brasília. I won among all social classes, though I had a slightly stronger margin among wealthier voters. Most astounding of all was this fact: It was the first time in my life that I had finished first in an election.

For my inauguration, we organized a concert of Bahian music on Brasília's main plaza. It was attended by more than 20,000 people. We also hosted a formal dinner for more than 5,000 guests. Rather than sit at a formal head table, as is traditional, Ruth and I mingled freely among the guests at a buffet-style event. The idea was to show that this would be a new democratic era for Brazil, where the old barriers between the government and the people were broken down.

Well before my inauguration, I met Itamar at the presidential palace as he was still clearing out his belongings. We hugged and chatted for a while, but something was clearly bothering him.

"I'm sorry," Itamar said, frowning, "but there is a wooden crucifix of mine that is still attached to the wall in your office. I've struggled with it but can't quite seem to take it down."

"Perhaps it would be better if you left it, Itamar. I'm not sure we need any stories about how I made you remove a cross. Plus, with this job," I said with a wink, "I could use all the help I can get."

REMEMBER EVERYTHING I WROTE

I t took me only three days as president to see that I was in big trouble.

On January 4, 1995, in what should have been just another dull bureaucratic procedure, I submitted my candidate for the new head of the central bank for approval by the Senate. The nomination failed—not on ideological grounds, but because, at the precise moment of the vote, a large group of senators left the floor of the legislature to go get a steaming cup of coffee.

They staged the walk out to show support for a senator who had recently used the official Senate printing press to manufacture thousands of calendars with his grinning picture emblazoned on them. The senator now faced charges of impropriety, and his comrades were lobbying for me to issue a presidential pardon to get him off the hook. No pardon, no vote. So out they went for their coffee, guaranteeing that there would be no quorum on the floor of the legislature. The central bank, and the very delicate six-month-old currency that it was charged with overseeing, would have to wait.

Days later, it was the lower house's turn. It approved a raise in the minimum wage to 100 *reais* (the plural of the currency, the real), then equivalent to about $100 per month. I, too, believed that Brazil's minimum wage was woefully low. However, there was no money to pay for such an increase in the budget, which was still under great strain as we struggled to keep the anti-inflation plan afloat. So I was obliged to veto the bill. The next morning, newspapers published blaring headlines about how the brand new president was a sworn enemy of the working class. Within three weeks of taking office, my approval rating plummeted to 36 percent.

Congress was certainly not to blame for all the shortcomings of my presidency. However, these initial missteps did illustrate the frustrating, particularly Brazilian nature of the resistance that I would face over the next eight years.

My presidency was, at its most basic level, about trying to turn Brazil into a stable country. For our entire history, we had lurched from one crisis to another, mainly because of our refusal to follow rules. I believed that the common thread of that instability was an all-too-frequent disregard for the rule of law. Presidencies, economic plans, and entire democracies had habitually been tossed aside on the whims of a few people. Amid such arbitrariness, the roots of a modern capitalist economy had failed to take hold, leaving much of our country mired in poverty. I believed that, if I could now establish a minimal degree of stability as president, then the foundations for a modern society—private investment, effective social policies, the reduction of poverty— would follow.

There were many people, Brazilians included, who believed such a change was impossible. They saw Brazil as the incorrigible land of the jeitinho, the artful little trick for getting around the system. This word, and the concept behind it, were supposedly intractable parts of our national identity, the products of a society that took deep pride in flaunting the law. Many observers had long attributed the jeitinho to a streak of tropical playfulness, adding to the stereotype of Brazil as a kind of lovable ne'er-do-well, mai tai in hand, possessed of an innately rueful inability to keep its promises. But I believed that the jeitinho revealed a hidden and far darker aspect of Brazilian society, one that went to the heart of our history and threatened my presidency.

Brazil's refusal to follow rules was, in reality, just another product of our deeply unjust society. Where others saw random chaos and improvisation, I saw a sublimely well-organized effort to maintain the status quo. The coups and other manifestations of instability in Brazil almost always served to benefit the tiny minority of people who possessed most of the country's wealth and power. Rules were broken not because of some pathological lack of discipline, but to benefit those interests. Each time a government or economic stabilization plan went out the window, the elite had almost always benefited most, or at least been damaged least. Inflation had been a perfect example of this. When half of the Senate walked out for coffee, they were trying to protect their own interests to the detriment of the nation at large. The same was true of the lower house's vote to increase the minimum wage. I believed that the jeitinho had no place at the table anymore in Brazilian politics.

Thus, my challenge as president was to establish rules and then force the country to stick to them. The policies concerning our currency constituted one set of rules. Trade policies were another set. Capitalism is little more than a system of rules. If these rules were respected, then we could build the foundations for lasting prosperity. Brazilians would finally have a more solid framework on which to build; they would then be able to use their formidable talents and make plans for the future—the very essence of economic and social development. But, in order to do so, we would have to fend off numerous well-organized attempts at sabotage by small, yet powerful interest groups eager to defend their privileges. We would have to change the very essence of the country.

Accomplishing this would have been extraordinarily difficult for any politician. It may have been just a little easier, however, for a sociologist.

Shortly before I took office, a Brazilian newspaper quoted me as having said: "Forget everything I wrote in the past. The world has changed, and today's reality is different." That quote was invented by the reporters; people who had been present at the actual interview confirmed that I had never said such a thing. But it caused quite a stir and—regardless of its veracity—is remembered as one of the defining quotes of my presidency. People still wince when they ask me about it, and all the other questions that always seem to follow: Had I betrayed the principles I'd embraced as a professor? How much had I changed over the years? Why did I govern the way I did?

I would contend that, even as I settled into my new job, I was still a sociologist at heart. My goals were mostly the same, even if my sense of how best to accomplish them had evolved. I still tried to see Brazil's problems with the same detached objectivity of the young professor in the white lab coat who had marched through the favelas of southern Brazil forty years earlier. Before making a decision, I struggled to collect all the relevant information and understand all points of view, as my old mentor from USP, Florestan Fernandes, had taught me. Methodology, more than ideology, was the true legacy of my academic career.

Sometimes, I was so eager to see Brazil with a sociologist's eye that I was shy with the use of power. This was surely one of the biggest flaws of my presidency. On some occasions, when the country needed a president, I was still too much of a sociologist. I was so keen to remain above the fray that I missed opportunities to convince other people of my beliefs or to take substantive action. I tended to see the big picture better than the small one, and my scientific instincts could make me seem aloof. Politicians from all sides would often leave meetings with me and gleefully declare to the press: "The president agrees with us!" This was often not true. I had simply listened to their complaints, expressed sympathy, and said I would try to help them. Not quite the same as agreeing, but looking back, I can understand why they were confused.

However, I believe that in most instances, my background served me well. Perhaps in a developed country like Germany or the United States, a sociologist would not have been such an asset as president; but in Brazil, where so many of the policy problems stemmed from social injustices, I was in an advantageous position. It was surprising how often a dilemma could be solved by taking an honest, objective look at the different groups involved and then imposing the fairest solution for everyone. A little common sense proved to be much more effective than throwing money at a problem—and a lot cheaper too. When a policy was well-considered and fair, it also became that much more difficult for the opposition to search for a jeitinho or some other trick to derail it.

One example was our strategy in addressing one of Brazil's most fascinating and controversial barriers to development: the distribution of land. This issue had been dominated for a decade by the Movimento dos Trabalhadores Rurais Sem Terra, known as the "Landless Movement" or MST. The MST had caught the attention of the world in the mid-1980s, when machete-wielding farmers began confiscating land in the Brazilian countryside. Large groups, sometimes numbering in the thousands, would march on to a plot of land, set up tents, and begin farming it themselves. From that period on, MST leaders have argued that, in a country plagued by such unequal land distribution, they have no choice but to resort to such confrontational tactics. They claim to seize only tracts of land deemed "unproductive," which are usually—but not always—fallow or improperly farmed sections of very large estates. After farming for a while, the MST claims ownership.

With the support of leftist intellectuals and the Catholic Church, the MST has become much more than a movement of the poor. It boasts 1.5 million members, including television stars, samba singers, and other celebrities at home and abroad. The American leftist Noam Chomsky once called it "the most important and exciting popular movement in the world." It has become a pop culture phenomenon. Through its Web site and a retail outlet in São Paulo, the movement sells products ranging from wine and cheese and organic seeds to rum, blue jeans, T-shirts, and desk calendars. The MST also has its own school system, with 3,900 educators working in squatter camps and settlements across Brazil. Each morning, students raise their fists as they belt out the MST's anthem: "We will wake up this sleeping nation, we will plant the world."

Not surprisingly, the MST's actions often end in violence. Since 1985, an estimated 1,500 people have been killed in land disputes in Brazil. Usually, these arise from landowners paying hired guns to eradicate members of the MST or organizations like it. The clashes tend to take place in far-flung corners of the country, where the rule of law is weak, if present at all. When violence occurs, police can be bought off, and the courts will often turn a blind eye.

One of the most abhorrent episodes took place in 1996, when twenty-three MST members were gunned down by police in the Amazonian state of Pará. The murders caused an international outcry, posing one of the first major crises of my government. I did everything I could: I dispatched federal troops to the region to prevent further bloodshed, and I sent officials from Brasília to oversee the investigation. Beyond that, I was restricted by Brazilian laws designed to keep the federal government out of such matters. I later tried to push a bill through Congress to give the president more jurisdiction over crimes such as this; however, the proposal threatened the hegemony enjoyed by powerful state governments, to which most congressmen responded. The bill failed.

I knew that the only effective way to avoid further bloodshed was to try and solve the problem at the root of the dispute. But doing so would mean addressing issues that had festered in Brazil for five hundred years.

The origin of the problem has a distinct irony—at the beginning of Brazil's history, it was almost impossible to give land away. When Portuguese explorer Pedro Álvares Cabral's fleet was blown off course and sailed into a Brazilian harbor in 1500, he and his crew found a relatively empty expanse of unwelcoming jungle. The indigenous population within our modern-day borders numbered only about 3 million, tiny for such a massive area. They practiced rudimentary shifting agriculture, fishing, and hunting. The Portuguese initially fared no better. For decades, Brazil was little more than a strip of fortified coastal garrisons, which mainly served to export monkeys, parrots, and a red dye extracted from a tree called the *pau brasil,* from which our country takes its name.

By 1580, a mere 50,000 settlers had trickled into Brazil. Meanwhile, Portugal's rival, Spain, was making quick headway in colonizing other parts of Latin America. So were the French and the Dutch, who would control a large swathe of northeastern Brazil for forty years. Desperate to halt the other invaders, the Portuguese Crown decided to make colonization of Brazil its top priority.

To populate the wild and hostile land as quickly as possible, the Crown granted unthinkably large tracts of land to a very tiny group of settlers. Choice plots along the coast often encompassed 20 to 50 square miles, and in the interior they could be ten or twenty times that big. Thus, much of Brazil was haphazardly given away in a few decades. Most of the people willing to leave Portugal, then at the apex of its unlikely rise to world power, were political exiles and common criminals. They became the first settlers of Brazil, and their new homes were enormous. As technology improved over the centuries, allowing the cultivation of cash crops such as coffee and sugar, many of these same vast landholdings then became the fabulously wealthy fazendas, or plantations, that were—and to some extent, still are—the backbone of Brazil's economy.

It is amazing how little mistakes can reverberate through history. That hurried decision by the Crown in 1580 was fundamental to so many of the problems that would later haunt Brazil: slavery, economic underdevelopment, and disrespect for the rule of law, just to name a few. History could have been different, of course. The United States had the Homestead Act of 1862, which enshrined small landholdings and laid the foundation for the world's most prosperous middle class. Brazil, in contrast, never shook its policy of unequal land distribution. Political alliances, most notably the military dictatorship of 1964–1985, ensured the continued survival of an economic scheme that was instrumental in creating one of the world's biggest gaps between rich and poor.

When I took office in 1995, this pattern was still as entrenched as ever. Data on the subject can be inaccurate or controversial, owing to overlapping claims, but this much is inarguable: Land distribution in Brazil is one of the most unfair in the world. One frequently cited statistic from the beginning of my presidency showed that 1 percent of the population controlled 45 percent of Brazil's arable land.

Because of this injustice, I had enormous sympathy for the MST and for the landless movement in general. I once declared publicly that, were I not president, I would probably be out there marching with them. They were calling attention to a cause that I believed was important; without the MST's activism, Brazilian society might not have felt such a strong need to solve the problem.

However, while I agreed with the spirit of their cause, I could not support the MST's methods.

In a modern economy, you can't seize other people's land. Property rights need to be respected. Although this may sound like a universally accepted tenet of capitalism, it was still being hotly debated during those years in Brazil. I had to explain to the country on numerous occasions that the image of mobs taking over privately owned farms would chase away investment, both local and foreign. This wasn't a hollow warning—industries such as meat packing and commercial agriculture did flee parts of the country where the MST was strong, fearing their businesses would be confiscated. To make matters worse, it was clear that small-scale subsistence farming had, sadly, become extremely difficult to maintain in a modern economy. Many of the MST settlements depended on government subsidies to survive. They could wave red Che Guevara flags and rage against the unfairness of global capitalism until they turned hoarse, but that was the reality we all had to live in.

I decided that the best policy was to seek sweeping land reform through rigorously controlled legal channels. There *was* a large amount of unused land in Brazil that could be distributed to people interested in farming it. The ability to do this was even enshrined in the constitution. But it had to be done in an orderly fashion so that it would not destroy the agricultural sector and take other portions of the economy with it. To that end, we imposed a new tax on unproductive land to encourage its sale. With the cooperation of multilateral organizations such as the World Bank and the Inter-American Development Bank, the Brazilian government purchased land that was then given to the poor via a legal and transparent process.

Meanwhile, I sought a balanced strategy of containment with the MST. While I did not evict them from their existing settlements, I did everything possible to discourage new ones, including the use of force if necessary.

No one liked my policies. The right said I was coddling criminals by refusing to remove the "squatters" from private land, and the left accused me of betraying my roots and violating the spirit of the constitution.

Meanwhile, the MST was outraged, and on one occasion its adherents went as far as to seek revenge, invading a farm that belonged to my family in the state of Minas Gerais. Television cameras rolled as hundreds of MST members sat in my living room drinking fortified cachaça. They ruthlessly slaughtered several animals on the farm as well. This was a working farm—they had no legitimate grounds to deem the land "unproductive," and their actions were nothing more than a political provocation. So I followed the same policy anyone else would have in a similar situation: I went to court and was granted a judicial order to clear the land. Police then went in and arrested people. This was done peacefully, and we did not press charges.

I didn't take their actions personally, though, and I never stopped being curious about the MST's methods. One time, I decided to go witness them for myself. I was on a vacation at that same family farm in Minas Gerais, which sat about 20 kilometers away from the nearest MST settlement. I knew that it was impossible for me to make an announced visit—it would be too politically charged, and the media would turn it into a circus. So I decided to go incognito.

A horde of journalists was camped out at the main entrance to the ranch, so I sneaked out through the back gate. I went with just two bodyguards in a small station wagon, dressed as a typical farmer in an open-collared shirt and thick mud boots. I was also wearing sunglasses. I think it was a Sunday, so when we arrived at the settlement, there were dozens of people just milling about, very relaxed.

No one recognized me at first—it was unthinkable, after all, that the hated president might be there among them. I spoke casually with several people, asking them about the condition of their crops and the weather. I resisted the temptation to ask them what they thought of Fernando Henrique Cardoso. In fact, I kept politics out of the conversation entirely.

"Do you want to see where we're living?" a young woman asked me.

I nodded, and she took me down to the shore of a creek. There was a community of large black tents, and people washing their clothes in the water. We entered one of the tents and sat down with her family. They served me coffee and we chatted for a while. I was reminded again of my days as an assistant professor. It was all very pleasant, very informal, but also informative.

Before long, more people had crowded into the tent to see the stranger. An elderly woman then asked, "Are you Fernando Henrique?"

She said it very calmly. All eyes turned to her, then slowly shifted back to me.

"Yes, I am."

What followed was not the pandemonium one might have expected. Indeed, I saw this on several occasions during my presidency: When you take the politics out of the equation, people are people. With no media around, and no camera lights to get them nervous, everybody stays relaxed; it is just another conversation. Once they found out who I was, of course, the nature of their questions changed. But throughout, everyone was very cordial. I invited them to come visit me on my nearby farm someday, and I left.

The only people who got angry about this encounter afterward were those in the press. They accused me of being patronizing, but that was not my intention. I was merely trying to gather information, to understand the unadorned reality of the situation, so I would know how to help. It was the same methodology I had always employed. I suspect the media was just upset that I didn't take them along for the ride.

Meanwhile, I went back to Brasília and quietly pressed on with my policy of trying to help those people get some land of their own.

Under land-reform projects during my eight years of government, implemented through the excellent work of Minister Raul Jugmann, we resettled about 588,000 families—double the number resettled in the previous three decades combined. My government granted titles to about 44.5 million acres, an area roughly the size of Missouri. This was all done via legitimate means, following the rule of law. After I left office, the *Wall Street Journal* deemed my efforts "one of the most ambitious land-distribution programs ever seen in the developing world." I consider it a testimony to my roots as a sociologist and one of the proudest achievements of my government.

If there was another cause where it didn't hurt to have a sociologist running Brazil, it was with regard to AIDS.

By 1990, Brazil faced a catastrophe. We had the same rate of HIV infection as South Africa, at just over 1 percent of the adult population. Our infection rate was the highest in Latin America, and our health-care system, long neglected by the military regime, was unable to cope. The United Nations predicted that, by 2002, Brazil would have 1.2 million cases of HIV. The impact of such an outbreak would have been devastating to our economy and our society.

Would we deny the existence of the problem, or face it head on? At the time, this was a legitimate question. Many other countries, namely those in Sub-Saharan Africa, were taking the former approach. They stuck their heads in the sand and pretended that if they did not talk openly about it, AIDS might go away. Governments allowed taboos about homosexuality, prostitution, and other sexual mores to keep them from putting together a coherent AIDS policy. This neglect, of course, caused the disease to spread much faster than it would have if these countries had put reasonable policies into place.

Brazil, where the large majority of AIDS cases resulted from sexual transmission, could have easily followed a similar path. While it is true that Brazilians have long had a more open attitude about sex than the people of most other countries, it was not customary for the government to reflect this attitude in its policies. Quite the contrary. Brazilians expected their government to be above such matters—a sober, even prudish counterbalance to society at large. Sex was just not something that elected officials talked about.

Under my government, we took the exact opposite approach. We decided it was better for society to blush a little bit than to watch thousands of people die. So we got the problem out in the open and tailored our response to the Brazilian reality. For example, with the help of nongovernmental organizations (NGOs), we started handing out 10 million condoms during Carnival season every year. We made AIDS warnings compulsory at the start of pornographic movies. In some schools, students were taught how to put on condoms. Students also received comprehensive sex education classes emphasizing the importance of honesty in relationships. In poor neighborhoods, the NGOs helped us to stage informal events, such as plays or workshops in community centers, to educate adults about the problem. With large billboards and blunt TV ads, we also designed individual programs for specific risk groups, including prostitutes, drug users, truck drivers, prison inmates, street kids, and indigenous people.

In doing so, we defied the conventional wisdom that the best AIDS policy was to teach abstinence and fidelity. In practice, we believed these messages to be confusing and ultimately counterproductive. They tended to create a false sense of security. For example, many women in stable relationships felt protected by the simple fact that they had a single partner. The sad reality was that women were one of the fastest-growing at-risk groups. The concept of abstinence simply did not correspond to the reality. So we pressed ahead with the message that condoms needed to be used in all sexual situations. In doing so, we gained support from a broad swathe of society. Newspapers and television stations granted us free advertising for public information announcements. The Catholic Church also supported the spirit of our message. By the end of the decade, many of the old taboos in Brazil had been completely shattered.

By far the most controversial aspect of my government's AIDS policy ended up having nothing to do with sex. In 1996, we passed a new law guaranteeing Brazilians free access to antiretroviral AIDS drugs. Anyone who wanted these drugs, which had begun making a positive impact, allowing patients to live longer, now had a legal right to get them. This was a truly revolutionary initiative, the first of its kind in any developing country. We would have to deal with enormously complex issues of cost, ethics, and trade and business practices. Doing so meant a confrontation with foreign pharmaceutical companies and governments, notably that of the United States.

To be able to afford universal coverage, we knew we had to lower the cost of treatment. Antiretroviral medicine was prohibitively expensive for poor countries, with a typical "cocktail" of drugs costing upward of $12,000 per year per patient—triple what an average Brazilian makes annually. We began encouraging Brazilian pharmaceutical companies to make cheaper, generic versions of foreign AIDS medicines that were not protected under local patents. For the drugs covered by patents, we intensely lobbied foreign pharmaceutical firms to slash their costs for the Brazilian market. If they refused, we threatened to break the patent and produce them as well.

This caused a huge international outcry. The pharmaceutical companies declared that lower prices would inhibit their ability to produce new drugs. Acting on their behalf, the U.S. government presented a complaint before the World Trade Organization (WTO), alleging that our policy was in violation of international property rights laws. We also had to confront numerous skeptics who said that poor or uneducated people would not have the discipline to follow a program that required taking a variety of drugs on a very specific schedule.

I understood most of these concerns. With regard to the issue of patents, I simply believed that the unique magnitude of the AIDS crisis justified our actions. Human lives took precedence over profits. It was clear that the free-market system would not be able to provide a solution by itself, so the government was needed as a mediator. We tried to reach a compromise, offering to pay the foreign pharmaceutical companies what we could. It was less than they wanted, but it was better than nothing—which is what they would have received if there had been no program at all. In one sense, we were creating customers rather than taking them away. And as far as the claim that the poor lacked discipline to take medicine was concerned, I have always had far more faith than that in people's abilities.

So, we set about explaining Brazil's point of view to the world. The point man on this issue was the health minister: José Serra, my old friend from exile in Chile and one of the most capable officials in my government. The contributions from the foreign minister, Celso Lafer; the ambassador to the WTO, Celso Amorim; and other diplomats were also instrumental.

Over the next few years, we steadily built a coalition of allies. We won people over to our position that life-saving technologies serve an overriding public interest. Leading NGOs, the scientific community, and organizations of people living with HIV mobilized world public opinion. United Nations agencies adopted resolutions defining access to anti-AIDS drugs as a fundamental human right and urged the WTO to be flexible in finding a balance between patent rights and public health priorities.

Victory arrived unexpectedly in June 2001, when a UN AIDS conference was due to open in New York. On that same day, the United States withdrew the complaint against Brazil from the WTO. I have no doubt that this favorable outcome was decisively influenced by global public opinion.

Since then, Brazil has become a model for developing countries' policies on AIDS. Our strategies on both prevention and treatment are now being replicated all over the world.

All success in terms of AIDS is relative, and the disease continues to be a grave threat for Brazil. But I do believe we averted a catastrophe. By 2002, the final year of my government, we had about 600,000 cases of HIV in Brazil—just half the number predicted by the UN a decade before. The government still spends about $300 million a year on the AIDS program—most of which goes toward treatment. The Brazilian "cocktail" of antiretroviral drugs costs about $4,500 a year per person, roughly a third what it does in the United States. The annual number of deaths from AIDS plummeted by nearly two-thirds during my government. Part of this decline in mortality was due to more effective drugs, but Brazil's policy played a role as well.

Unfortunately, no imagination is needed to see what might have happened to Brazil otherwise. Today, some studies show that at least 20 percent of the adults in South Africa are infected with HIV or have AIDS. In Brazil, that rate is now about 0.3 percent and steady. Their destiny could have easily been ours. Instead, our infection rate is more similar to that of the United States. This was one case where a common sense policy saved innumerable lives.

Before I took office as president, I took a long trip to the Pantanal, an amorphous expanse of southwestern Brazil whose name translates roughly as "the big swampy place." In a country best known for its beaches, a murky wetlands area might not have seemed like the most obvious vacation spot. However, knowing that years might pass before I could properly relax again, I intentionally chose a place famous for its anonymity and vast nothingness. I rented a tiny flatboat with an outboard motor, donned a bathing suit and a worn old pair of sandals, and puttered around the flooded plain by myself for hours at a time.

It is a weird and wonderful place, probably my favorite in all of Brazil. The few cattle ranchers resilient enough to live there seem to have almost as many words for "mud" as the Inuit do for "snow." A handful of tourists come to fish, and to see the area's spooky nocturnal jaguars and myriad species of birds, but the Pantanal is otherwise blessedly empty. It stretches across an area more than a third the size of France, its boundaries shifting with every rainstorm. Parts of the Pantanal stretch well into Bolivia and Paraguay, although there are no visible borders. Even if somebody was crazy enough to build a fence, it would soon sink into the tea-colored water, which smells like candy and inevitably conquers everything.

The water is shallow enough in many areas that I could just jump out of the boat and wade around. One day, accompanied by Ruth and a bodyguard, I moored the boat and picked a random spot on the horizon, and we started sloshing aimlessly toward it. This probably wasn't a brilliant idea, given my notorious sense of direction. Within minutes, we were hopelessly lost, with no sense of how to find our way back to the boat.

We trudged along for about half an hour until we saw a flag.

"That's strange," Ruth said. "Why would *that* flag be here?"

After another half hour of walking, we saw a tiny village of muddy huts on the horizon. As we approached, a soldier emerged from the shadows, aiming his rifle at us.

"*Alto!*" the soldier cried.

And then we knew. The word meant "Halt!"—and his accent was not Brazilian, but Hispanic.

"You have crossed the border into Bolivia!" he said sternly.

I had brought no identification of any kind—my swimsuit had no pockets.

"My name is Fernando Henrique Cardoso," I declared, extending my hand, "and I am the president-elect of Brazil."

Judging by the skeptical look on his face, I might as well have told him I was Queen Victoria.

It took a good half hour of explaining, soothing, and pleading, but we finally managed to convince the Bolivian soldier of my identity. He was a nice, good-humored, if lonely young man. He said that his post was usually pretty boring, and that we were the first people he'd ever had to stop from crossing the Brazilian border, then apologized if he had scared us with the gun.

Before we left, I asked the soldier to help me play a little joke. I asked him to send a telegram to his military headquarters, with instructions to pass on a message to Gonzalo Sánchez de Lozada, the president of Bolivia and an old acquaintance of mine.

"Please tell him that Fernando Henrique Cardoso's first trip abroad as president-elect was to Bolivia."

The soldier laughed and vowed to send the message. He kept his word, and believe it or not, the message eventually got through to its recipient.

This inconsequential episode illustrates a larger truth: Brazil's fate will always be irrevocably connected to the rest of South America. We share a border with all but two countries on the continent: Chile and Ecuador. Elsewhere, in the Pantanal and through vast reaches of the Amazon, most of our borders are unguarded, and often blurred. The implications of our proximity on economic, trade, and political matters are enormous. That makes it even more crucial for Brazil to concentrate on building better relations with countries around the region.

That may sound like common sense, but it is worth noting that it was not always the prevailing philosophy in Brazil. The concept of "South America" was still relatively new, and had yet to be properly reflected in our foreign policy. The military dictatorship, for example, spent far more energy on its relations with countries in Africa and the Middle East than it did on relations with its neighbors. This was due to a rather bizarre formulation of Third World power politics. The military believed that by extending ties to poor African countries, it could cheaply gain allies and help Brazil realize its long-stated dream of becoming a strategic world power. Brazil often financed purchase of exports or provided funds for construction projects in those regions. In some cases, Brazil even granted millions of dollars in direct foreign aid, which was preposterous, since we also had people starving at home.

Simultaneously, the Brazilian dictatorship had seen South American countries, particularly Argentina, as strategic rivals. The whole region was beset by a mutual antagonism, fueled by military rulers who were obsessed with the doctrine of geopolitics and seemingly hell-bent on creating a South American Cold War. During the 1960s and 1970s, the Brazilian military regime was in the embryonic stages of developing a nuclear arms program, believing the Argentines were doing the same. It has been said that when the Argentine dictatorship launched its misguided war against Britain in 1982 for the Falkland Islands, Argentina did not send its best troops to the islands because leaders feared this would expose the country to an invasion from Brazil. By the 1990s, with democracies firmly installed in both countries, such mistrust had largely receded. But even when I was foreign minister, I often had difficulties convincing some Brazilians to work with the Argentines. The wounds had not yet completely healed.

I knew I had to change this as president; we had to be friends with our neighbors. I received a memorable push in that direction from an unexpected source: Helmut Kohl, the chancellor of Germany. In person,

Kohl was a powerful presence, like a rock. He was a man of great vision, and I felt a deep admiration for him, even though our political philosophies were quite different. During one of our meetings, he looked at me gravely and declared: "You Brazilians have a historic responsibility."

I asked him why.

Kohl explained that he had grown up near Bonn, in an area that was occupied by the French following World War II. "I hated the French when I was younger," Kohl told me. "But I finally realized that, if this rivalry continued, my children would go to war as well. It became clear to me that unless we integrated France and Germany economically, the cycle would never end. And that is why I have spent much of my adult life as a passionate proponent of the European Union.

"In Brazil," Kohl continued, "your responsibility is to do the same with Argentina. You must put your past behind you. Your historic mission is to make a great union in the Southern Cone."

Thankfully for us, the degree of historical enmity between Brazil and Argentina was not even remotely comparable to that of Germany and France. But Kohl's overall point was still valid: We were living in an era when broad economic integration was replacing old rivalries. If South America did not launch a similar project, we would be left behind, both economically and politically.

The main manifestation of this strategy was the attention we paid to developing the Mercosul trade bloc, which encompassed Brazil, Argentina, Paraguay, and Uruguay. Chile and Bolivia were associate members. Through the Mercosul, which became the world's third-largest trade bloc, with a combined gross domestic product of nearly $1 trillion, we were able to greatly increase trade among member countries.

Our focus on Mercosul sometimes vexed the United States, which had plans to create its own trading bloc: the Free Trade Area of the Americas, or FTAA. That bloc would have encompassed thirty-four countries across the entire Western Hemisphere. It was scheduled to come into existence on January 1, 2005, but as of the writing of this book, it has yet to come to fruition. This was no accident. I was always concerned that the terms of trade as dictated by Washington would be damaging to Brazil, particularly with regard to agriculture. My government would have been willing to negotiate a trade pact under favorable terms. As it was pitched to us, however, I admit that we had a strategy of dragging our feet in negotiations for the creation of the FTAA.

When prudent, Brazil also acted as a mediator in regional disputes. I played a significant role in negotiating the peace treaty that ended a border conflict between Ecuador and Peru. My government also granted exile to several leaders from Paraguay to help end the constant turmoil there. We believed, however, in using "soft power" to expand our influence in the region; we didn't want to become the new *gringos* of South America. Brazil operated instead through simple diplomatic channels, employing measures such as sponsoring cultural events at Brazilian embassies abroad. Under my government, Brazil would never attempt to use a heavy hand to become a regional power. I have always believed in the concept of national self-determination, and we refused to meddle in other countries' affairs.

This philosophy contrasted with that of the United States, which often brought us into conflict over another complex regional matter: what to do about Cuba.

I always had a relationship of mutual respect with Fidel Castro, and I still receive a box of Cuban cigars from him every now and then. I met him when I was foreign minister, and he visited me in Brazil on several occasions. Prior to that, of course, I had seen only the public Fidel, the man who gives dull, repetitive, and uninspiring six-hour speeches. This widely held image of him is a shame, however, because in private I was always surprised by how polite, curious, good-humored, and soft-spoken he could be.

One time in Brasília, Castro and I spent almost five hours together over lunch. He peppered me with extraordinarily complex questions about our oil policy and asked why our interest rates were so high. Then he started asking me about my daily routine.

"How do you start your day, Fernando Henrique?"

I told him I began each morning with a swim: "There is a pool here. Then, I go up to my office and I usually spend the rest of the day working and meeting with people."

Castro took a long drag on his ubiquitous cigar and slowly shook his head.

"When I first became president of Cuba, I was doing as you do now. I received many, many people. I nearly worked myself to death. But now," he said with a smile, "I don't bother with such things. I stay at home, reading. To cultivate my mind. When I need to speak to someone, I just call them on the phone. And the country works!"

I laughed. "Well, Fidel, how long have you been in government? Forty years now? I'm here for four at a time. So if I suddenly decided to just stay at home and read, my government probably would collapse the next day!"

Castro thought this was very funny.

Whether Cuba was really "working" by that point, as he asserted, was an entirely different matter. There had been a time when Cuba was an inspiration to a generation of aspiring leftists, including myself as a young man. Castro had shown that it was possible for a Latin American country to liberate itself from an oppressive dictatorship. The problem was that he had replaced one authoritarian regime with another.

I visited Cuba once during the 1980s to attend a meeting of a committee charged with granting a cultural award. This was well before the Soviet Union cut off foreign aid, but the island was already in obvious economic trouble by that point. Havana seemed like it was on the verge of simply falling down. Old buildings had rotted; the paint was peeling everywhere and floors were bowing. I was a senator by then, but I managed to move about the island anonymously and quite freely. I visited a Catholic church that was open, but it was eerily empty. I was, of course, impressed by the advances in health care and education in Cuba compared to other Latin American countries. But the country had an equally obvious aura of unhappiness and lack of freedom. Censorship had reached a comic level: Every day that I picked up a newspaper, a new version of the same story appeared on the front page, about a cow that was capable of producing an enormous amount of milk. I remember thinking how odd it was to see a country in the tropics, full of warm and spontaneous people, but living a life as gray and threadbare as I remembered it being in Warsaw Pact Romania and East Germany.

Since then, nothing much has changed. The years seem to have passed Castro by. He still believes he is living in 1985, and that is the way he runs Cuba. Deep down, Castro may realize that the world is different now, but for political reasons he can't admit it, not even in private. When the subject of Cuba comes up, he becomes very quiet, very protective. He never allows open debate of his policies.

A spectacular example of this was at an Ibero-American summit that I attended in 1999 in Havana. These are meetings of the heads of state and officials from Latin American countries plus Spain and Portugal. Generally, nothing much of consequence happens during the conference itself. Things can get very interesting, however, at lunch, when the heads of state are left alone. There are no aides, no press—just about a dozen of us, usually, seated at a table.

On this particular afternoon, good red wine was served. I will always remember the brand: Vega Sicilia, from the famous Unico vintage. The conversation was civil at first, covering everything from trade policy to everybody's favorite beverage. But then things got a bit heated—perhaps because of the wine, perhaps because of the complicated political divisions that have always marked Latin America.

One of the leaders present rose to his feet. Protocol dictates that I cannot tell who it was, but I can say that he was a leader from an influential country. He pounded the table and said: "Damn it, Fidel! What are you going to do about this lousy, piece-of-shit island of yours?"

Castro's jaw dropped.

"We're sick of apologizing for you all the time, Fidel," the leader continued. "It's getting embarrassing. We're the only friends you have left! What are you going to do?"

Castro kept his head bowed and said nothing.

Six or seven other heads of state out of the dozen present then took turns making similarly heated challenges. It was all done with relatively good humor, but the underlying message was very serious. This went on and on for at least twenty minutes. I kept silent and watched as Castro sunk further and further into his chair. The whole time, he did not say a word.

When the others finally finished, Castro stretched, moved his fork around on his plate a bit, and smirked like an adolescent.

"Well, you know," he said softly, "all of you have much more power than I do. I hardly know what's going on in Cuba anymore. You guys know how it is. Ours is a collective government. I'm the last one to find out about anything." He sighed, and then smiled ironically. "Poor me."

We all laughed, and the conversation turned to other matters. But no one believed Castro's grandstanding that night, nor any other, for that matter.

The incident perfectly illustrates why I do not support the long-standing U.S. regional policy toward Cuba. Washington wastes a tremendous amount of energy trying to get other Latin American countries to oppose Castro. One of the instruments is an annual resolution presented before the United Nations condemning Cuba's human rights record. Under my presidency, Brazil abstained from these votes. We also declined numerous requests to serve as a go-between for Washington and Havana. Quite often, the United States expends so much political capital on this issue that it overwhelms all other American interests in the region—trade, drugs, property rights, and other much more important issues take a back seat to Cuba. Washington has chosen to pander to a small but influential group of Cuban exiles in Miami rather than show true leadership in the region. Many opportunities have been squandered.

No country in Latin America wants to follow Cuba's path anymore. That truth was especially evident at that lunch in Havana, but it has been crystal-clear for about two decades now. There is no real risk of another Cuba. Even the recent leftward shift in Latin America's politics does not mean that everybody wants to be like Castro; the region has moved on from such Cold War–style thinking, even if the United States has not.

There has been much fuss about the new generation of left-leaning leaders in Latin America: as well as Lula, men like Hugo Chavez in Venezuela, Nestor Kirchner in Argentina, Tabaré Vazquez in Uruguay and Evo Morales in Bolivia.

Each of these leaders had historic ties to the left, and some continue to rage quite publicly about the injustices of free-market capitalism. But all of them have, in practice, worked with the system. This is not by accident; they all are smart enough to know that no other feasible path exists in today's world. Even the most extreme leaders recognize this.

Chavez is possibly the boldest of them all. He is a bit of a wild card. He railed against Bush. But he knows that the market for Venezuela's oil is the U.S. He cozies up to Castro but actively courts foreign investment. I always thought his eccentricities were intended to appeal to his domestic audience and not an expression of ideology. I always tried to understand him. My view is that as long as Chavez respects basic democratic principles, he is not a threat to the region. Venezuela's right and left wings were at each others throats for decades. Each side has committed its sins. When a society becomes that polarized, it is difficult for anyone to rule effectively.

Like most Latin Americans, Chavez has a deep sense of humor. I remember an episode between the two of us in Quebec, during a summit meeting of America's heads of state in 2001. Just before the summit, I had met President Bush, who expressed his worries about Chavez possibly behaving aggressively at the conference in Quebec. I told Bush that there was no reason for his concern, but that, in any case, since Chavez was coming to Brazil first, I would counsel him to act with moderation. Indeed, when I welcomed Chavez a few days later in Brasília, I suggested to him that the best way to approach Bush was to be polite and gentle: this would be the opposite of Bush's expectations and would disarm him.

Chavez then replied: "You know me, Fernando Henrique. Sometimes I let my emotions take me over. When I go to OPEC meetings and I start to give an indication that I am about to say things that I should not, a friend of mine, the Emir of Qatar, to stop me from sounding as if I'm proclaiming a republic in the Gulf, signals to me with his hands—which he presses together as though in prayer—so that I can restrain myself from destroying his monarchy! Fernando Henrique, you can be my friend in Quebec and do the same."

In my opening statement of the Quebec Conference, I made clear the Latin American conditions for progress in the FTAA talks. I had to use strong words. Suddenly, out of the corner of my eye, I saw Chavez jumping up from his seat with his hands pressed together as if in prayer, staring intently at me. I realized that my message to the U.S. had been expressed robustly enough since Hugo Chavez, of all people, was gesturing to me that I should tone it down!

Chavez and some of the current leaders in Latin America have political views that are closer to the traditional nationalism and anti-Americanism of the past. However, U.S. foreign policy, especially after 9/11, has done little, if anything, to dispel the resurgence of old ideologies in Latin America. The U.S. unilateralism and the way the war against Iraq was waged reinforced Latin America's fears.

Nevertheless, Latin American leaders are obviously capable of judging what is right or wrong for themselves. When Cuba cracked down on dissidents in 2003, that was the last straw for many of us. I have had no contact with Castro ever since. And I strongly suspect that when Castro does finally pass away, the ultimate sign of his outdated philosophy will pass into history as well. Of their own accord, Cubans will surely follow the same path as the rest of the world and open the country to democracy and capitalism, as they should have done years ago.

Castro is a warning to any politician not to cling to power when your moment has passed. But while I had no appetite for trying to match Castro's forty-year record, I also felt that four years as president weren't quite enough. Our currency, the real, was still vulnerable, and I had not been in office long enough to make the deep structural reforms that I believed the country needed. So, barring any unforeseen circumstances—such as, perhaps, an exploding cigar—I decided to seek a second term.

For once in my life, my timing could not have been worse.

CHAPTER

II

THE SAMBA EFFECT

ONE OF MY BIGGEST challenges as president was to keep everybody from panicking. I don't like panic.

To that end, I always tried to cling to a semblance of a normal life. Over the years, I zealously held on to the same circle of friends I had known since my university days. I enjoyed an occasional round of poker; after all, diplomats usually make pretty good bluffs. Opera and classical music have always been passions of mine, and late in life I developed a taste for bossa nova. I continued to read voraciously, immersing myself in the same mix of literature and academic work that had always captivated me. I returned as often as I could to my family home at Ibiùna in the countryside outside São Paulo, near several of my old friends.

Perhaps more than other countries, Brazil needed an overtly steady hand. Given the mercurial nature of many previous presidents, a big part of my job was to restore faith in the office itself. I had to show people that I was no Jânio, that their president was a decent and level-headed man. Achieving stability in Brazil was therefore not just a political question—it was also personal, whether I liked it or not. There was, of course, a certain amount of theater involved in this; often I had to suppress my personal feelings in order to project a certain image.

That said, appearing calm often required a performance worthy of a master thespian.

Throughout my presidency, Brazil was constantly threatened by a mysterious outbreak of a kind of financial flu. All over the world, emerging market economies like ours were collapsing with a virulence that had rarely been seen before. Nobody quite understood why; we only knew that, if a country fell ill, its government and millions of its citizens would surely end up bankrupt. It all started in 1994 with Mexico. Then came Thailand, followed by all of East Asia. Then Russia. All of these crises consisted of some awful combination of stock-market crashes, debt defaults, currency devaluations, and mass layoffs that left shattered economies. By the time I started running for a second term as president, many economists were loudly predicting that the next victim would be Brazil.

At home, I had my own headaches. My economic reform agenda had stalled in Congress. The first accusations of corruption against my government were starting to pop up in newspapers. Running for a second term as president—against Lula, yet again—presented legal and political pratfalls. There were also mounting fears that the real, the financial anchor and biggest symbol of my presidency, had become unstable.

I didn't fully comprehend it at the time, but it is clear now that all of these challenges, inside and outside Brazil, were profoundly connected.

The seeds of the so-called Samba Effect were planted in 1989, when the Berlin Wall collapsed. The resulting unbridled euphoria far surpassed the boundaries of Germany or even the old Eastern bloc. It was as if all of the barriers to commerce around the world had fallen at once. With the Cold War over, and with the advent of new technology, countries suddenly found that they could integrate their economies like never before—the phenomenon that became known as "globalization."

This new world was like a big club that countries clamored to be admitted to, with the tantalizing possibility of economic prosperity behind the gilded doors. Trade agreements, foreign aid deals, and deep-pocketed multinational companies awaited new members. But in order to gain entrance to this club, many countries first needed to recalibrate their economies in the mold of the "winners" of the Cold War, namely the United States and Western Europe. The recipe for this was no secret, involving policies that are largely accepted nowadays around the world as common sense. That is: Tariffs needed to be slashed, some state-run enterprises sold into private hands, and, above all, private property rights needed to be respected. When I became president, this transformation had already begun occurring across most of the world, including Latin America, and specifically, Brazil.

I had first started to notice these changes in the 1960s—my book on dependency theory addressed the first signs of globalization—but with the collapse of the Wall and, with it, communism as a viable alternative, the transformation kicked into overdrive. Countries everywhere realized that some version of free-market capitalism was the only path to prosperity. Perhaps keeping the economy closed had been a good idea in the past, but it wasn't possible anymore. Even China had come around. By the mid-1990s, only Cuba and North Korea had truly closed economies—and that was because the United States wouldn't let them participate in the global economy, not by their own accord.

My task, therefore, was to overhaul Brazil's economy so it could compete more effectively in a globalized world. Many of these same reforms also met my goal of creating a less unjust society. This was no coincidence. Free-market capitalism had proven itself to be the best system for creating a society that was more wealthy, prosperous, and fair in the long term. A more healthy economy, in tandem with more effective policing and a better judicial system, would also help combat the scourge of crime. By making our economy open to the positive effects of globalization, we would simultaneously be doing away with many of the privileges that a minority of elite Brazilians had enjoyed for too long. This linkage, unfortunately, also explained the fierce, shortsighted, and self-interested resistance reform often faced.

Brazil's state-run telephone company, Telebrás, was emblematic of this struggle. Telebrás had proven woefully unable to meet Brazil's needs at a moment in history when communications were of paramount importance because of the spread of the Internet and a global services industry. The day I took office, Brazil had only 8.4 telephones per 100 people—below the Latin American average (11) and light years behind the United States (66). This was less because of Brazilian poverty than because of Telebrás's own lack of resources. In some fast-growing parts of Brazil, there was a two-year waiting list to get a phone installed. Nationwide, some 17 million people were thought to be waiting for a phone line. With its unwieldy bureaucracy and empty coffers, Telebrás simply could not keep up with demand.

Faced with this dilemma, we had two options. Either the government could provide the capital needed to make further investments, as had been done in the past, or we could sell Telebrás to the private sector, possibly to a foreign company. Given the cold reality of the times, it didn't seem like much of a choice. The Brazilian government had limited amounts of cash, which of course had produced the problem in the first place. Meanwhile, we knew that an independent, private company would be in a unique position to inject new funds and expertise on a managerial and technical level. Service would improve, and more people would have access to telephones, the Internet, and other basic necessities of a modern economy.

I took great pains to explain to the public why privatization was the option that would benefit most Brazilians. However, change threatened a noisy minority of people who were afraid of losing their privileges. Telebrás employees knew that if a privately run company took over, they stood to lose benefits and possibly their jobs. Other people in similarly privileged positions—namely, labor union leaders and employees of other state-run companies—saw that if Telebrás was privatized, their own status quo might be endangered as well. So when the government decided to move ahead with the sale of our share of Telebrás in July 1998, all hell broke loose.

At first, labor unions filed more than a hundred lawsuits in court to halt the privatization. When that did not work, opposition politicians began screaming about supposed irregularities in the sale. Lula accused me of rushing to sell Telebrás so I could use the proceeds to finance my reelection campaign—an outrageous assertion that led me to file defamation charges against him in court. On July 29, as the auction of Telebrás took place on the floor of Rio's stock exchange, street battles broke out just a few hundred yards away between thousands of rock-throwing protesters and riot police. About a dozen people were hurt.

Ultimately, the sale of Telebrás netted the government $18.9 billion, making it the largest privatization in the history of Latin America. The final price was much higher than expected, despite our prior decision to split the company into twelve separate legal entities; I was opposed to any kind of monopoly, whether public or private. Perhaps the sale price would have been higher if we had sold Telebrás as a whole, but we wanted to do everything possible to encourage competition. Ultimately, the results spoke for themselves. During my presidency, the number of telephones per 100 people in Brazil jumped from 8.4 to 30. The gross number of telephones nearly quadrupled to about 50 million lines. The number of cell phone uses jumped from 800,000 to 81 million in eight years. The resulting improvement to Brazil's economic infrastructure had benefits far beyond the sale price that Telebrás fetched on the open market.*

Despite the obvious benefits, we still had to fight similarly epic battles over every single reform my government proposed. Opposition often seemed to come not just from the special interests that had the most to lose, but from society at large. My opponents accused me of

---

*The communications minister, Sérgio Motta, played an instrumental role in privatization and in other modernization efforts.

being a "neoliberal," a negative buzzword used so widely in Latin America during the 1990s that its meaning became somewhat blurred. In the most general terms, a neoliberal usually meant someone who wanted to dismantle the entire state and let the private sector control everything. This was certainly not my intention; public spending actually increased during my government. I also believed that some companies could be effective in state hands as long as they were not used as a repository for cronyism; Petrobrás, the state energy company, and the Banco do Brasil were examples of well-run state companies. Neither the International Monetary Fund (IMF) nor many of Brazil's right-wing interest groups were ever comfortable with my seeming refusal to follow the prescription for free-market reform to the letter.

I was accustomed to simultaneous criticism from both the left and the right, and usually took it as a sign that I was doing my job effectively. But in truth, the name-calling and the debates about privatization were usually part of a much greater battle against change that was particularly difficult to undertake in Brazil.

To understand why, my thoughts often drifted to a familiar topic: coffee. Brazil produced more of the dark brew than any other country in the world; it was generally of excellent quality and very competitively priced. Yet many foreigners rarely asked for the Brazilian "brand" of coffee by name. For example, Americans tended to believe that Colombian coffee was preferable. Even Guatemalan and Kenyan coffees usually registered a degree of recognition. Patriotism aside, I would venture that Brazilian coffee was superior in quality to coffee produced in any of those other countries. But, when John Smith walked into a Starbucks in the United States, he was not nearly as likely to request a Brazilian blend of coffee as one of those other types. Why was this?

For decades, Brazil's economy had been a fortress unto itself; companies could focus almost exclusively on selling to the domestic market. Since high tariffs shielded most Brazilian companies from foreign competition, they essentially had a large and dynamic group of consumers all to themselves. Exports were usually an afterthought. Even with a product like coffee, of which a large amount was exported, few companies put much energy into concepts such as marketing or branding, especially abroad. Brazil had no equivalent of Juan Valdez, the mustached farmer with the trusty burro who peddles Colombian coffee in newspaper and television ads all over the world. Juan, a creation of a Colombian coffee growers' association, had been around since 1959. Coffee was just one example of an industry in which much of the world had a giant head start on us. In factories and the services industries, the gap was even bigger.

Catching up would prove very difficult, not just for Brazil but for many countries in Latin America. Next door in Argentina, where the transition from a closed to an open economy was particularly abrupt—and poorly managed—President Carlos Menem referred to the whole process as "surgery without anesthesia." In Brazil, we strove to make the transition significantly less traumatic, lest we lose the patient on the operating table. But there were some harsh realities about globalization that were inescapable. Competing in a global environment meant that the potential payoff for success was far greater than ever before. But it also meant that many companies would also fail, as would many people.

Essentially, we were asking Brazilians to make a leap of faith. If the country tolerated a certain amount of pain in the short term, the long-term benefits could be tremendous. This was difficult for many people to accept. I understood why. Brazilian governments had made similar promises in the past and then failed spectacularly. This left many Brazilians cynical, and they preferred to stick with an old economic system that, while restrictive and largely broken, was at least familiar. Many Brazilians simply distrusted capitalism. I am sure that my father, with his distaste for profit and financial markets, would have been skeptical of my reforms, had he still been alive. We were proposing much more than any one isolated reform—we were promoting a fundamental overhaul in the relationship between people and their government. It wasn't just the sheltered elite who had so much at stake; it was the whole country.

It was this resistance to change—from both special interests and society at large—that made us so vulnerable to the financial panic sweeping the world during the 1990s. If foreign investors saw that a country like Brazil was not doing enough to modernize its economy, they could turn their backs on us overnight. This was the dark side of globalization: If billions of dollars could flow into Brazil, they could also flow out. In order to attract investment, a country like ours had to allow capital to enter and exit with equal ease. The consequences of this could be dizzying. Money sloshed around the world like water in a fishbowl. If investors on Wall Street, in London's City, or elsewhere believed a country was vulnerable, an economy like ours could see the rug pulled out from under it with frightening speed.

We had already seen how devastating—and random—this panic could be. When the Mexican government had devalued the peso four years earlier, the Mexican economy collapsed—but that was not the end of the fallout. Foreign investors were burned by an emerging market for the first time in this heady new post–Cold War era. Many on Wall Street had rushed to invest in places like Mexico, eager to harness the high local interest rates, which were above anything that could be offered in the United States or any other developed economy. But these same investors had not fully realized that interest rates were high for a reason: Young democracies and recently opened economies could pose a great risk.

These investors responded to the Mexican crisis by pulling their money out of not just Mexico, but *all* emerging markets. Overnight, billions of dollars stampeded out of countries that had absolutely nothing to do with Mexico's troubles. Half a world away in Argentina, the banking system was nearly overwhelmed. We felt ripples from the crisis in Brazil as well, although the lingering euphoria over the real meant we were relatively insulated. Other countries were not so lucky. All across the world, money rushed out of bank deposits, risky currencies, and sovereign bonds. The pattern repeated itself several times during the 1990s, often without rhyme or reason. Once Wall Street decided a country was in trouble, there was little that could be done to save it; it became a kind of self-fulfilling prophecy. The emerging market crises of the era were due to foreign investors' immaturity just as much as the countries' own problems.

The seemingly random contagion from Mexico's troubles became known as the "Tequila Effect." This phenomenon recurred after Thailand's currency collapsed—the ensuing fallout was called the "Asian flu"—and again when Russia defaulted on its debt in August 1998.

Rather than glibly talking about vodka, however, much of the world had already moved on to worrying about the Samba Effect.

No matter how far I traveled from Brazil, there was no escaping the constant drumbeat of crisis. On a trip to Colombia, I visited a gorgeous colonial-era church with the president, Ernesto Samper. He was facing tremendous U.S. pressure to act in the so-called war on drugs, and after a long and weighty discussion, we took a much-needed break to tour the church. We were just approaching the altar when I received a phone call from Brasília.

It was Pedro Malan, my finance minister. To avoid causing a stir, I apologized to Samper and hid behind the altar to take the call. Malan told me that the real was under attack yet again. We deliberated whether I should return to Brasília immediately, but, as I peeked around the corner to see if any reporters were nearby, I whispered to Malan that I did not wish to create the impression that we were panicking.

I reemerged from the shadows and told Samper, somewhat unconvincingly, that everything was fine. Nevertheless, just a day later, I had to prematurely leave an Ibero-American summit in Venezuela to attend to the financial panic back home.

There was no denying that Brazil was vulnerable. Our budget deficit in 1998 climbed to a dangerous level equivalent to 7 percent of our gross domestic product; 3 percent was considered healthy. This was due largely to the lingering legacies of inflation, which had not been completely solved. The Real Plan had provided only a short-term fix to the fundamental problem: that the government still spent far more than it earned. The reforms that might have remedied the deficit were stuck in Congress, which was a microcosm of the broad resistance to change that characterized Brazil. So, in order to cover the deficit, we were forced to rely on a constant influx of foreign capital. To attract funds, we depended on high interest rates and a strong currency. We knew that if the flow of foreign money was cut off, the fundamental pillars of our economy—including the real—might collapse.

Rough-and-tumble politics further complicated our efforts. The Constitution of 1988 had limited future Brazilian presidents to just one term in office. Like the rest of the document, this clause had been written with two decades of military rule in mind; every step had been taken to prevent a future authoritarian ruler. While I had misgivings about modifying the constitution, I also understood the document's shortcomings. I decided that there would be no institutional harm in bringing Brazil's presidential system in line with that of the United States and many other countries. Polls showed that a clear majority of Brazilians wanted me to run again. Unfortunately, some legislators in Congress proved more difficult to convince. Although Congress eventually passed the reelection amendment by a healthy margin—80 percent of the Senate voted in favor—the fallout would resonate for a long time to come.

Soon after the amendment passed, I was accused of bribing congressmen to assure its passage. This was senseless; apart from the fact that I never engaged in corruption, Congress had approved the bill by such a wide margin that no bribes would have made a difference anyway. These allegations were soon compounded by the even more absurd "discovery" of documents underneath a highway underpass in São Paulo. The blatantly falsified papers purported to show the existence of a secret offshore bank account shared by myself and three top officials in my party—José Serra, the health minister; Mário Covas, the governor of São Paulo; and Sergio Motta, the communications minister. The men responsible for the forgery were later jailed. I was occasionally held hostage by my own policies regarding corruption investigations. I refused to interfere with action by the courts—even when their targets were people close to me. Many Brazilians believed that I needed to take justice into my own hands and decide who was guilty or not. I usually retorted that that would have been autocracy, not democracy. There *were* corrupt politicians in Brazil. But I knew that the only proper way to deal with them was to build regulatory and judicial institutions and then let these institutions operate freely. This conviction, which I believed was key to building democracy in Brazil, also meant that even the most baseless accusations sometimes caused a huge stir.

Many Brazilians assumed that where there was smoke, there was fire. Some foreign investors, who by that point were monitoring our every move under a microscope, fell victim to the same belief. They were all too willing to see yet another corrupt Latin American leader. As a result, these frivolous and baseless accusations pushed us further toward the brink.

The election itself became nearly an afterthought. A majority of Brazilians supported the progress we had made so far and trusted me to handle the problems to come. They voted overwhelmingly in favor of continuing down the path we were on. On October 3, 1998, I was elected to another four years in office with 53 percent of the vote, good enough to avoid a runoff. Lula took 32 percent.

The anticlimactic nature of the vote, and the task that awaited us, were clear in the next morning's newspapers. *O Globo* proclaimed, "Re-election with record amount of votes gives Fernando Henrique strength to face the crisis." *O Estado de São Paulo* almost skipped mention of the vote altogether, noting, "FHC, reelected, prepares to defend the real." There was little appetite in Brazil for analyzing the positive aspects of my government so far, a task undertaken by the British weekly *The Economist*: "Mr. Cardoso has at times been accused of not moving fast enough. He can well ask why. In just under four years he has done roughly what Britain's Margaret Thatcher—no famous ditherer—did in nearly 12." After citing a long list of the problems that confronted us, the magazine concluded, "In an ideal world, Mr. Cardoso would have ended all these evils at the stroke of a wand; in the real one, he has laid the bases of a richer and so, in time, a better society."

Maybe so, but it was little consolation at the time.

In the aftermath of the election, Lula was livid. Upon learning that I had defeated him by such a wide margin, he stormed out of his apartment and confronted the TV cameras outside. "Fernando Henrique Cardoso is the executioner of the Brazilian economy, responsible for one of the greatest economic disasters in the history of Brazil," he declared. "I find it almost incomprehensible that the victims voted for their own executioner."

We had not spoken face to face in nearly five years. Our personal relationship, which had been so close when we were fighting together for democracy in the 1970s and 1980s, was now deeply strained. I had tried to contact him on numerous occasions, but his party ridiculed my requests. Now he had lost to me twice and been defeated in three consecutive presidential elections. Lula had spent the previous decade as Brazil's leading opposition figure, loudly criticizing anything and everything—at a time when Brazilians clearly valued a constructive leader. He had called for impeachment on God knows what grounds and said I was destroying Brazil. None of it had worked.

I could never admit it at the time, but I often felt particularly stung by Lula's criticism. It wasn't the substance of his attacks that bothered me; I knew that Lula had no viable alternative to the policies that I promoted. I was confident in my policy choices. Rather, Lula represented in my mind a segment of the Brazilian population that I had thus far been unable to win over. Years before, I had shared some of their beliefs; why hadn't they come to the same realizations that I had? Sometimes I worried that their opposition was due to my own inability to win them over on a philosophical or intellectual level. I also knew that Lula was a symbol; if he could ever be convinced of the merits of a modern, capitalist system, then I would truly have won the broader ideological battle. But in the meantime, it frustrated me that he, like much of Brazil, clung so passionately to the past.

Now, Lula seemed fatigued, vaguely aware that he needed to change, but unsure how to do it. Though he had long been regarded as an inevitable part of Brazil's destiny, it now seemed that he might just fade away into history. He had to either reinvent himself or disappear.

About two months after the election, with the financial crisis raging, I received a very strange message. A visiting businessman passed along word that Lula wanted to have a meeting, and he gave me a telephone number to call. I was intrigued. Why didn't Lula come to me directly? He certainly knew where I lived . . .

I assumed he wanted to be discreet about our communication. So I waited until late one night and called the number myself, from my private residence in the presidential palace. But Lula is a man who is never at home, and I failed to reach him for several nights in a row. Finally, just as I was about to give up, I managed to contact him.

"It would be a good idea for us to meet," Lula said, sounding subdued.

I agreed, of course. We decided to keep our meeting secret to avoid a media frenzy. We arranged for him to come with the governor of Brasília, Cristovam Buarque, who was from Lula's party but also a relative moderate, and an old friend of mine. It took several weeks before finally, one night, the two of them showed up. Guards escorted Lula and Cristovam into the library, and I gave Lula a big hug when I saw him.

Lula said he had never been to the presidential palace before.

"Maybe one day you'll be living here," I said with a grin.

Lula smiled politely, lowered his eyes, and nodded.

I gave him and Cristovam a brief tour. We walked around the main floor of the palace, chatting amiably, and then went upstairs to my personal living quarters. I poured us all some scotch and we sat down to talk. Politics was notably, almost uncomfortably, absent from the conversation. Instead, we spoke of how Lula and his family had once used my beach house for a vacation back in the 1980s. My family adores the house, which is very isolated and rustic, but Lula's family was very uncomfortable there because of the lack of amenities. We laughed about that for a while, bantering back and forth.

At one point, Lula got up to go to the restroom. When he left, Cristovam looked at me, bewildered. "When was your last face-to-face talk with Lula?" he asked.

"Many years ago," I answered.

Cristovam sighed. "It seems like it was yesterday."

When Lula returned, we got down to more serious business. "Lula," I said, "I think it's important that we stay in touch. Brazil is in a very difficult situation."

"Yes, it's very difficult," Lula said, slowly. "It's very bad. I think we are heading toward a tremendous crisis."

He said this with a certain glee. It was subdued, but I could see the romantic glint in his eyes as he said the word "crisis." Something about it made me furious, and I recalled all the frustration of the past four years. I leaned forward in my chair and stared at him.

"Lula, you're not taking into account the fact that my government will act," I said sternly. "We will try to control the situation. We will do everything we can. You can count on that.

"But," I continued, "let's imagine, just for a moment, that we fail, and a tremendous crisis occurs. Then, what will happen? In your past, you were never a socialist. But Cristovam was a socialist," I said, nodding at the governor, "and so was I. We were taught, years ago, to expect there would be a tremendous crisis, the uprising of a new society, a new political system, and the working class taking power. That is what I sense you are expecting. Still.

"All that is gone, Lula. The Berlin Wall is gone. So is the Soviet

Union. There is no historical alternative now. So if there is a crisis in Brazil, after that there will only be disaster. The crisis will be pure misery. You still have intellectuals in your party who think otherwise, but they're guiding you down a disastrous path. If you're expecting a true crisis to solve the problems of Brazil, you're wrong, Lula. A crisis would destroy both you and me."

Lula protested, saying I was not willing to listen to his ideas, and he only wanted what was best for Brazil. We argued a little while longer, and then the late hour led us our separate ways.

My hope was that our conversation that night would produce a change in Lula, that he would abandon his devisive rhetoric in favor of language that would be more broadly appealing to the whole country—and would bring him success at the polls. But initially nothing seemed to have changed.

A few months later, word of our meeting finally leaked. When Lula was confronted about the nature of our conversation, he simply shook his head and declared, "It's senseless to speak to Fernando Henrique!"

Around that time, I was speaking regularly with President Clinton by telephone. During one of our conversations, Clinton complained to me that the Republican Party was conspiring against him, desperate to sabotage his presidency at any cost. I replied that, in Brazil, my problem was not so much an organized opposition as a disorganized group of supporters.

Clinton's support had been instrumental in convincing the International Monetary Fund to grant Brazil a $40 billion aid package shortly after the election. The money, which would be made available in stages, was an attempt to give us a "cushion" so we could continue to finance ourselves despite the panicked world markets. The package was granted over the objections of some officials in the IMF who were never happy enough with our efforts to cut spending. The irony of my being so widely labeled a neoliberal in Brazil was that my reform agenda often did not move fast enough to please the IMF or the World Bank. I found myself explaining on numerous occasions that I was not a dictator; that there was a democratic process in Brazil that had to be respected; and that if our Congress refused to pass austerity measures, then my hands were largely tied.

The IMF's confusion was understandable, to a certain extent. On paper, the coalition of parties that formed my government enjoyed a comfortable majority in Congress. But therein resided the paradox about which I told Clinton: The parties were so undisciplined, and the pressures on them so intense, that the line between opposition and pro-government politicians was often blurred or nonexistent. So when the IMF conditioned its aid package on future spending cuts totaling billions of dollars that needed to be approved by Congress, it marked a tremendous challenge. If Congress refused, then the loans would be off the table. Therefore, although the aid package had the potential to see us through the crisis, it was also a gamble; the stakes had been raised so high that if we failed, we would fall even harder than before.

The beginning of the end came on December 2, when the lower house rejected a bill that would have saved us nearly $5 billion by raising the pension contributions of government workers with high salaries. By a vote of 205 to 187, Congress essentially torpedoed our deal with the IMF. The privileges of a few Brazilians had yet again triumphed over the greater good. The dissenting voters included members of Lula's party and also members of my coalition. It was an instant tragedy. The next day, the stock market in São Paulo plummeted almost 10 percent. The vote was read, correctly, as a sign that Brazil was not willing to swallow the tough medicine of fiscal austerity. Even the New York Stock Exchange fell by more than 2 percent over renewed concern that Brazil could implode and bring the world economy down with it.

From that point on, we were never able to convince anyone on Wall Street that Brazil was seriously committed to fixing its problems. No amount of foreign reserves, IMF cash, statements of support from wealthy countries—nothing else—would stem the panic. To make matters worse, some disgruntled IMF officials, believing we had gone over their heads to negotiate the aid package, began whispering to the market that Brazil was on the verge of collapse.

Each of the crises that swept the world during the 1990s took a different shape. Even though the fundamental causes were often the same, the symptoms varied from one patient to another. In some countries, such as Russia, the meltdown took the form of a debt default. In Brazil, it had been clear for years that, if we were to fall, it would be because of a currency crisis, a devaluation of the real.

We had resisted devaluing the real for years, despite intense pressure. There was no question that the currency had become overvalued with time, as the central bank acted to maintain its value within a narrow price band against the U.S. dollar. In retrospect, I realize that it would have been best to implement a controlled devaluation of the currency during a period of relative calm; the problem was that, with the constant onslaught of crises abroad, calmness was in short supply. Panic always seemed to be in the air, even when Brazil was doing everything right. Under the circumstances of late 1998, my economic team and I feared that, if the real was suddenly allowed to trade at its actual market value—to become a "floating currency," in economic parlance—the transition would be so abrupt and violent that many Brazilians would panic. They would lose faith in the real, and that old Brazilian bogeyman—inflation—would return with a vengeance. So, before devaluing the currency, we kept waiting for a semblance of calm to return. It never did.

After Congress failed to approve the pension reform, many people believed that it was just a matter of time until the real suffered a messy collapse. If we didn't act, the market would do it for us. Since August, the central bank had spent $30 billion of its currency reserves to prop up the currency's value as investors, local and foreign, bought U.S. dollars to protect themselves from what they believed was inevitable. More than $50 billion, in total, had left the country. This pace could not continue, even with the IMF aid. We had become a juicy target for speculators, and we had lost the confidence of most Brazilians at home.

I didn't find it amusing at the time, but I suppose there was some irony in the fact that the last straw for the real was an act of sabotage by one of its founding fathers. Itamar Franco, the former president who had appointed me finance minister in 1993, had returned to politics as the newly elected governor of Minas Gerais state. Itamar had always been unpredictable; now that he didn't have to worry about the whole nation's fate anymore, he was even more so. On the night of January 4, 1999, Itamar went on national television and announced the unthinkable: Minas Gerais was bankrupt and therefore was defaulting on the $13.5 billion state debt it owed the federal government.

"If I borrow 100 reais from a pawn broker, I am in debt to the pawn broker," Itamar explained. "But if my child gets sick, I will give the 100 reais to my child and say to the pawn broker, 'I don't have your money now, sir, so you will have to wait a bit.'"

The analogy was absurd, of course. We had just negotiated an overly generous deal for states to finance themselves at rates up to 10 percentage points below the federal government rate. The problem was the same old lack of discipline that had carried over from the era of inflation in Brazil. For decades, state debts had been financed by printing money—now, with that option closed, states had not subjected themselves to the same rigorous (if insufficient) budget controls as the federal government. Itamar, of all people, should have understood that. By 1999, a stunning 77 percent of the state budget in Minas Gerais was being used just to pay the salaries of government workers. It was the same ugly, entrenched interests rearing their heads again.

Sadly, Itamar wasn't alone. His actions emboldened other governors to join him in revolt, tantalized by the possibility of whitewashing their own fiscal mismanagement and blaming it on me. Following his example, six opposition governors issued a joint press release denouncing my "cruel and unjust" economic policies and demanding a renegotiation of their debts. "If I have to choose between paying wages or paying the state debt, I'll pay wages!" exclaimed Anthony Garotinho, the governor of Rio de Janeiro. "We don't want crumbs!" said Olívio Dutra, the leader of Rio Grande do Sul state. In Minas Gerais, the state's secretary of finance got into the act: "Minas Gerais has nothing left," he moaned, "except maybe this palace."

Never one to be upstaged, Itamar didn't stop there. He surrounded his palace with special elite troops from the Minas Gerais military police. Itamar dressed them up in combat uniforms and even made them wear masks, saying he was going to "defend Minas" from an imminent federal attack. It was as if he had traveled in time back to the era of the nineteenth-century regional revolts in Brazil.

As could be expected, world financial markets went absolutely crazy. Money started leaving Brazil at the pace of about $1 billion a day. Fears that the federal government would have to pick up the tab for Minas Gerais, and thus shatter our own dubious finances, resulted in a huge worldwide sell-off of Brazilian bonds and currency. Lost in the shuffle was the fact that it was technically impossible for a state to declare default; the federal government could just withhold tax transfers and the balance would be even. By that point, however, the panic was so intense that no one would listen to reason.

Through the whole crisis, Itamar was gloriously unrepentant. "I'm really worried," he said mockingly, "about my shares in Tokyo, Hong Kong, and New York."

On January 13, 1999, we declared that we would expand the narrow band in which the real had been trading—effectively allowing it to devalue. That day, the real lost 8 percent of its value, more than it had depreciated in all of 1998. The stock market plummeted 10 percent, and nearly $2 billion left the country. Brazilian bond prices fell so sharply that trade was suspended all over the world. On January 15, we abandoned the trading band altogether.

The real, the biggest symbol of my government and the anchor of our economy, was left to fend for itself. All of Brazil held its breath.

Depression followed, but not the kind most people had expected.

Things looked bleak at the start. Between mid-January and the beginning of March, the real lost nearly two-thirds of its value. Economists darkly predicted that the Brazilian economy would spiral into recession, and that GDP would contract as much as 6 percent. Inflation would reach 90 percent, they forecast. But, to the surprise of nearly everyone, both the currency and the economy quickly bounced back. Our GDP actually ended up *expanding* in 1999, albeit a meager 0.81 percent. Our biggest fear—that massive inflation would return to haunt Brazil—also failed to materialize. Prices rose just 8.9 percent in 1999; not great, but not a catastrophe either.

At the beginning of April, I received a phone call from the IMF's number two official, Stanley Fischer, who said, "Congratulations, Mister President. You won. Inflation is coming down, and the economy will recover soon."

I'm not sure that we really "won"—the crisis wrecked many lives, at least in the short term. But we could take some solace in the fact that the reforms we made, the ones that were not blocked by Congress, had helped to save us from a much greater disaster. Local industries had become more efficient by adopting modern infrastructure, thanks to the strong currency and lower tariffs. Greater inflation had been avoided in part because the Real Plan had removed indexation from the economy. We also approved new measures to see us through the crisis, such as tax breaks for companies that created new jobs.

The most lasting legacy of the crisis was not nearly as easily measured as inflation. But it was perhaps just as damaging. All across the country, there was a sinking sensation that Brazil had done everything right in recent years and still had little but crisis to show for it. This feeling was wrong on both counts—we hadn't made all the reforms we needed, and there had indeed been some substantial progress. But that was hollow consolation, and people didn't want to hear it. Even in 2000, a visiting foreign journalist wrote of a "strangely stubborn mood of depression" that continued to haunt Brazil.

I sometimes felt the same way. There were only two years during my government that Brazil did not experience some kind of financial crisis. Part of me hated having to deal with such matters; I would have preferred to inherit a stable economy at a time of global tranquillity. But that was precisely the point—I had inherited neither of those. The transformation that Brazil experienced during my presidency was absolutely necessary to the long-term well-being of the country. Many of the bumps along the road were the inevitable products of a rapidly changing and still immature global economy. Some of it was Congress's fault, and the rest of it was my own.

Still, it could have been a lot worse. Argentina had been going down much the same road to modernization as Brazil, and with a great deal more fanfare. It had embraced the policy prescriptions of the IMF with much more zeal than we ever did, and it was often touted as the world's star pupil of free-market reforms. Like Brazil, Argentina entered a recession in 1998 following the Russian debt default—but then did not recover for four full years. During that period, Argentina's economy shrank by a fifth, unemployment soared to nearly 30 percent, and people saw their life savings confiscated by the government. About 6 million Argentines were plunged into poverty, and the country has still not fully recovered to this day. Other crises, while not as dire, also shook Venezuela, Paraguay, and Uruguay in the years ahead.

Despite all the crises, home-bred and otherwise, Brazil's economy averaged 2.7 percent GDP growth per year while I was president. That may not have been spectacular. But, if nothing else, it was stable. In a way, that was remarkable enough.

THE LAND OF THE FUTURE

DURING A VISIT to Brazil, Pope John Paul II delivered a marvelous sermon on the plight of our country's indigenous people. I greeted him at Rio's airport, and thousands of flag-waving Brazilians listened as the pope spoke passionately of the need to set aside land for the Indians "so they might live their culture in dignity."

The next day, the pope granted me a private audience at the old presidential palace in Rio. We sat together side by side, surrounded by my family. He looked down at me with his kind, serene smile. I remember he trembled a little bit, even back then. I told him, "Your Holiness, that was a wonderful sermon. The problems of the indigenous in Brazil are deeply rooted in our society and we are doing everything possible to change that.

"But," I added, inching closer to him, "as pertinent to our history is the legacy of slavery and the struggle of the blacks."

I held out my arm and placed it next to his. The contrast in color between his skin and mine was evident.

"As you can see, almost all of us in Brazil have a bit of African or Indian blood in us. But this hasn't stopped us from being discriminatory. Discrimination against blacks, both social and economic, is one of the biggest problems we face."

As president, I was in a unique position to address the injustices of Brazilian history, among them the struggles that had impassioned me since my youth. Ever since I was an assistant professor, few issues had captured my imagination quite like the plight of the blacks in Brazil.

Poverty has a different face in each country. On the streets of Moscow, one can see how the legacy of Communist rule and the breakup of the Soviet Union have shaped the lives of the poor. In India, the lingering effects of the caste system are quite clear. In Brazil, meanwhile, there can be no doubt about how, even to this day, the nature of poverty has been defined by slavery.

There is a peculiar isolation to poverty in Brazil. The concept of the favela itself suggests a stark divide—between rich and poor, between black and white, between those who have a stake in society and those who do not. Many people in large Brazilian cities are homeless, sleeping beneath underpasses or in plazas; in some other parts of Latin America, even in countries that are poorer than Brazil, the unfortunate at least have a place to sleep. When I walk the streets of São Paulo, I see the legacy of a centuries-old problem that was never quite resolved. Brazilian society never did quite enough to integrate the people it had once subjugated, or their descendants, into society.

By the time I became president, most Brazilians had at least stopped propagating the old myth of racial democracy. But the country remained largely unaware of the sheer magnitude of the divide between blacks and whites. My government conducted a survey on race in 1999 that shocked even me. Though they made up 45 percent of the total population, blacks constituted 64 percent of people below the poverty line. A twenty-five-year-old white Brazilian had an average of 8.4 years of schooling, while a black Brazilian of the same age had just 6.1 years. Illiteracy among whites over fifteen years of age was 8 percent; it was 20 percent among blacks.

Meanwhile, blacks were still hardly ever seen among the country's political, economic, and media elite. In newspaper classified ads for jobs, the phrase *boa aparência*, or "good appearance," was known to mean that black people need not apply. In 2003, only 9 of the 513 deputies in Congress identified themselves as black. When I became president, people of color were perhaps most notably absent from the foreign ministry. Only one black Brazilian had headed a diplomatic mission abroad—that was in Ghana, and the man was a journalist rather than a career diplomat. We continued to present Brazil abroad as a white country; it isn't, and it never was.

No amount of apologizing or policy hocus-pocus was going to completely atone for past sins. But I realized quite early that a system broadly similar to affirmative action programs in the United States could be effective in Brazil. The decision to pursue such a system came quite late in my administration; I wasn't sure, for a long time, that the political support for one existed. The mere idea of racial quotas had long been scandalous in Brazil, in part because of society's refusal to accept the existence of the problem. By 2001, however, that was changing. A study on racism in Brazil was commissioned prior to the World Conference on Racism to be held in Durban in September of that year. A subsequent study suggested that quotas would not violate the Brazilian constitution. At that point, we decided to go ahead with an eclectic mix of affirmative action policies.

There were a few problems with implementation that were unique to Brazil, chiefly: How could we define who was black? There had been so much mixing of the races over the years that racial identity was often extremely subjective. So we decided to address the issue in that spirit: We allowed people to declare their race. If someone said they were black, then so they would be in the eyes of the government.

Government agencies at all levels began announcing a wide variety of affirmative action policies. The agriculture ministry, for example, launched a program establishing a 20 percent quota for black employees and in firms seeking official contracts. The justice ministry established a similar quota for blacks (20 percent), women (20 percent), and handicapped people (5 percent). The general principle was also established that, in government, if there were two people with equal qualifications to name to a post, one being black, we would choose the black person.

We tried to design a system that was more effective and creative than mere quotas. For example, with regard to the foreign ministry, we decided to offer twenty fellowships for blacks to enter a training program for the diplomatic corps, and those who were successful would have an opportunity to become foreign service officers. In doing so, we were trying to avoid the problem sometimes seen in U.S. universities that use a pure quota system: Black students end up gaining admission, but then can't finish school because they were not adequately prepared. Other institutions were also given the freedom to address the fundamental problem as they saw fit. My old alma mater, the University of São Paulo, refused to accept a quota system. However, it did create 5,000 spots for courses for poorer students to prepare them for the university.

I thought this was an adequate solution. Black in Brazil had equaled poor for too long. I hoped that these policies, along with others more generally aimed at poverty, would one day make that connection pass into history.

In 1995, I apologized on behalf of the Brazilian government for the atrocities committed during the 1964–1985 military dictatorship. Compensation was granted to the families of the dead as well as to the victims who had survived. While the gesture could never have completely atoned for the campaign of state terror, it was long overdue and widely welcomed by society as a way to further heal wounds from a divisive era.

It was a deeply emotional topic for me, and brought all the memories of my exile, and the fight for democracy, rushing back to my head. One woman asked me to write a letter certifying that her late husband had given Portuguese classes to my children in Chile, so that she could receive the compensation. The wife of Rubens Paiva, my friend who was killed by the regime, came to my office. There is a beautiful but sad photo of my military chief of staff embracing her.

The wounds from that era may never fully heal. But much has changed. The military is now a responsible and modern contributor to society, respectful of our democracy. Society would never tolerate another dictatorship. Brazil has learned from its mistakes. That is the best possible legacy from that awful era.

Of all the misguided quests that Brazil had undertaken over the years, few rivaled our efforts to attain our dream of world prominence.

"We are doomed to greatness," Juscelino Kubitschek famously proclaimed during the high-flying 1950s. Getúlio Vargas said, "We are marching toward a future different from all we know." As Fernando Collor's government reportedly embezzled millions, he boldly predicted that Brazil would "soon join the First World." I suppose it should not be a surprise that the most outrageous comments on this well-worn topic came from Jânio Quadros. "This is the land of Canaan, unlimited and fecund," Jânio once declared, adding, "In five years, Brazil will be a great power." That was in 1961.

It was good to dream big. I always felt that Brazil's thirst for greatness reflected a deep-seated belief in progress that, if harnessed, could be a tremendously positive modernizing force. But a history of awful follow-through meant that, in retrospect, such declarations always ended up looking rather brash.

Instead of adding myself to this pantheon of big talkers, I decided to quietly put together policies that would change the way the world saw us. Brazil was so much more than the land of soccer, coffee, and the Girl from Ipanema. Most governments knew this, but they were not always acquainted with the new Brazil: a rapidly maturing democracy, an expanding if somewhat volatile economy, and a growing force in international trade. Of course, the best way to change antiquated perceptions was for us to take care of business at home. But our domestic efforts could be complemented by a responsible, active foreign policy.

Brazil's foreign service is highly professionalized and of world-class quality, so much of this work was done via formal diplomatic channels. But I also believed that it was perhaps just as important to cultivate good personal relationships with prominent world leaders from both rich and poor nations. It was truly amazing how many foreign policy issues could be resolved over a cup of coffee.

During my presidency, the United States consolidated itself as the world's only superpower. So, it was quite logical that much of our foreign policy would focus on our U.S. relations. And that was how I had the great pleasure of getting to know Bill Clinton.

I felt a connection with Clinton from the first moment I spoke with him. We met in Miami in December 1994, when I was still president-elect. It was a gathering of heads of state from the Americas, and we all took a scenic boat cruise off the coast of downtown Miami one night. Clinton bounded happily around the deck, eager to speak with everyone, as is his custom. But there was a rather significant language barrier; several of the leaders present knew only rudimentary English. I was one of just a few people capable of holding a real conversation with him, even though I am not completely fluent myself. That night, we spent a long while leaning over the railing of the boat, looking at the skyline and chatting very informally about Brazil and foreign affairs. Ever since then, Clinton has always called me just "Henrique"—I suppose it is easier for him to pronounce than my full name.

Our next meeting was much more formal—at least at first. Soon after becoming president, I made a state visit to Washington. These are different from a regular foreign visit—they have a special protocol and involve a tremendous amount of decorum: National anthems are played, flags are displayed, and gifts are exchanged. Some of the events can be rather dull, and they usually drag on for hours.

When all the formalities finally ended, our aides streamed out, and it was just Clinton and I sitting there in his office in the White House. He folded his hands, leaned across the table, and said, "After all that, you probably need to use the restroom, don't you?"

After accepting his offer, I returned and we got down to business. "What can I do for you and Brazil?" he asked with a smile.

An elegantly simple question, and a difficult one to answer. Brazil's relationship with the United States had always been characterized by extreme highs and lows. During the previous half-century, the United States had too often treated Brazil as just another anonymous pawn in the global power game of the Cold War. When Ronald Reagan visited our capital in the 1980s and declared "I'm very happy to be in Bolivia," it seemed to confirm all of our worst fears. Nothing stung Brazilian sensibilities more than not being properly recognized by the bigger and much richer continental giant in the hemisphere.

Brazil had certainly committed its own sins in the relationship. Up until the 1980s, and especially during the military regime, Brazil had viewed the world in general as a threat rather than an opportunity. This was a reflection of our country's fortress mentality during troubled times. The government erected barriers to trade and foreign investment, building a kind of wall around the country. Much of the suspicion was directed at the United States, which, to be fair, had done its share of unwanted meddling in our politics. Washington's enthusiastic support for the coup of 1964 had left a bad taste in the mouths of an entire generation of democratic leaders. The end result was a dysfunctional relationship between two countries that should have been friends—that wanted to be friends, by all accounts, but couldn't figure out how to begin.

I explained this to Clinton and expressed my desire to break with the past and explore a new relationship with the United States. I told him that Brazil would continue to defend its interests, but that we needed to get over our mutual history of petty sniping and move on to something more substantial that befitted the United States' new role as the only world superpower and our post–Cold War role as a major emerging market.

Clinton enthusiastically agreed. "I will do everything I can," he promised, "to help Brazil achieve its great hope."

In coming years, he kept his word. He made numerous visits to Brazil, one as president and others after he left the White House, and helped boost our profile on the world stage. Ruth and I were once invited to spend a weekend at Camp David, which is unusual for a Brazilian leader. Clinton was instrumental in marshaling approval for the multilateral aid packages that underpinned our economy during difficult moments. He was unfailingly perceptive of my needs during key moments; for example, during my 1998 reelection campaign, he asked me if his endorsement would help me or hurt me. I told him it would certainly help me, but I appreciated the sensitivity of the question. His eye for detail, his passion for policy, and his extraordinary personal skills made Clinton, without a doubt, the most impressive all-around politician I have ever met.

Clinton and I had our share of disagreements at the policy level, of course. Trade was a particularly contentious issue. Clinton also urged us to become involved in the situation in Colombia; I said that violated our principles of national self-determination, and politely declined. We also did not always see eye to eye on the subject of Cuba. Brazil's production of generic AIDS drugs was a sticking point. Unlike in the past, however, these differences were handled with a tremendous amount of respect.

It often seemed like Clinton could deal with a thousand issues at once, even when he was under siege personally. On one of his trips to Brasília, Clinton and I had a one-on-one conversation in which I told him about the importance of Mercosul, the trading bloc that we had worked so hard to build with Argentina, Paraguay, and Uruguay. His secretary of state, Madeleine Albright, had recently criticized us publicly, saying that Brazil should focus more on the Free Trade Area of the Americas pact, or FTAA. I told Clinton that we needed to make progress first on integrating the Mercosul before we could be ready politically for any other trade deals.

Clinton listened to all this with great interest. "Do you think that if I make a statement to that effect in the press conference, it would help you?"

"Of course," I said.

We walked out together into the gardens of the presidential palace, where hundreds of journalists, many of them from the United States, awaited us. Rarely had the world's media ever been so focused on Brazil; it was a tremendous opportunity for us. Clinton didn't let the moment pass by: He unambiguously stated that the Mercosul and the FTAA were not incompatible, and that the former would eventually lead to the latter. I was stunned, and immensely grateful.

At that same press conference, most of the questions focused on Clinton's mounting legal troubles back in Washington. As we walked back into the palace library, where Ruth and Hillary were waiting, Clinton smiled and said, "You know, those journalists, they have good relations with me. It's not their fault. They're just doing their job."

Clinton kept visiting Brazil long after he left the presidency. On one such trip in June 2005, I organized a dinner for him. At the request of José Serra, mayor of São Paulo since January of that year, I invited an official who was in charge of disabled persons' affairs for the city. This woman suffered from total paralysis as the result of an accident, and she wanted to talk to Clinton about stem-cell research. I introduced them, and they spoke about the issue for no less than twenty minutes. He knelt by her wheelchair and listened to everything she said, then responded with a sterling command of every detail. He has a way of making whomever he speaks with feel like he or she is the only person in the entire universe. I remember being absolutely astounded.

My friendship with Clinton has blossomed further since we both left office. Ruth and Hillary enjoy a warm relationship, not surprising given their similar personalities and interests. We continue to see each other quite often, and we have collaborated on numerous projects, such as his global initiative to alleviate poverty, the first meeting of which I attended in New York in September 2005.

I have had much less contact with George W. Bush. Our governments only overlapped for two years.

After September 11, 2001, Bush seemed to care very little about Brazil. Brazil immediately asked for a meeting of the Organization of the American States to condemn the attacks on Washington and New York City. We declared that an attack on one member country was the same as an attack on all of us. We did this to express our immediate support for the United States. After that meeting, I met with Bush and a small group of officials, including Condoleezza Rice, who was then his national security adviser.

Bush had recently been to a mosque in Washington to show his support for the Islamic community. I congratulated him for the gesture.

"We can't confuse religion with terrorism," I commented. "Our world is a world of diversity. In Brazil, we have 10 million Arabs, and they are overwhelmingly peaceful."

Bush nodded. "It sounds like you've got a real diverse country down there."

"Oh, yes," I said. "We are truly a melting pot." I told him about all the immigration Brazil had from Italy, Germany, Ukraine, Japan, and so on. "We also have one of the world's largest populations of blacks, you know."

"Do you have blacks in Brazil?" Bush asked.

At that point, Rice chimed in. "Of course, Mister President," she said, and we quickly changed the subject to other matters.

It didn't bother me that Bush knew so little about Brazil. Instead, what shocked me was that all he wanted to discuss was energy in Venezuela, and especially who was friends with the Venezuelan government and who was not. I found it disappointing that a man who had campaigned so heavily in 2000 on improving regional ties—"Those who ignore Latin America do not fully understand America itself," he had said—ended up being interested in basically one aspect: energy. I understand that American foreign policy focus changed forever after 9/11, but that didn't give America carte blanche to turn his back on the rest of the world. I have always said, only half-jokingly, that all people on earth should get to cast a vote for the U.S. president, because he ultimately affects all our lives so much.

In April 2001, a U.S. spy plane made an emergency landing in China. The plane had collided with a Chinese fighter while gathering intelligence off the mainland, and the twenty-four-member U.S. crew was detained by the Chinese when they landed. The incident resulted in a diplomatic standoff at a time when relations between the two countries were already tense. Beijing demanded an apology, while Washington wanted the return of the plane and the liberation of the crew.

By coincidence, Chinese President Jiang Zemin was scheduled to make a trip to Brasília in the very midst of the confrontation. The night before Jiang's arrival, Bush telephoned me. "Could you please put in a good word for him to release our troops?" Bush asked. I promised him that I would try my best.

The next day, I briefly ended up alone in my office with Jiang. I had always had a warm relationship with the Chinese president, whom I found to be a very educated, sophisticated man. Jiang spoke fluent English, and we usually conversed in that language. "You know," I told him, "President Bush wanted me to ask you for the return of those troops."

"I see." Jiang leaned back in his chair and folded his hands in thought. "Do you know how many times Bush has telephoned me regarding this incident?"

"Several times, I imagine."

Jiang smiled and held up a solitary finger. "Only once!" He laughed. "Do you remember when the Chinese embassy was bombed in Yugoslavia? Well, President Clinton tried to telephone me five or six times. Only *then*, we spoke. So why should I answer Bush on the first call?

"It's bizarre," Jiang continued. "How old is the United States? Two hundred years old. Well, China is five thousand years old, and they must learn to respect us! I will release these American troops, but it will take some time. I will make them work for it. This new president needs to learn how the world works. Bush senior was in China for a long time, and he was a gentleman. This Bush junior is a young man, unaccomplished. It is difficult for us to deal with him."

Eventually, the United States backed down and gave China what it wanted: a letter saying it was "very sorry" for entering Chinese airspace. The U.S. troops were released after eleven days in captivity, and the confrontation died down.

I later told Bush about what Jiang had said. Bush still didn't seem to understand the cultural significance of the incident. Under the current administration, the U.S. policy toward Latin America has become what E. Bradford Burns once characterized as "benign neglect." We are not high on Washington's priority list, though this has in one sense been positive—we are free to pursue our own destiny. On the other hand, it would be far better for all parties if the United States was more actively engaged. There is much work to be done on matters such as trade. I worry that, if Washington continues to focus too much on security—building new barriers instead of tearing them down like we did in the 1990s—then many of the gains that have been made will be lost. If there is any lesson to be drawn from the history of the last decade, indeed the last century, it is that exclusion from the world only causes more problems.

There was, of course, a vast world beyond Washington. My presidency occurred during a crucial moment in history when countries were organizing themselves into new alliances following the end of the

Cold War. Brazil needed to actively participate in this process. However, we had to be selective; we only had a limited amount of time and energy. So I decided to focus on places that could offer the best opportunities for investment and trade.

This was sometimes wrongly seen at home as a diplomacy of the "First World." I was inevitably accused of pretending that Brazil was a rich country. But I had a responsibility to make a practical decision. Roughly a quarter of our exports went to the United States, a quarter to Europe, and another quarter to Latin America, with the rest divided up among other countries. My foreign travels needed to reflect that economic reality. Of course, I spent a great deal of time visiting our neighbors. I also visited places as diverse as India, South Africa, China, Russia, Japan, Indonesia, and Malaysia. I knew that I had a unique opportunity to raise Brazil's profile across the world, and I spent much of my time as a traveling salesman, peddling our country as a kind of brand. Everywhere, I found that the personal connections I made were just as important as the official ones.

I made several trips to Britain. When I was still foreign minister, I once met Princess Diana. She had visited Brazil before and was friends with our ambassador in London. I found her very poised and possessed of a vibrant sense of humor. "My impression is that the Brazilian men are vain," she told me with a sly smile. "It seems they are always rearranging their hair!" This was perhaps a bold thing to say to a country's foreign minister, but it made me laugh, especially given my own reputation for vanity back home. I was very saddened when she passed away.

As president, I made an unforgettable state visit to London, where I stayed at Buckingham Palace for a few nights. Queen Elizabeth and Prince Philip received Ruth and me at Victoria Station. Then, the four of us rode together to the palace in a gilded carriage through the streets of London—a surreal experience. When we arrived, the queen herself gave us an exhaustive tour of our private apartment. She even showed us how to open and close the drawers where we were meant to store our clothes. She was impeccably polite and personable, and Ruth and I were bewildered that the queen of Britain would take the time to show us such trivial things!

My favorite royal was the Queen Mother, who was already ninety-five years old but blessed with more energy and lucidity than Ruth and I combined. There was to be a formal banquet during our visit, and protocol dictated that we pay her a visit beforehand. So we entered the Queen Mother's palace, where she was all alone in an elegant drawing room, pouring tea for the three of us.

I had brought her a present: a sculpture of a Brazilian bird made of silver and precious stones. She opened it and giggled with childlike delight. "What kind of bird is it?" she asked, her eyes twinkling.

Her unexpected question stumped me. I have never been able to remember the names of birds. So I panicked. The only species of Brazilian bird I could think of was the jaburú, which I knew only because it was the name of a palace in Brasília. There seemed to be a passing resemblance, so . . .

"It is a jaburú," I told her, rather unconvincingly.

The Queen Mother squealed with happiness. "A jaburú!" she declared, relishing the pronunciation. "Oh, I absolutely love it! A jaburú! Jaburú, jaburú, jaburú!"

As I sat there, watching a beloved British royal gleefully repeat the name of a bird that was most certainly incorrect, I must admit that I felt a bit sheepish. Ruth just stared at me, bewildered. As to why I felt compelled to invent a name rather than just confessing that I didn't know, well, I suppose I didn't want to disappoint her.

Later that night came the formal dinner. I ate at the main table with the royal family, seated between Queen Elizabeth and the Queen Mother. Tony Blair, who had recently been named prime minister, sat at another table, which I found a bit odd. The queen gave a mesmerizing appraisal of all the British prime ministers she had known since Winston Churchill. She said that she believed Margaret Thatcher had lingered in power for too long; I thought, my God, the queen has been around quite a lot longer!

While Queen Elizabeth was still speaking, my eyes wandered over to the Queen Mother. She beamed at me, winked, and silently mouthed, "Jaburú!"

I still smile when I think of the Queen Mother. While I was pained when I heard of her passing, I deeply admired her for leading such a rich, long, and meaningful life.

In the following years, I was also fortunate to develop an excellent relationship with Tony Blair. He is enormously intelligent and well-traveled, a true man of the world, with a keen interest in Brazil. He believed that our country was on an upward track, even during the most difficult moments. We shared a broadly similar governing philosophy, and I participated in his initiative on the "Third Way" exploring the future of progressive governance in the twenty-first century.

After a conference we attended in Madrid in 2002, Blair invited Ruth and me to spend a night at Chequers, the country home outside London that has been used by British prime ministers for a generation. I slept in a bedroom once used by Churchill, which was quite a thrill.

Clinton was no longer president, but he attended the Madrid meeting and also accompanied us. One evening, the five of us—Bill, Tony, Cherie, and Ruth and I—sat in the living room and spent a long, pleasant evening chatting. Tony sat on the floor and unfurled a giant map of the Middle East across the coffee table. He was about to make a trip to Israel and Palestine, and he wanted to discuss the situation there. He and Clinton spent hours talking in enormous detail about the peace process—I remember they even knew about issues such as water supplies—and discussing potential solutions. I felt flattered to be in such rarefied company.

From that retreat, I proceeded to Paris, where I became the first Latin American president ever to address the French parliament. It was an honor, and the sight of me on such a grand stage caused a stir back in Brazil. While there, I met with Jacques Chirac, with whom I always had a warm friendship.

My other travels focused on Latin America, Europe, China, and other places where Brazil needed to build strategic ties. I came into contact with numerous leaders who impressed me: Felipe González, Gerhard Schroeder, Mário Soares, José Maria Aznar, King Juan Carlos, Lionel Jospin, Ernesto Zedillo, Vladimir Putin, Romano Prodi, Massimo D'Alema . . . there are too many to list here. All of them appreciated what we were trying to do in Brazil and granted us generous support at crucial moments.

During my trip to China, I saw things that reminded me of both Brazil's past and its future. The growing economic strength of China, and its demand for products that Brazil exports, will be a central fact of life for both countries for decades to come. However, while I am optimistic about China's long-term prospects, I do believe that Brazilian history offers some important lessons about the years ahead. China is now embarking on a transition from a largely rural to an urban society; caught up in the hype of its rapid transformation, many observers seem to have forgotten how turbulent and unsteady such social change can be. China has not yet made the transition to democracy; when that inevitably happens, there may be fireworks. It remains to be seen whether China's transformation in the twenty-first century will be as problematic as Brazil's was in the twentieth.

Some of my most emotional visits were to Chile, where I saw many of my old friends from exile. Now that Lagos was president of Chile, we were able to relive old times and learn from Chile's new triumphs. After Pinochet finally left power in 1990, Chile was able to quickly regain its historical identity as a thriving democracy. The vibrant society that I had once known made a dramatic comeback after years of oppression, and I was heartened to see that Chile was returning to its perch as a model of stability for the rest of Latin America.

When I think of the leader I admired most on a personal level, there was no contest: Nelson Mandela. Brazil, as one of the only countries in the world to consistently and rigorously oppose apartheid over the years, has always enjoyed a unique relationship with South Africa. Because of our large black population, in Brazil we have always tended to see traces of ourselves in that nation, and I believe South Africans feel a similar affinity to us. Mandela reflected his country's warmth toward us with a mix of elegance and earthy spirituality that I have not witnessed in any other senior political figure.

On one trip, Ruth and I walked together through the streets of Soweto, the old black township outside Johannesburg. We stopped at a plaza with a plaque commemorating a youth who had been murdered during the fight against apartheid. There, we were surrounded by hundreds of people who sang in homage to Brazil. We proceeded to the house of the legendary Walter Sisulu, who had led the fight against white oppression during the 1950s and then spent twenty-six years in jail with Mandela. He had later been a congressman, but by the time I met him he had receded from public life, and he rarely received visitors.

"I just wanted to thank you," Sisulu said, his voice frail, "for Brazil's help at a time when no one else would support us." By the end of the conversation, both of us were in tears.

Almost everywhere I traveled, I felt that by the time I left, people were looking at Brazil with new eyes. Success in foreign policy can be difficult to measure in the short term. One way to gauge it, however, is by looking at foreign direct investment. During my presidency, Brazil received more than $100 billion—only China received more. Our exports also increased by almost 50 percent during my government. Far more important, though not as easy to quantify, was the issue of respect.

Another long-standing dream of Brazil's is to have a permanent seat on the Security Council of the United Nations. I supported this initiative. But I always mused that it would be more useful for Brazil to aspire to a seat in a different body: the G7, or Group of Seven, composed of the largest economies in the world. If Brazil succeeded in growing its economy and alleviating poverty, then power and influence would come naturally. As we tried to accomplish this most difficult of goals,

I thought of my travels, and I often found myself thinking of New York City—the way it used to be.

I had made several trips to the Big Apple in the 1960s, 1970s, and 1980s, when vast swathes of the city still resembled a war zone. New Yorkers believed back then that their city was basically ungovernable and that, despite the city's good points, crime and poverty were intractable facts of life. I remember accompanying an American friend of mine to his grandmother's house in the South Bronx. The buildings there looked burned out, with the abandoned shells populated by desperately poor people. My friend's grandmother was a tiny, sweet Puerto Rican woman who could not go outside unaccompanied because the gang violence was so intense. We spent a long afternoon cooped up in her cramped fortress of a house, protected by a half a dozen locks and a wooden barricade across the door. When we wanted to leave, a "friendly" gang member had to escort us to our car.

I frequently found myself in similar districts of New York, usually because of my notorious talent for getting lost. One time, I came out of the wrong subway stop and started walking around a neighborhood where dozens of young men were staggering about, clearly high on drugs. I was dressed in a coat and tie and must have looked quite out of place, because a taxi immediately screeched up next to me. "Are you crazy, man?" the driver yelled, gesticulating wildly. "You can't stay here!" I gladly hopped in and we sped away. On another occasion, I accidentally found myself in Harlem, where a group of enormous youths started running circles around me, dribbling basketballs and yelling in my face. That time, it was a police car that drove up and took me away to safety.

I remember thinking: Here I am in the biggest city of the world's richest country, and this kind of poverty exists?

These days, New York seems like a different world. Economic development and responsible management have done absolute wonders for the city. Now, Clinton has his office in Harlem! This was unthinkable when I first started traveling there. I returned recently to the South

Bronx, and although there is still poverty there, the situation is not nearly as dire as before. There are new shops and clean streets; the people themselves look healthier. An outsider like me can walk around just about everywhere. This spectacular transformation, which can also be seen in other U.S. cities, has taken place in only a quarter of a century.

I mention this not to trivialize our problems in Brazil, but to show that poverty can indeed be significantly alleviated in a single generation. People tend to be overly cynical about this. While São Paulo is admittedly not Manhattan, there are other places that have made major progress in a short period of time. Thirty years ago, Ireland and Spain were impoverished countries, and it seemed unlikely that they could ever become prosperous. But with good policies, democratic governments, and a vibrant business sector, they were able to make a quantum leap. Millions were lifted out of poverty; the changes in Dublin or Madrid are perhaps as striking as those in New York. The truth is that no place is ever ungovernable, nor should poverty ever be thought irreversible.

We knew that repeating such an experience in Brazil was never going to be as easy as in some other countries. First of all, we were starting from a much lower point. We also did not have the benefit of European Union subsidies or favorable terms of trade with the rest of the world. Rather, Brazil's constant financial troubles meant that the government was severely limited in terms of what it could spend. Our neighbors were often just as deep in crisis as we were. I would have loved to be able to spend billions of dollars on health care and education, but we just didn't have the money. For Brazil to climb out of poverty, it would be a long, unglamorous road. The results would not come quickly or easily.

With education, the problem truly was not a lack of funds. In fact, Brazil's overall spending on education was equal to about 5 percent of its GDP, above that of many rich countries. The real problem was the way the money was spent, and who the existing structure favored. In Brazil, tuition to public universities is "free"—that is, it is funded by the government. At my alma mater, the University of São Paulo, students paid not a dime to attend. Because of this system, a quarter of Brazil's overall education budget went toward these universities, even though only 2 percent of the country's students attended them.

Meanwhile, the average Brazilian university student was much wealthier than society at large. Gaining a coveted spot at a public university usually requires families to spend thousands of dollars on a top-notch private school—this exacerbates the income gap even further. The bottom line was that most students could afford to pay at least part of their tuition. Instead, we were spending ungodly amounts to pay it for them. According to the World Bank, Brazil's spending per university student, when compared to the size of our economy, was by far the highest in the world. Put another way: The government was paying for relatively wealthy students to attend college for free at the expense of primary and secondary schools serving a relatively poor majority.

Thus, my challenge regarding education was the same as in other areas: to redesign the Brazilian system to more fairly serve the *whole* population. In practice, this meant spending less on universities and channeling more money to primary and secondary schools. This caused an uproar. People asked how a former university professor could "destroy" the system that had nurtured him, and I was highly unpopular on public university campuses. There were numerous strikes by students and professors alike. Of course, they couldn't attack me publicly for trying to help the poor—that would not have been politically correct—so instead they renewed the accusation that I was a "neoliberal." They accused me of wanting to sell the universities to foreign investors. This was ridiculous. I challenged them: "Who in their right mind would want to buy a public university in Brazil?"

Our biggest victory on education was a constitutional amendment that forced state governments to spend more money on primary schools. In the poorest parts of Brazil, they had to allocate at least $300 per student per year. That, in essence, instituted a minimum salary for teachers. It was a simple but effective way to guarantee that states would spend enough. With the rule in place, they had to cut other entitlement programs to make sure they met the limit. Somehow, they almost always did.

We also took two problems—poverty and education—and linked them to each other in an effort to solve both. We established a program called *bolsa escola* that guaranteed a modest income to poor families—as long as they sent their children to school. Brazilian governments had experimented in the past with directly handing out food aid, but this caused enormous problems. Corruption within the food distribution system had been rife, and there were logistical nightmares as well—including one classic case where macaroni was sent to an indigenous tribe, and they had no idea how to cook it. So we decided it was best to give money directly to people. As long as their children attended school 85 percent of the time, they were eligible for the *bolsa escola*. In another interesting twist, we gave the cash directly to the mothers instead of the fathers—we found the women to be rather more responsible.

This system was controversial at first. Besides the conventional claims that a welfare system would discourage people from working, we were also accused of essentially bribing parents to send their kids to school, which some saw as morally questionable. Indeed, the system was imperfect—the 85 percent attendance rate was difficult to enforce. Anytime a government gives handouts, it creates an easy avenue for clientelism and corruption. However, we also believed that we were directly addressing the problem: In vast parts of Brazil, children traditionally dropped out of school because their families needed them to work. So we aimed to replace the money they would have earned, and put the students back in the classroom.

Executing all of this was a mammoth task. We had to implement special programs to reduce child labor, which was customary in sugarcane fields and in the coal-mining industry. We needed to build schools where there had been none before—and then sustain them. There was an old Brazilian tradition of building marvelous, monolithic school buildings and then not filling them with teachers and supplies.

All of this had to stop. It involved a change not just of policy, but of culture. Under the leadership of Paulo Renato Souza, the minister of education, Brazil underwent a silent revolution.

Some of the results were immediate. By the end of my term, the percentage of Brazilian children not attending school dropped to 3 percent, compared with about 20 percent a decade earlier. The improvement was even more pronounced among black students. Meanwhile, high school enrollment more than doubled. The universities also prospered—in fact, the annual number of students entering college doubled. Illiteracy fell by more than 30 percent. We made similar progress on health care, and infant mortality experienced a 25 percent decline during my presidency.

Some of the most important work against poverty during my presidency came from nongovernmental organizations, including the one run by Ruth. She spent much of my presidency traveling to the most distant corners of Brazil, quietly doing work to help the poor. She was not a traditional Brazilian first lady; everything she did was in association with NGOs, outside the realm of government, with no access to public funds. It is estimated that her organization Comunidade Solidária worked with more than 1 million adults to teach them how to read. Ruth has always detested publicity, and most Brazilians never knew about the good deeds she performed. She helped people out of a deep sense of duty and did not expect to be rewarded or recognized for her efforts. I think that is the very definition of a hero.

The real results of these efforts will take time to come to fruition. The progress may not be as fast or dramatic as what happened in New York City—in Brazil, a generation may pass before the positive economic impact of these policies becomes clear. But I hope that Brazil will look back one day, twenty or thirty years from now, and see my health-care and education policies as positive and enduring legacies of my government.

It was only fitting that, before I left the presidency, I would have to deal with one last financial crisis. This one was different from all the others, however, and could be summed up in three words: "Lula, Peace and Love."

After losing three straight presidential elections, Lula had a new strategy. Gone was the screaming union leader who, during campaign speeches, had often worn a T-shirt that said "I'm not in a good mood today"; the new "Lula Lite" had flecks of gray in his beard and spoke in soothing tones of brotherhood and reconciliation. He became more subdued in his anti–free market rhetoric, positioning himself as a moderate who was friendly to foreign investment. "I think that I've changed, changed a lot," Lula told skeptical middle-class audiences, "and I think that the Workers' Party is also much more mature, much more conscientious." This sweeping makeover was summed up by Lula's warm and fuzzy media campaign slogan of, yes, "Lula, Peace and Love."

There was one problem: Wall Street didn't believe him. The possibility of a Lula presidency terrified investors just as much as it had before.

I did not believe that Lula was the best candidate for president in the 2002 elections. That distinction belonged to José Serra, whom my party chose as its official candidate. Since the first time that we met in that classroom in Chile, I knew that Serra would make a superb leader. He had spent the past several years as my minister of health, heroically leading our AIDS program and other effective initiatives. Serra was a brilliant administrator with a sharp eye for detail. Though he was not always the most charismatic public speaker, he did have a gift for political deal-making. He also represented the best opportunity to deepen the reforms initiated by my government. I believe that Serra would have made a very good president had he ultimately been elected.

As the vote drew close, however, it became apparent that Lula's moment had finally arrived. After years of grueling and often painful change in Brazil, voters yearned to try something different. Meanwhile, Lula had successfully convinced the public that he wouldn't be *too* different. Polls consistently showed Lula with more than 40 percent support, with Serra and two other major candidates evenly splitting the rest of the vote.

I knew that I would have to lay the groundwork for a smooth transition, or everything I had worked for in the past eight years might be lost. My last great task as president would be to make myself replaceable.

Foreign investors said they were most worried that, if Lula came to power, he would keep his old promise to default on Brazil's foreign debt. With every percentage point that Lula rose in the polls, there was another massive sell-off of Brazilian bonds and currency. But the truth was that Lula was only a small part of the problem.

Despite all of Brazil's progress in the previous decade, some outsiders continued to see us and all of Latin America according to the paradigm of the Cold War. They saw us as the same old land of dictatorships and guerrillas. Thus, they refused to believe that a leftist, no matter how reformed, could ever be trusted in power. Many on Wall Street feared that, if elected, Lula would lead Brazil down a radical path. In believing this, these foreign investors were, ironically, committing the same mistake as the handful of grizzled old Latin American Communists who still rear their heads from time to time. That is, they mistakenly believed that there was an alternative to capitalism.

Only Nixon could go to China, and only Lula could show the world that the Latin American left could run a stable modern economy. But, for him to get there, the world needed to be convinced that Brazil had matured to the point that no one could take us back to our unstable past. I toured the capitals of the world one last time, touting the economic and social successes of my government. It was like a final exam on my way out the door.

I passed. The IMF granted us a $30 billion aid package and declared that Brazil was "on a solid long-term policy trend which strongly deserves the support of the international community." In return, all four of the major candidates for president—most crucially, Lula—agreed to uphold the spirit of my economic reforms if they were elected. This was an unprecedented sign of Brazil's newfound maturity. After that vote of confidence, which amounted to overwhelming support by all of the world's richest countries, the last financial crisis of my government, this time the sole result of the external perception of Lula and his party, drew to a close.

On January 1, 2003, in a ceremony in Brasília, I removed the presidential sash from my chest to give it to Lula. As I pulled it over my head, and flashbulbs popped everywhere, I accidentally knocked my eyeglasses to the floor. Without hesitation, Lula bent over, picked the glasses up, and handed them back to me. We smiled at each other, a brief moment of understanding between two old friends, and then I slipped the sash over his head.

Despite my reservations, I was pleased to see Lula wearing that sash. I felt as if a cycle had completed itself. The man who had once been my main opponent was now promising to carry on my policies. I felt validated by his election, and I was optimistic at the time that he would do an adequate job.

As Ruth and I prepared to leave the presidential palace for the last time, Lula accompanied us to the elevator. As the doors opened, tears ran down his cheeks and he enveloped me in a giant bear hug. "You leave here a friend," Lula said, clapping me on the back. "You leave here a friend."

EPILOGUE

I HAVE ENJOYED few moments in my life more than when, in January 2003, I left a friend's house in Paris, strolled down the street, and climbed aboard the subway—alone.

Immediately after handing power over to Lula, Ruth and I boarded a plane for France. We spent a quiet three months there living in relative anonymity, enjoying basic pleasures like going to the Louvre, visiting the Chartres Cathedral or walking along the shores of the Seine. For the first time in more than ten years, I could do these things without a bodyguard or anyone else looking over my shoulder. Very few people recognized us, and we relished the trappings of the normal life we had once known.

Since that briefest of breaks, however, I have immersed myself in the busy life of a former statesman. I still travel as often as I did as president. Much of my time goes toward international conferences on topics such as global democratic governance, protection of democracy, conditions for economic growth, poverty alleviation, and AIDS. I have accepted many international assignments, including being the chairman of the Club de Madrid, which gathers almost sixty former heads of state around the cause of enhancing democratic rule. I am the co-chairman of the Inter-American Dialogue, a Washington-based think tank on hemispheric issues, and a board member of several non-profit organizations including the Rockefeller Foundation. I was invited by UN Secretary General Kofi Annan to prepare a report on the relationship between the UN and civil society. I have finally resumed my academic life, at least in part; I usually spend about five weeks each year at Brown University in the United States as a professor-at-large.

In Brazil, I have stayed very involved in politics, and I continue to serve as the honorary head of my party, the Brazilian Social Democracy Party (PSDB). However, I have no intention of running for president again. Although the Brazilian Constitution does allow presidents to seek a third, non-consecutive term, I believe that the country would be better served by a new generation of leaders. Plus, being president of Brazil is tough enough—for the sake of my heart, if nothing else, I think two terms were quite sufficient.

Instead, I have spent much of my time building my own institute, the Instituto Fernando Henrique Cardoso, which is modeled on the presidential libraries of the United States. That we needed to follow a foreign model highlights the fact that I am now in largely uncharted territory. For a good number of former Brazilian presidents, retirement mostly meant deciding which plane or boat to take into exile, and then starting to plot a comeback. Honorary degrees, presidential libraries, and, yes, memoirs are an entirely unexpected consequence of our new-found stability.

I was pleasantly surprised in April 2005 when Lula invited me to accompany him to Rome for the funeral of Pope John Paul II. We chatted easily on the presidential plane, and for a fleeting moment it seemed like old times. But the true shock of that trip came at the funeral itself, when *four* Brazilian presidents were reunited in the same place. José Sarney, now a senator, had also joined us on the plane ride over, and Itamar Franco was serving as Brazil's ambassador to Italy.

The four of us were standing around, talking amiably, when Jacques Chirac happened to walk by. "Ah, Fernando, how are you?" Chirac asked, gallant as ever, speaking his silky French. "Are you enjoying your retirement?"

I nodded and we bantered for a moment. "You know, we've got four current and former presidents here today."

Chirac beamed at us and declared, "A historic moment for Brazil!"

Historic indeed. There have been few, if any, moments when so many Brazilian presidents have been brought together in one place. In fact, it is hard to imagine any other Brazilian presidents who could have tolerated it. If such a reunion had taken place in the past, it certainly would not have been under such civil circumstances. That all four of us present had become president through democratic means was testimony to the new era in which we were living.

Brazil is maturing. Just how far it will progress in coming years remains to be seen. I frequently said as president that I didn't know if my government represented a new era or just a pause in Brazilian history. I am still not certain. There is always a possibility that some future president or unforeseen event could undo the gains that we made. I am less optimistic about my children's generation than I am about my grandchildren's—people now in their adolescence. I believe that some tough transformations still await Brazil before the country can achieve true prosperity.

Nevertheless, it seems more probable, as time goes by, that the newfound political and economic stability will be lasting. Ironically, the recent bout of tough times since I left office has been proof of this. I would never have imagined what a disappointment Lula would be as president. His term in office was marked by administrative incompetence and by allegations of serious corruption among his inner circle. But, through all the scandals, the economy has stayed remarkably stable. Lula has governed with largely the same policy agenda as my government, even though he has failed to institute meaningful new reforms. If nothing else, Brazil's stability is an overwhelming sign that the ideas of my government should endure. The foundations for a richer, more prosperous country—and perhaps, one day, a world power—seem to be firmly in place.

As I left office, *The New York Times* referred to me as "Brazil's great stabilizer." "Mr. Cardoso's greatest achievement," wrote *The Economist*, "has been to make Brazil look governable." In a nationwide poll a month before I left office, Brazilians named me the best president in our country's history, just ahead of Getúlio Vargas. Another article published by *Veja* magazine asserted that my "record in social areas is arguably more important" than my legacy in the economic field. I also received, in 2002, the first United Nations award for world leaders promoting the advancement of human development in their respective countries.

As someone who arrived in the presidency thanks to no small amount of luck and circumstance, it would be arrogant for me to take all the credit. Brazil was greatly served by the numerous talented and visionary professionals who worked in my administration. Some previous presidents also did their part, and I credit Brazil as well. Historical change results from processes deeply rooted in society, not just from one man. While those processes produced me, they also produced a country that craved change and had the courage to elect an inexperienced, former university professor as president—twice. In that sense, perhaps I wasn't such an accident after all.

I feel that my true place in history may only be known fifty years from now. When that time comes, if people can look back at Fernando Henrique Cardoso as the first in a modern era of Brazilian presidents who helped the country realize its dream of prosperity, that would be the most positive legacy that I can imagine.

Whatever history determines, I am proud of the way I lived my life. There are very few people who can say that they accomplished almost everything they wanted. I am lucky enough to be one of them. I helped reestablish democracy in Brazil, and I helped improve the quality of life of my countrymen. Along the way, I enjoyed a rich family life and endeavored to improve myself as an intellectual and as a man. I am thankful for the luck that I enjoyed. I hope that my actions would have made my parents and grandparents proud, as I struggled to fulfill their dream: that a Cardoso would bring Brazil just a bit closer to being not the land of tomorrow, but the country of today.

ACKNOWLEDGMENTS/PHOTO CREDITS

I am deeply grateful to Brian Winter. Without his work, this book would simply not exist. His first draft, extensive research, and skill as an interviewer were irreplaceable. In addition, he read the manuscript of the book I am myself writing in Portuguese on the eight years of my presidency. Brian's excellent work made my editing task much easier and simpler than I had anticipated.

For the editing of the book, I have relied on the valuable and relentless help of José Estanislau do Amaral.

Danielle Ardaillon was responsible for selecting the illustrations and for providing Brian Winter with documents from the Instituto Fernando Henrique Cardoso's collection, of which she is the curator.

I would also like to thank my friends Boris Fausto, Celso Lafer, Sergio Fausto and Tarcisio Costa. They were attentive readers of the book and made several comments and factual corrections that contributed immensely to the improvement of the book.

Finally, I would like to thank Sergio Machado, my publisher in Brazil, who introduced me to Peter Osnos of PublicAffairs, where I also had the privilege of Clive Priddle's support and advice.

FERNANDO HENRIQUE CARDOSO

The co-author would like to thank: Clive Priddle, Peter Osnos, and everyone at PublicAffairs for the opportunity to work on such a unique and fulfilling project; Paul Bresnick, my agent, for believing in me;

Mario Andrada and Kieran Murray, whose encouragement made my participation in this book possible; Nick Shumway, Ted G. Goertzel, Kenneth Maxwell, and Roderick J. Barman for their insight into Brazil; Danielle Ardaillon, José Estanislau do Amaral, and everyone at the Instituto Fernando Henrique Cardoso, for their patience and assistance; Stephen Brown and Adrian Dickson, who helped launch my South American adventures; Laura López and Sebastián Pla, who took me in; my parents, for their support; Erica Baker, my muse; and, above all, thanks to Fernando Henrique Cardoso, for his unwavering faith in this most "accidental," or at least unlikely, of partnerships. It was Brazil that was truly lucky.

BRIAN WINTER

PHOTO CREDITS

Insert page 1
   1A   Courtesy of President Fernando Henrique Cardoso
   1B   Heitor Hui/AE
   1C   Courtesy of President Fernando Henrique Cardoso
   1D   Courtesy of President Fernando Henrique Cardoso
Insert page 2
   2A   Courtesy of President Fernando Henrique Cardoso
   2B   Courtesy of President Fernando Henrique Cardoso
Insert page 3
   3A   Courtesy of President Fernando Henrique Cardoso
   3B   Courtesy of President Fernando Henrique Cardoso/Divulgação
   3C   Domício Pinheiro/AE
   3D   Courtesy of President Fernando Henrique Cardoso
Insert page 4
   4A   Courtesy of President Fernando Henrique Cardoso

4B   Clóvis Cranchi Sobrinho

4C   Courtesy of President Fernando Henrique Cardoso/Divulgação

Insert page 5

5A   Courtesy of President Fernando Henrique Cardoso/Divulgação

5B   Claudine Petroli/AE

5C   Courtesy of President Fernando Henrique Cardoso/Divulgação

Insert page 6

6A   Courtesy of President Fernando Henrique Cardoso/Divulgação

6B   Antônio Milena/Abril imagens

6C   Ricardo Stuckert

Insert page 7

7A   Wilson Pedrosa/AE

7B   Courtesy of President Fernando Henrique Cardoso/Divulgação

7C   Courtesy of President Fernando Henrique Cardoso

Insert page 8

8A   Renato Castro/AE

8B   Courtesy of President Fernando Henrique Cardoso/Divulgação

8C   Courtesy of President Fernando Henrique Cardoso/Divulgação

8D   M.Klein/Présidence de la République Française

INDEX

FERNANDO HENRIQUE CARDOSO was president of the Federative Republic of Brazil for two consecutive terms from 1995–2002. Born in Rio de Janeiro, he is married with three children and lives in São Paolo.

PublicAffairs is a publishing house founded in 1997. It is a tribute to the standards, values, and flair of three persons who have served as mentors to countless reporters, writers, editors, and book people of all kinds, including me.

I.F. STONE, proprietor of *I. F. Stone's Weekly*, combined a commitment to the First Amendment with entrepreneurial zeal and reporting skill and became one of the great independent journalists in American history. At the age of eighty, Izzy published *The Trial of Socrates*, which was a national bestseller. He wrote the book after he taught himself ancient Greek.

BENJAMIN C. BRADLEE was for nearly thirty years the charismatic editorial leader of *The Washington Post*. It was Ben who gave the *Post* the range and courage to pursue such historic issues as Watergate. He supported his reporters with a tenacity that made them fearless and it is no accident that so many became authors of influential, best-selling books.

ROBERT L. BERNSTEIN, the chief executive of Random House for more than a quarter century, guided one of the nation's premier publishing houses. Bob was personally responsible for many books of political dissent and argument that challenged tyranny around the globe. He is also the founder and longtime chair of Human Rights Watch, one of the most respected human rights organizations in the world.

For fifty years, the banner of PublicAffairs Press was carried by its owner Morris B. Schnapper, who published Gandhi, Nasser, Toynbee, Truman, and about 1,500 other authors. In 1983, Schnapper was described by *The Washington Post* as "a redoubtable gadfly." His legacy will endure in the books to come.

[signature]

Peter Osnos, *Founder and Editor-at-Large*

CPSIA information can be obtained
at www.ICGtesting.com
Printed in the USA
LVOW04s2141070616

491656LV00013B/151/P